A PREHISTORY OF ORDINARY PEOPLE

A PREHISTORY OF
ORDINARY
PEOPLE

MONICA L. SMITH

The University of Arizona Press   Tucson

The University of Arizona Press
© 2010 The Arizona Board of Regents
All rights reserved

www.uapress.arizona.edu

Library of Congress Cataloging-in-Publication Data

Smith, Monica L.
  A prehistory of ordinary people / Monica L. Smith.
    p. cm.
  Includes bibliographical references and index.
  ISBN 978-0-8165-2695-6 (hard cover : alk. paper)
  1. Prehistoric peoples. 2. Social archaeology. 3. Antiquities,
Prehistoric. I. Title.
  GN470.S65 2010
  930.1—dc22   2010024011

15 14 13 12 11 10   6 5 4 3 2 1

Contents

List of Figures   vii

Preface   ix

Prologue: A Chance Encounter   xiii

1   The Origins of Multitasking   1

2   Individuals and Food   53

3   Individuals and Goods   98

4   Individuals and Work   134

5   Multitasking and Social Complexity   175

References   183

Figure Credits   213

Index   215

Figures

1.1   Making stone tools   3

1.2   Food, goods, and energy expenditure in small groups   5

1.3   Manufacture of pottery   14

1.4   Sources of parameters for individual action   17

1.5   Relationship between creative actions and habituation   24

1.6   Marking identity on the body   31

1.7   Relationship among food, goods, and work   49

2.1   Early European images of plowing   59

2.2   Food storage area at Çatalhöyük   60

2.3   Types of waste   72

2.4   Decision-making parameters for agriculturalists   76

2.5   Bowls, jars, and cups as common vessels for liquid foods   83

2.6   Statuette of woman grinding grain   87

2.7   Food and political activity in the Moche culture   92

3.1   Making an Acheulean hand ax   99

3.2   Rock art panel of South Asian Buddhist worship   114

3.3   Uses of broken pottery by the modern Tzeltal Maya   124

4.1   Manufacturing involves both specialized and routine tasks   136

4.2   Work includes experiencing as well as creating objects and symbols   140

4.3   Steps in stone tool making   143

4.4   Flower seller in the Aztec *Florentine Codex*   163

4.5   Multitasking is done by managers as well as by workers   172

Preface

As an archaeological investigation of ordinary people, this book has been in the making for a long time. Along the way, I have benefited enormously from the generosity of my friends, family, and colleagues in sharing the richness of the social world that we as a species have inherited. The observations about human interactions with food, goods, and work that form the basis of this book have come from a rich variety of experiences that I have been privileged to have.

My youthful summers were spent in France with my village-born grandmother, whose lifespan went from the nineteenth century to the rocket age and whose observations about cuisine and food provided a warm impetus to the present work. While doing archaeological fieldwork, I have had the opportunity to live in rural, and sometimes very remote, parts of Egypt, Turkey, Bangladesh, Madagascar, and India where patterns of work and consumption have provided insights about the relationship between people and goods in a variety of different contexts.

One story stands out: in the summer of 1998, I was in a small shop in far eastern Turkey where I watched a traditionally dressed man make purchases. He filled his basket with potatoes, onions, tomatoes, and other basic staples that he would provide to the family kitchen. Those who prepared the meals would have to accept the goods brought and make the best of them in a way that would lead to the production of a proper meal. But the man's final item gave me pause: it was a shiny orange packet of branded detergent. It is highly unlikely that the man was washing his own clothes, meaning that the purchase was at the request of others in the family. The careful addition of this relatively costly item to a repertoire otherwise signaling a household of modest income made me realize how consumer goods, including those designed to be disposable, play a large role in the expression of individual identity.

My subsequent observations of both archaeological sites and contemporary behavior led me to assess the way in which deliberate decisions, manifested in small and incremental actions, are initiated by specific individuals acting on specific understandings of the world around them. People engage in these selection processes through the investment of limited wherewithal, even under very restricted conditions of consumption and distribution, and even when consumption takes place by proxy through a third party. Social scientists have wrestled with the concept of free will versus social constraint since the inception of philosophy. By identifying the individual as an autonomous cognitive entity, I show how the archaeological record is a cumulative process of individual decision making on two levels. On the level of analysis, the individual is the acting entity of stasis and change, and we can count individual people one by one as acting at the household, neighborhood, and community levels. On the level of lived experience, people consciously make some decisions about mundane activities that serve to reinforce and manifest thought processes about social actions; in other words, by doing things, they create the shared culture that we can observe both in the archaeological record and in the world around us.

The material in these chapters has been viewed and commented upon throughout the process of the construction of this volume. Many of the ideas in chapter 1 were first publicly discussed as part of a symposium at the Amerind Foundation led by Michael E. Smith in 2008. Chapter 2 is an outgrowth of the general processes of food preference first developed in a paper for *American Anthropologist* in 2006. Portions of chapter 3 had their genesis in the seminar "Relational Concepts in Archaeology: An Agenda for Theory," which Adam Smith and I co-organized at the 2000 Society for American Archaeology meetings in Philadelphia. I thank all of the many participants of these sessions for their insightful comments and leading questions that have contributed to the growth of the arguments presented here.

I also am greatly indebted to the many friends and colleagues who have listened to and helpfully critiqued the ideas that have coalesced here. First and foremost, I thank Michael Schiffer for a decade's worth of long discussions about consumption and material culture. His pioneering work on behavioral archaeology has paved the way for others to consider the processes by which human social systems evolve and are sustained. Allen Johnson of UCLA's Anthropology Department provided important early support for my career there. James Skibo and Cathy

Cameron encouraged my outrageous foray into modern material culture for the *Journal of Archaeological Method and Theory*, supporting my view of the links between our current world and the archaeological past. Along the way, I know that many others have sheltered in the anonymity of peer review to encourage, challenge, and foster the thought process. I hope that they can see the improvement that they wished for me and that they will forgive my failure to take some of their good advice.

The final assembly of the manuscript was undertaken during a wonderful sabbatical leave as a research associate at the School for Advanced Research, Santa Fe, in 2007–8. I would like to thank James Brooks and the warm, welcoming staff of that institution for the intellectual hospitality of this unequalled environment. I would also like to thank the spirited and gracious group of scholars with whom our family shared meals and companionship during that fall and winter.

My "home" is a moveable feast of people, goods, and places, but the focal point is always my family. James and Aidan have shown to me how wonderful ordinary life can be, and to them I convey the greatest thanks of all.

Prologue
A Chance Encounter

About 5,300 years ago, a middle-aged man traveling in the Alps finally succumbed to his injuries and died on a high mountain slope far from his village.

About 2,300 years ago, a forty-year-old woman met with a violent end, and her body was tossed into a peat bog in Denmark.

About 600 years ago in western Canada, a young man from the coastal region trekked to a high mountain pass but died before he could finish his journey.

We know about each of these individuals because their bodies were preserved through accidental means. They were not accompanied by any history, as famous leaders might have been, nor were they formally buried by others who might have added or removed bodily adornments. Instead, the stories that we can tell about these individuals are generated through the analysis of their physical remains and the objects that they had with them. They were ordinary people caught unawares, providing us with an opportunity to analyze their actions and environments through archaeological remains.

Scientists have named the first individual Ötzi and treated him as a time traveler from the Neolithic era. Along with an avuncular name and intriguing tool kit, Ötzi's continued popularity is ensured by his custom-built museum facility and a cottage industry of medical investigations that seem to produce new autopsies every few years speculating about his death from exposure, injury, or violence (e.g., Holden 2001; Rollo et al. 2002; zur Nedden et al. 1994). Ötzi's personal history can be read at several time scales, from the structure of his bones and skin that show the accumulated aches and pains of a long hard life in the mountains, to his last few hours in which his stomach and intestines show the ingestion of several different meals (Oeggl et al. 2007).

Ötzi's New World counterpart is Kwäday Dän Ts'ìnchí, a frozen body found in a Canadian glacier (Dickson et al. 2004). Graced with a name that links him to a nearby descent community, the young man's body has been studied to learn about his environment and his life. The mineral signatures of his bones and hair show that he had grown up in the coastal regions eating seafood, but in the year or so before he died, he had moved about eighty kilometers inland, where his diet had slowly changed. Still, he retained some habits from his childhood, as migrating people often do—he had two pieces of fish with him, and the hat found with his body was a style popular on the coast.

Exceptional conditions of preservation likewise have enabled us to interact with the dead woman as if on a first-name basis. We call her the Huldremose Woman, a title that reminds us of other individuals found in peat bogs, such as Tollund Man, Lindow Man, and the Windeby Girl. In those bogs, the formation of soil has preserved bodies and hairstyles as well as clothing, ornaments, and the flesh itself. The Huldremose Woman was wearing several items of clothing, including a check-pattern skirt and scarf and two skin capes, with another wool garment found nearby as well. Analyses show that the clothing was made of fibers that were not locally available and that the woman herself might have been a foreigner to the area (Frei et al. 2009).

The chance discoveries of Ötzi, Kwäday Dän Ts'ìnchí, and the Huldremose Woman remind us of the intense humanity of the individual, whom we recognize through the naming process. Our desire to attach identity to our long-ago relatives stretches even further back in time to the earliest recognizable human ancestors. They include the diminutive skeleton of an australopithecine named "Lucy" and the juvenile *Homo erectus* skeleton known as the Lake Turkana Boy. In the archaeological and popular literature, they have each come to represent whole eras and lifeways. Preserved in flesh and bone, they somehow seem more "real" than the aggregate statistics of human endeavor that usually constitute our data set.

In this book, I want to examine the life processes of those whose bodies have not been so fortunately preserved. The goal is to write a prehistory of ordinary people whose lives are usually traced only in the collective. The archaeological record is the result of millions of individual actions, a factor that compels us to recognize the impact of the everyday decisions made by ancient people. They were as conscious of life and death as we are, and their activities over the course of a lifetime produced the material remains that archaeologists see today as "cultures." In their deliberate actions generated by both creativity and habituation, our most ancient ancestors embodied a history of cognitive autonomy that was the basis upon which cities, states, and empires were eventually made possible.

A PREHISTORY OF ORDINARY PEOPLE

CHAPTER 1

The Origins of Multitasking

THE HUMAN PAST is the collective story of individuals. Just like us, ancient people were born and lived within a social context framed by family, community, and ideology. Each day, they acted on basic human needs for food and shelter and made an impact on their surroundings by using tools, acquiring resources, and discarding waste. With their minds and hands they constantly transformed their world in both large and small ways, using their time and energy to contribute to their own biological and social survival and to the maintenance of the household and community.

Although the past two million years are a blink in evolutionary time, they represent the era in which humans have gone from being merely one type of clever but vulnerable primate to being the only species whose conscious actions with material objects continually shape the landscape. The archaeological record of this transition shows that nearly everything about our species has changed over time: we do not eat the same things as our Paleolithic ancestors, we do not speak the same language as medieval people, and we do not wear the same styles of clothing as our grandparents. These changes were collectively incremental, but from the perspective of the individual they involved conscious actions with material goods and the surrounding environment.

Archaeology is the ideal discipline through which we can examine the generative quality of individuals' decisions and actions in forming cultural patterns both in the past and in the present. Although we think of it as being the study of ancient people and artifacts, archaeology can be defined more broadly as the discipline that evaluates the relationship among people, material objects, and space (see Reid et al. 1975:864). What it means to be human is manifested in the conscious manipulation of our surroundings through the use of resources and creation of objects. People also transform their surroundings through spatial modifications, with a rich and nuanced understanding of the landscapes around them. As point-specific locations of behavior, archaeological sites are the end product of many acts carried out by anonymous persons who have left their houses, their pottery, their hearths, and their burials for us to find.

The recovery of these artifacts and features shows that there were many different ways to engage with the material world. What makes an object useful as a tool? How much energy investment is required to make it "finished" enough for use? Does the completion of the object involve decoration, and if so, of what type? Even the act of constructing a simple dwelling involves a number of steps in which the linear process of construction is interwoven with situational, fluctuating conditions of the surrounding physical and social landscape. Where to build the house, and of what materials? When to start, and how much to complete before it could be lived in? How to integrate with seasonal tasks such as hunting, planting, and harvesting and with daily tasks such as taking care of children and the elderly? What forces, both human and supernatural, to placate in the construction of the dwelling? How and when to modify it in the course of the residents' lifetimes? What tasks are to be done inside, outside, or far away from the dwelling? When to abandon it, to whom, and for what compensation?

In this book, I argue that the individual human cognitive capacity for memory and planning in everyday activities set the stage for the eventual development of social complexity. Deep in the prehistoric past, humans already were engaging in flexible, information-based decision making and selective energy expenditure through multitasking. As early as the beginnings of *Homo erectus* 1.8 million years ago, creative capacities at the individual level enabled our ancestors to compete successfully with other predators, to migrate across diverse and ever-changing landscapes, and to cope with seasonal and long-term changes in the environment (fig. 1.1). In much more recent times, the human capacity to engage with material culture, modify space, and engage in multiple simultaneous acts of energy expenditure made successively larger social configurations possible. As Kyle Summers (2005:108) has observed, the past ten thousand years of human evolution have not changed gene frequencies sufficiently to account for new behavioral patterns. Instead, preexisting cognitive frameworks provided individuals with the capacity to develop and adjust to new technological and social environments, in which the demands of home and family life were augmented by the requirements of permanent political leaders and an increasingly elaborate community life in cities, states, and empires.

FIGURE 1.1. Our earliest ancestors' deliberate actions with the environment included making tools from stone as well as from perishable materials such as wood, plant fibers, feathers, and fur.

While we may see in an archaeological site the collective effects of a social group, it is the individual who actually feels the sensations of hunger, thirst, fear, cold, pain, and pleasure. It is the individual who wears clothing, who eats food, who discards waste, and who sleeps and wakes. It is the individual who operationalizes the pace of energy expenditure: walking slowly or quickly, eating slowly or quickly, working slowly or quickly. Over the course of a day, it is the individual who wakes, rises, and prepares to interact with the household and community. Over the course of a lifetime, it is the individual who grows, matures, and acquires skills.

Most artifacts recovered through archaeological investigation are representative of individual activities. Eating, for example, is facilitated by one-person items such as cups, bowls, and spoons. Clothing and headgear are made for an autonomous human body, in which items are attached through an individual's deliberate acts of draping and fastening. From spears and digging sticks to baskets and bags, the human repertoire of tools is designed to be used one person at a time. Until about ten thousand years ago, most artifacts also were made by one person from start to finish. In each event of creation, an individual assessed the suitability of raw materials and aspects of decoration and determined when the object was "finished" enough to be utilized. Similarly, most features in a domestic context are only large enough for one person to use or manipulate at a time. Hearths, storage bins, cooking jars, and grinding tools are configured for individual use, signaling the way in which human energy expenditure is an individual phenomenon with cumulative archaeological effects.

The archaeological impact of the individual can be examined through three basic categories: food, goods, and work. It is in these three aspects of the daily realm that we can perceive how individuals use their autonomous cognitive capacities to address biological and social needs through selective applications of energy expenditure. Food is a daily physiological requirement, consumed by each individual with reference to personal expectations and preferences as well as to the social parameters of acceptability in both raw materials and the manner of preparation. Goods encompass the physical realm modified by people, most often in the form of portable artifacts but also in the use of architectural space and the landscape. Work consists of energy expenditure, which can be undertaken for the direct consumption of natural resources as well as to acquire wherewithal that can be expended on social activities.

The three realms of food, goods, and work intersect in a dynamic way at the scale of lived daily experience. Individuals recognize cause and effect in the physical world and make predictive calculations about the expenditure of time and energy to modify those effects. The food quest can be addressed through many different allocations of time to the natural environment, with steps that include the acquisition of nutrients (through hunting, gathering, fishing, or farming) and the treatment of those raw ingredients through preparation by boiling, roasting, baking, or fermenting. Each of these methods of food collection and food preparation requires the use of tools that are made with the expectations of particular uses but can be modified and used idiosyncratically. Goods and work are interconnected in other ways as well, as the creation of objects requires deliberate planning for the acquisition of raw materials. Once materials are gathered, the craftsmaker also decides the way in which energy will be applied to making a basket, a pot, a meal, or a metal knife. The same deliberation also applies to activities that may leave few physical

FIGURE 1.2. Individuals' interactions with food, goods, and energy expenditure in small-group settings constituted patterns that were retained and augmented in the subsequent development of social complexity.

remains, such as the narration of stories, the singing of songs, and the intricate steps of dance.

The individual cognitive autonomy that we see in the archaeological record, exercised in the interactions with food, goods, and work starting more than a million years ago, constituted the underpinning of communal activity that eventually culminated in political formations such as cities and states (fig. 1.2). Although the state is the dominant form of political organization today and plays a role in patterns of everyday action through laws and boundaries, it is a configuration that emerged only a few thousand years ago. Elites in these contexts provide new types of parameters for emulation and behavior, but the vast majority of actions even in the most totalitarian states take place away from the gaze of elites. The development of institutionalized political hierarchies added onto, but did not obscure, the underlying individual capacities for decisions about what to eat, what to wear, and when to work. Through the cognitive processes of planning, memory, and multitasking inherited from our ancestors, we have the capacity to be profoundly innovative in using the world around us.

The Individual in the Social Sciences

The social sciences constitute the study of humans at both the individual and the group level through specific domains such as psychology, sociology, anthropology, and often, economics and history. These disciplines have engaged with many different approaches to the study of the individual in the present, which have in turn generated considerable thought about when the individual emerged as a social entity in the past.

We must first distinguish between the "individual" and the concept of "individuality." Scholars generally suggest that "individuality" is a Western concept that emerged in the Enlightenment era and cannot be successfully applied to understand eras before our own (e.g., Fowler 2004; Hodder 2000:23). A modernist perspective on individuality grants primacy to our contemporary world, with the result that ancient people are viewed as having a kind of herdlike mentality, as succinctly noted by the psychologist D. W. Winnicott (1971:70, citing his debt to Michel Foucault's 1966 *Les mots et les choses*): "One could suppose that before a certain era, say a thousand years ago, only a very few people lived creatively. . . . A body of science was needed before men and women could become units integrated in terms of time and space, who could live creatively and exist as individuals." There is, furthermore, a link perceived between "individuality" and the development of the state, such that the ethos of individuality was developed as the direct result of increasingly rigid hierarchies and their political and class distinctions, with the ironic result that people cognized their "individuality" only at the moment when it was subject to loss.

This perception of individuality has filtered through into archaeology to promote the idea of a great distinction between modern and ancient humans; Chris Fowler (2004:3), for example, proposes that "[p]eople in past societies were not necessarily individualized in the same way as those of modern people, and past identities may have been temporary, contextual, and community concerns." A natural extension of this particular approach has been the analysis of Great Individuals, who constituted the group of the "very few" who lived creatively and whose grand actions propelled a particular form of political or social action. The discovery of spectacular tombs such as those of the Mesopotamian Queen Puabi or the Egyptian King Tut further reinforces an image of distinct individuals whose control of their societies explains the trajectory of an ancient, enigmatic civilization. Rulers, shamans, and other notable people were often buried or housed in ways that mark them as having been distinct in the social hierarchy, providing to archaeologists the material basis for explanatory models of sociopolitical complexity that focus on how "chiefs come to power" (Earle 1997). For periods in which we have written texts, those rulers' own words further reinforce this view, as their life histories emphasize singular moments of action such as battles and conquests that led to their political success (Smith 2005a).

In the "great leader" model, individuality and individual autonomy are the prerogative of powerful political figures who establish and maintain hierarchies that extract labor, distribute goods, and dictate the terms of political engagement. Moreover, these elites are viewed as setting the parameters of consumption in ways that promote coercion and cohesion, such that "materialized ideology molds individual beliefs for collective social action" and "the materialization of ideology creates a shared political culture over time" (DeMarrais, Castillo, and Earle 1996:16, 17). These materialized ideologies in turn enable the analysis of economic systems through the evidence of craftsmakers and the supply chains of raw materials for the textiles, metals, and pottery manufactured for living contexts as well as for burial ceremonies.

Another approach, closely related to the idea of the Great Individual, views individuality as applicable to a slightly larger number of people but only under circumstances of social growth and progress. In this view, individuality is a consequence of conditions under which social betterment is possible. Textual sources provide a glimpse into ancient societies in which individual actions could be rewarded (for example, in Rome, where freed slaves could achieve legitimate social status, or in China, where the examination system for the civil service enabled persons from modest backgrounds to achieve an elite rank [e.g., Thompson 2003; Kracke 1947]). Expanding the notion of mobility to the ancient Maya, Joyce Marcus (2004:255) proposes that "[i]t seems likely that hard-working commoners would become influential actors, particularly those individuals who showed initiative and great skills."

In the elite-centered and progressive explanatory models alike, social scientists tend to treat the remainder of the population of ordinary individuals by subsuming them into groups labeled "subalterns," "commoners," or the "disenfranchised" who act collectively in response to the dictates of Great Individuals and high-achieving social opportunists. Elites make rules to which non-elites respond in one of two ways: either an acceptance through a process of "false consciousness" in which non-elites allow themselves to be convinced that the dominant order is morally correct and that they are somehow deserving of oppressed status; or a complete rejection that sharply defines whole groups in a process of "class struggle," through which non-elites attempt to collectively thwart, augment, or change the will of the social and political hierarchy. In his seminal *Weapons of the Weak*, James C. Scott (1985:xvii) argues that large-scale peasant uprisings (in the style of the French Revolution, for example) are relatively rare compared to the ubiquity and effectiveness of actions on a smaller scale: "[I]ndividual acts of foot dragging and evasion, reinforced by a venerable popular culture of resistance and multiplied many thousand-fold, may, in the end, make an utter shambles of the policies dreamed up by their would-be superiors in the capital. Everyday forms of resistance make no headlines. But just as millions of anthozoan polyps create . . . a coral reef, so do the multiple acts of peasant insubordination and evasion create political and economic barrier reefs of their own."

One of the limitations of the "resistance" concept, however, is the implication that the social agenda is always set by some higher authority to which non-elites merely react. Research on contemporary groups shows that people create alternative authorities and subvert centralized planners not merely against a dictum but proactively as a means to create their own environments (e.g., Colombijn 1994; Myers 1996; Streicker 1997). The ascription of proactive construction of cultural parameters to individuals is, however, relatively underappreciated by archaeologists. Archaeologists have traditionally studied group-level behaviors, in which the individual is subsumed into "cultures." Actual individuals are viewed as either invisible in the archaeological record (Gamble and Porr 2005:3) or a source of idiosyncratic behavior that should be filtered out of systems-level analyses (Hill and Gunn 1977).

Archaeologists' interpretation of individuals in the aggregate mirrors the "resistance" perspective of the anthropological literature. As Marcia-Anne

Dobres and John Robb (2000:8) have observed, many aggregative models—such as Darwinian models, game theory, evolutionary ecology models, and optimal foraging models—also borrow from the physical sciences. Individuals have been analyzed in their collective capacity under the rubric of "self-organizing" systems (e.g., McIntosh 2005; Spencer 1997). These "analytic individuals" (see Redman 1977) have value as the minimal component population unit of archaeological systems, but rarely have they been perceived as the prime movers and creators of cultural traditions. Archaeologists focused on historic periods, when texts can help us identify groups, similarly have relied on aggregate descriptors when they analyze the development of identities related to ethnicity, occupation, or geographic origin (e.g., Mullins 1999 and Gradwohl and Osborn 1984 on African Americans, Saitta 2007 on coal miners, and Voss 2005 on overseas Chinese communities).

New approaches to the understanding of complex societies, as well as the increasing robusticity and diversity of archaeological data sets, provide scope for a renewed focus on the individual as a generative component of culture across deep time. One important discipline-wide transformation is the development of postmodern—usually called postprocessual—archaeology. In contrast to structuralist explanations in which individual actions reflect manifestations of rules based on systems of order such as kinship (Manning and Cullum-Swan 1994), postprocessual adherents "are concerned with individuals, specifically how the social negotiations of individuals affect social structures represented by the archaeological record" (VanPool and VanPool 1999:38).

The actualization of the individualist, postprocessual paradigm has, however, proven to be a challenge, as the resulting analysis often still focuses on group-level functions. Ian Hodder, for example, proposes that "rather than starting with 'individuals' we need to see how 'individuals' and other wholes such as sites, cultures and exchange networks are constructed, not solely by large-scale processes and hegemonic groups, but through the intentionality within particular and individual events" (2000:25). He suggests that to investigate those events we "build up these fragments into the fullest possible accounts of individual lived lives, by grouping together events and sequences of events wherever possible" (Hodder 2000:26). One approach has been to identify particular individuals as an illustrative reference point, whether through the analysis of a single individual body as a record of cumulative events and "small-scale drama" (e.g., Hodder 2000:27) or through the imaginative re-creation of a particular event such as a hunt or a meal (e.g., M. Jones 2007:45–48). In a statement that summarizes the challenge of accommodating an individual approach with archaeological data sets, Lynn Meskell (1998:209) concludes that "[p]ostprocessual archaeology has placed great importance on individuals and social interaction, though in practice this often proves a difficult project to realize."

In other words, archaeologists want to study the individual, but they are not sure how this might be achieved or why it is necessary other than fulfilling the postmodern goals of looking for agency in the past. I would suggest that to capitalize on postprocessual theories of the individual and understand how agency is manifested in the archaeological record, we need to examine the detailed components of individual lives from the cognitive perspective. The building blocks of individual cognition can be traced from infancy to adulthood to senescence, resulting in sequences of daily actions that indicate the capacity of individuals to act creatively both to modify and to sustain parameters of behavior.

When might the individual first be recognizable in the archaeological record as a distinct, creative entity? Richard Bradley (2005), following the work of Colin Renfrew (2001), proposes that the effects of the individual can be discerned in the Neolithic period, when humans first permanently settled into villages and there was a dramatic increase in the types and varieties of material culture. But in a provocative volume that examines the earliest human material evidence, Clive Gamble and Martin Porr (2005:4) have urged that we consider the individual as a "foreground principle in our evolutionary history" and not merely a background idea to be immediately subsumed into group-level interpretations. They emphasize the visibility of the individual from the earliest time of the Paleolithic starting 2.5 million years ago, when we can first discern how our human ancestors distinguished themselves from other mammals through tool manufacture and use.

Gamble and Porr's insights suggest that the impact of the individual in the long time frame of human adaptations is found not merely in the actions undertaken within the framework of complex societies but throughout the period of human social evolution. A definition of simple and complex societies from the perspective of ordinary people assists with analyzing this transition and the way in which the actions of ordinary people constituted the foundation for the development of social complexity in the form of cities, states, and empires.

Simple societies (such as villages) share the following characteristics:

1. Everyone knows everyone face-to-face.
2. Everyone knows where the next meal is coming from.
3. Leaders can occasionally organize people to do something spectacular.

Much of our human history was encompassed within this category of "simple" societies. Our mobile hunter-gatherer ancestors had group sizes well under one hundred people, and even the earliest villages would have housed relatively modest populations. Small group size would have facilitated face-to-face interactions for most social and economic transactions. This high level of familiarity did not preclude the ability to interact with new people, such as those joining the group and strangers met during population movements. The second point concerns food access: in simple societies either with or without storage capacities, individuals are within sight of their next meal and the chain of provisioning is clear. Social obligations, knowledge of and access to surrounding resources, and often the physical foodstuffs themselves are immediately apparent. Third, the phenomenon of leadership in simple societies involves energy expenditure for specific actions, such as a hunt, a burial, a feast, or a skirmish. The leaders can be different individuals depending on the activity, and there is considerable fluidity in the assignment of leadership from one event to another.

Even in simple societies, activities such as interacting with others, acquiring food, and expending energy would have required significant levels of cognitive skills on the part of the individual, including memory, planning, and language and other forms of communication. Individual cognitive capacity and actions as the basic building blocks of social organization remained essential to the development of complex societies, which added to this repertoire of social interactions through increased levels of energy investment in food, goods, and work. The increase of population and the development of hierarchical political networks starting around six thousand years ago resulted in the development of what archaeologists used to describe as "civilization"—now, more commonly referred to as "complex societies." In complex societies,

1. Individuals do not know everyone face-to-face and have to have other mechanisms of recognizing people with whom interaction is appropriate.
2. Individuals do not know where their next meal is coming from but have some assurance that it will be there.
3. Leaders organize people to do a variety of ordinary and spectacular tasks.

Complex societies build upon the capacities expressed in simple societies but at a much larger scale and with a greater quantity of material goods, provisioning streams, and time investments. The higher population density in cities, states, and empires means that face-to-face interactions must be supplemented through physical means of communication, often in the form of decorative elements that are themselves labor intensive. These markers of communication and belonging can include hairstyles, clothing, ornaments, tattoos, and other forms of personal embellishment, each of which is deliberately incorporated into the daily repertoire by individuals on an autonomous basis.

In complex societies, access to food involves numerous logistical steps. People often live in population centers that are densely inhabited, meaning that it is impractical to store large amounts of food or house large numbers of domestic animals. Instead, individuals rely on mechanisms of distribution such as markets, itinerant vendors, and ties with kin in the country who supply them with food as it is needed. Other distribution mechanisms are sponsored by civic or temple authorities who compensate people for their services with food through long-term contractual agreements that include payment for services rendered, bonds of indentured servitude, and even outright slavery. Each of these mechanisms, ranging from markets to custody, contains implicit and explicit expectations about a steady chain of supply.

The development of permanent, all-purpose leadership is the most distinctive component of complex societies (Feinman and Neitzel 1984; Spencer 1987). Leaders involve themselves in multiple activities simultaneously, including ritual activities, food production, and the accumulation of power through display, conquest, and resource concentration.

Within complex societies, however, people still face all of the same problems of basic maintenance at the individual and household level, such as preparing and serving food, using and handling goods, and engaging in communication and other social interactions, including ritual interactions. Although the mechanisms for achieving outcomes are more diverse and vary in scale, the capacity of individuals to discern and act upon their social and natural environments remains essential to individual and household viability. The capacity of individuals to critically assess and use their physical and social surroundings, which was already well developed in simple societies, was exercised in complex societies through the addition of communal tasks beyond the individual and household repertoire.

Recovering the Individual in the Archaeological Record

As archaeologists, we do not excavate "social systems" or other abstract configurations. Instead, what we dig up are the specific instances of human activity: a burial, a trash heap, a fortification wall, a tomb, a temple, a house. The process of identifying the individual in the archaeological record can be linked to contemporary social science theory through examinations of how anthropologists move from the interview of single individuals to the creation of large-scale generalizations about human behavior and culture. A consummate example of this process can be found in "person-centered" ethnography, with its reliance on open-ended interviews of just a few individuals in a manner that allows the researcher to evaluate both individual perceptions and the frame of cultural norms. Seeking to avoid the creation of overly simplified abstracts of large-scale behavior, a "primary focus of person-centered ethnographies is on the individual and on how the individual's psychology and subjective experience both shape, and are shaped by, social and cultural processes" (Hollan 1997:219). Like person-centered ethnography, a person-centered archaeology should be considered a way of analyzing the actions undertaken by real, discrete individuals that result in a materialization of both stasis and change.

An assessment of the types of information that archaeologists already gather shows the potential for expanding our understanding of individuals and their actions. The development of ethnoarchaeology in the 1950s

FIGURE 1.3. The manufacture of goods such as pottery was accomplished through many deliberate physical actions, learned and undertaken by individuals as they observed others and engaged in processes of trial and error.

was a particularly important shift in the development of the potential for evaluating individual actions. Seeking to expand their understanding of the production process, archaeologists studied modern craftsmakers using anthropological methods such as participant observation and interviews (David and Kramer 2001). While anthropologists have often lived with and talked with people to find out about social activities and kinship, archaeologists took up ethnography to specifically examine the "variability in material culture and its relation to human behavior and organization among extant societies, for use in archaeological interpretation" (Longacre 1991a:1). Researchers wanting to understand the steps involved in making items such as pottery, iron, and baskets learned by watching individuals make them using low-technology approaches similar to those used in ancient times (fig. 1.3). By getting to know real people, archaeologists realized that individual decisions were affected by and integrated into households, markets, and trade networks. This humanized the process of understanding mechanistic archaeological "systems" and showed that individual variation was generative rather than aberrant.

Archaeologists studying living craft production observed that people were not interchangeable: some were more skilled, more successful, and more respected in the community, while others were disregarded or ignored. Some of these individuals were socially marginalized even when respected for their craft skills or other forms of specialized knowledge. And some individuals were socially celebrated despite their lack of economic standing. Ethnoarchaeologists also observed divisions of labor, status, and knowledge within communities along the lines of ethnicity, age, and gender. The study of gender in particular showed that even straight-forward aspects of the production process could be perceived differently by different individuals. For example, William Longacre (1991b:102–3) noted in the course of his Philippine research that women in a community of potters could tell who made a particular vessel but men could not. Ethnoarchaeological research showed that women and men, in addition to having different bases of knowledge, often have different roles in the production process as well as in the acquisition of raw materials and the marketing of the finished product. The authority to make decisions about production, whether based on gender or family lineage, usually carries over into other realms of life such as household organization, social and ritual interactions among households, property rights, and matters of inheritance.

The diversity of data currently available from household excavations, environmental studies, and settlement surveys means that archaeologists now have the capacity to theorize large-scale cultural change from the perspective of individual actions. One region from which new perspectives are emerging is the Maya region of southern Mexico and northern Central America, where more than a century of research projects has provided data not only on massive temples and pyramids but also on the households and rural communities that sustained ceremonial centers (e.g., Ashmore, Yaeger, and Robin 2004; Ford, Clarke, and Raines 2009; Hutson 2010; Joyce, Bustamante, and Levine 2001; Lohse and Valdez 2004; Robin 2002, 2003). As Joyce Marcus (2004:268) has noted, this abundance of data enables the detailed examination of the impact of individual choices: "[I]n the past, when our data came from more limited testpits in house mounds, commoner households looked more similar than they do today. Small testpits yield incomplete inventories, no information on spatial clustering of artifacts and activity areas, and few data on the size of the house and labor investment in its construction." Other regions of the world in which there have been substantial numbers of projects providing information about the diverse variety of human adaptations include the American Southwest, the ancient Near East and Mesopotamia, the Valley of Mexico, and the Andean region of South America.

The Mechanisms of Individual Action

It is challenging to create an explanatory rubric for social activities that applies to human behavior in the broadest possible sense. Few approaches are inclusive enough to be applied to modern humans as well as to ancient ones, to foragers as well as urbanites, and to our earliest ancestors as well as to twenty-first-century people. Focusing on the individual as an independent cognitive entity fulfills this goal, as the inception of cognitive capacity in individual actions related to the manipulation of artifacts and landscape dates to at least 1.8 million years ago, the date of our ancestor *Homo erectus*. As a cognitive entity, the individual engages in daily activities that create, sustain, and reaffirm a conscious identity. Through these quotidian activities, the individual also creates and sustains social roles that are consciously and subconsciously interwoven with the actions of other people.

Change has been the hallmark of human evolution and social science investigation, but how does that change actually occur? To a certain extent, it is generated through changes in the environment and changes in scale (more people means more ways to interact) and even psychological changes in the population as certain individuals are replaced by others. However, the actualization of change in material culture comes from the deliberate actions of individuals who experiment with, adopt, or dismiss innovations with material culture at a variety of time scales and emanating from a variety of sources (fig. 1.4). One marker of the relationship between creativity and habituation is the fact that, as Brian Loasby (2000:55) has observed, change has to occur within a context of some stasis to be effective or even noticeable: "Everything may be subject to change, but not everything can change at once. . . . [W]e can not even recognize change unless there is something which does not change." Viewed from a perspective of individual cognitive creativity and habituation, both stasis and change require purposeful inputs of thought and energy. Because change is a continual component of the natural world, human efforts towards stasis may require even more consistent energy investment than the cognized or habituated acceptance of that which is new.

Change requires cognitive intent, and this intent is expressed through material culture. Archaeologists mostly have been interested in change

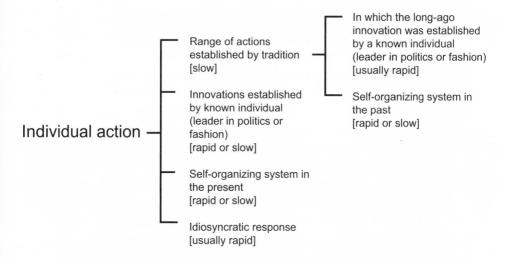

FIGURE 1.4. Sources of parameters for individual action. Origins of the parameter can be either incremental (slow change over time) or tied to a specific, known event resulting in rapid change. Regardless of whether their initiations were slow or rapid, each of these parameters is brought into existence and sustained by the actions of individuals.

as it is promulgated by elites, but change as a human phenomenon is evident in the autonomous cognitive processes of all individuals, not just high-ranking ones. Like ancient people, we all experience change in our own lifetimes that provides for us a general principle of human behavior; not only do our own bodies change through the aging process, but we also witness subtle environmental changes on an annual and lifetime basis, and we continually experience the introduction of new technologies, stories, music, and linguistic terms, as well as new acquaintances through birth and population movement.

Many years ago, V. Gordon Childe (1951:173) discussed the way in which social evolution took place and proposed the idea of the "socially approved need." This concept can be applied to the decision-making process required as part of adopting new tangible technologies, objects, and processes, as well as intangibles such as innovations in art, music, and language. Many inventions have failed to find a public acceptance because there was no perceived benefit in the adoption of the new technology.

The history of the bicycle provides a compelling case because it is so recent in the human technological repertoire (Herlihy 2004). One might wonder, for example, why the Romans did not invent the bicycle—they understood the concept of gears, and they had roads. But they did not have a socially approved ethic that individuals should power their own vehicles. Over a thousand years later, another potential technological turning point was reached in the late 1400s, when a notebook associated with Leonardo da Vinci (who was experimenting with the design of pulleys and gears at the time) showed a kind of two-wheeled vehicle that was apparently never built (Bijker 1997:20). Although the bicycle was to revolutionize personal transport in the late nineteenth and early twentieth centuries, the true pedaled vehicle did not emerge until the 1860s—many years after the steam engine, the railway, and the telegraph.

The development of new technologies requires not just the end user's acceptance but the development of an entire coordinating sphere of individuals whose inputs affect each aspect of the decision-making process, from the acquisition of raw materials to the use of the finished product. Michael Brian Schiffer (2005) discusses this sequencing event as an "invention cascade" that incorporates many distinct instances of decision making, each of which reacts to, and simultaneously affirms and modifies, prevailing social parameters. He notes that the life history of a technological development has numerous stages, from the "creation of a prototype" to the "replication or manufacture [and] use and maintenance" of the item (Schiffer 2005:488). Although Schiffer's article explicitly focuses on what he calls "complex technical systems" such as the telegraph, his model can be applied to a wide range of human technological developments. Returning to the example of the bicycle, we can see that its eventual development and adoption required not only the creation of a prototype (evident hundreds of years earlier in the Leonardo drawings) but also a social ethic of self-directed displacement, a fluidity of labor markets and trade activities in which individuals perceived a reward in displacement, and the need for a mode of transport that reduced dependence on the horse at a rapidly industrializing moment.

The sequencing of work inputs and calculations of benefit similarly can be applied to other technological suites ranging from architecture and agriculture to pottery production, textile manufacture, and the manufacture of stone tools. In an example drawn from the agricultural realm,

Jack Goody (1976) discusses the decision-making strategies affecting the adoption of different farming technologies in ethnographically observed African village societies. Agriculturalists made decisions about whether to use a hoe or an ox-drawn plow on the basis of many calculations beyond the simple factor of equipment cost. Hoes and plows have different scales of use that affect whether an individual will make use of a plow even if one is available; for example, small plots are awkward for oxen and plows to negotiate. The use of oxen for plowing entails significant costs in upkeep and maintenance but also provides the reward of manure, which can dramatically increase yields (Goody 1976:106–11). Following the work of Esther Boserup (1970), Goody notes that the division of agricultural work along gender lines also shifts when new technologies become available: a single decision such as the adoption of a plow entails other shifts in individual decisions about property and the function of agricultural work as a component of household energy expenditure.

The earliest agriculturalists would have each faced many of the same decisions regarding the adoption of animal traction, including the need for a whole new suite of material culture (harnesses, plows), features (stables, manure piles, feeding troughs), activities (castration and training of young cattle), and commitments of energy allocation (humans have to tend oxen every day, even if the oxen themselves work only periodically). Andrew Sherratt's (1987) discussion of technological changes in prehistoric Europe shows another case of the extensive linkages evident in the adoption of new agricultural technology and the implications not only for field crops but also for large-scale landscape alterations. Starting around 3500 BC, clearance of forest and use of the plow were accompanied by the increased potential for raising sheep. Sheep's wool could be used for a wider range of garments than other clothing fibers, and it could also hold a wider range of colors through dyeing. Sherratt (1987:89) suggests that this shift in fibers even affected burial customs, as the change from crouched to laid-out burials may have been prompted by a desire to display the clothing of the deceased for performative advantage.

In the Americas, the trajectory of changes in food production did not involve domesticated beasts of burden but did include shifts of decision making related to crops. Corn, beans, squash, and potatoes became the starchy staples of the diet, accompanied by new strategies of storage and year-round allocation of seasonally harvested crops. Researchers have documented the many different ways that hunter-gatherers utilized their environment and have observed that the diversity of approaches multiplied when deliberately tended crops were added. The highly precise chronology provided by tree-ring dating in the American Southwest, for example, lets researchers see how changes in tool use varied considerably from place to place even within broadly similar geographic regions, leading Patricia Crown (2001:246) to suggest "the importance of individual decisions and strategies in adopting new technology."

In sum, the decisions of whether and how to adopt technical innovations in material culture rest on the sequence of individual actions. A person chooses whether to follow a new fashion or a traditional one with each act of energy expenditure directed towards the making of an object in a particular style or shape. The use, display, and discard of that item further represent the materialization of decision making in form and design. The context for human action at each moment of creation and use are subject to natural and social alteration, with the source of moment-by-moment changes found in the landscape, environment, climate, weather, material availability, level of skill, and presence of helpers. Creative cognitive adjustments can capitalize on these shifts, but even habituated categories of action require the calculation of multivariate inputs. The dynamic interplay between creativity and habituation is in turn affected by the natural stasis and change of the environment and by the cultural parameters of stasis and change that are reinforced with each individual act.

Even for individuals who have very little means, there is an engagement with the physical surroundings that invests agency into the physical world: whether to braid hair in one plait or two, whether to slice the potatoes thinly or thickly, whether to wear clothing long or rolled up. The presence of individual cognitive autonomy does not, however, mean that people cognize each and every action all of the time. Archaeological discussions of agency and practice have fallen short precisely because they assume that individuals are constantly acting "consciously" to achieve particular results. This view of activity is seen in Gamble and Porr's (2005:9) expression of the relationship between individual actions and the establishment of parameters: "Practice is both a reaction as well as action. The agent not only responds, he or she also actively manipulates the material environment, which, in turn, necessitates further actions and reactions." The cyclical relationship is not, however, always active; it also consists of a level of cognizable habituation that is as important a component of human cognition as is active creativity. Anthony Giddens addressed this problem from a psychological point of view, characterized by his articulation of "structuration theory," in which people are both active agents and subject to habituation. In his view, the concept of habituation (what he calls "recursive actions" and "routinization") "is vital to the psychological mechanisms whereby a sense of trust or ontological security is sustained in the daily activities of social life" (Giddens 1984:xxiii).

Although Giddens points out the observed duality of creativity and habituation, his reliance on a psychological distinction results in a highly static division between cognized and habituated actions. Instead, human cognition as it results in activity or "practice" is a constant interplay between creative input and habituation. Humans can choose to cognize their actions, but they cannot cognize all actions and retain enough creative potential to address the new situations that are a constant component of the landscape and social dynamics. Perpetual creativity would exhaust the cognitive mechanism and result in the inability to process new information effectively. Perpetual habituation would result in the stagnation of very basic patterns of action in which all change would be the result of nonhuman environmental shifts. Instead, human cognitive processes are segmented and sublimated to enable rapid adaptation to many different circumstances and environments. This segmentation and sublimation was probably first demonstrated deep in our human ancestral past, when *Homo erectus* migrated from initial homelands in Africa to other parts of Eurasia to successfully exploit new environments. The physical conditions of these new locations required high levels of active cognition to extract resources from new landscapes, capture new forms of prey, and avoid new competitors. The ability to simultaneously habituate some actions and creatively address others was essential in enabling humans to modify their environment as a contrast to what other species do, which is simply to accept or migrate from the surrounding environment.

The human cognitive mechanism is structured to accommodate both stasis and change. Basic information processing is a sequential and segmented process, as seen in a 1998 study by Alex Martin. His research showed that the human brain does not store information as complete packets but instead assembles information through networks. For example, information about the characteristics of an animal (such as its color, shape, size, and mode of locomotion) is stored in several different places and reassembled in the brain each time the information is needed. This is the process that enables an individual to quickly envision the difference between a kangaroo and a kangaroo rat even though they are similar in all qualities except size. The ability to network together these physical components of an animal also likely enabled a ready understanding of new animals as our ancestors moved to new locations: a quadruped such as an elk or a deer was, on the cognitive level, different from gazelles in only one or two aspects of color, with shape, size, and manner of locomotion quickly identifying the animal as something edible.

Other kinds of cognitive shortcuts exhibited by humans involve functions of memory. Research shows that an individual's memory can have an effect on preferences, even if the person does not remember having seen the choices before (Zajonc and Markus 1982). Like the ability to link together packets of information into as-needed networks, the ability to make use of subconscious memories probably had adaptive significance, as it allows for the use of prior experience without requiring active conscious decision making. Memories related to landscape perception were probably a very early activation of this subconscious process, enabling people to make repeated use of familiar surroundings as well as successfully migrate into unfamiliar ones (see Rockman and Steele 2003). Subsequent memory and habituation processes could govern a wide range of natural and cultural interactions, from resource extraction to social interactions, in a way that conserved energy and active thought.

Memory as a means of subconscious information storage is an important guide for the repetition of previously successful behaviors. It also is the way to efficiently make use of bad or negative experiences lacking specific causality (an example might what happens if you get sick after eating an unfamiliar food in a new restaurant; you would be inclined to avoid both the food and the restaurant even though only one of the components was likely to have caused the illness). Because humans have a very high diet breadth, filtering out the exact cause of a negative experience is not necessary; communication with other individuals enables people to pool their collective experiences, through which individuals filter the "real" cause of negative outcomes, which can then be avoided on a case-by-case basis.

Both conscious acts and habituated responses have an impact in the physical and material record, because in performing them humans leave a material trace. Brian Wansink's work on human interactions with food shows that habituation has a variety of physical consequences. In several studies evaluating the context, containers, and companionship of eating, Wansink and his colleagues have demonstrated that we eat more when food is abundant, when the portion size is greater, or when the serving dish is larger (Wansink 2006; Wansink, Painter, and North 2005; Wansink and Sobal 2007; see also Geier, Rozin, and Doros 2006). We can extrapolate this "mindless" factor to other daily actions with material culture and space, such as personal hygiene, trash deposition, listening to music, interaction with animals, and movement along familiar pathways. As Brian Loasby (2001:17) notes, "Reasoning is expensive in time and energy, and should therefore be used sparingly. . . . Civilisation advances by extending the number of important operations which we can perform without thinking about them." Humans have the capacity for a large number of cognitive shortcuts built in, leaving "expensive" reasoning time to be devoted to choices among similar objects, divergent tasks, goals of different time lengths, decisions about landscape modification, decisions about cooperation (or conflict) with others, and the subtleties of choosing among different types of foods, goods, and energy expenditure.

As a result, individual processes of cognition are heavily intertwined with deliberate decision making and actions according to parameters that are set but flexible. The maintenance of traditions, and the engagement with stasis as a deliberate activity, is an often-overlooked component of the archaeological record, as noted by Henry Glassie (2000:75) and Michael Smyth (1998:43). But stasis is the result of as much dynamic interaction and deliberate energy investment as change is: each act of eating the same thing, wearing the same thing, or doing the same thing constitutes an often-conscious validation of a social norm by individuals engaged with their surroundings. As summarized in figure 1.5, both cognition and habituation are part of the human energetic portfolio that allows for dynamic interaction between stasis and change. When prompted, people can and do cognize habituated actions, regardless of the length of time that the actions have been perceived as the "norm."

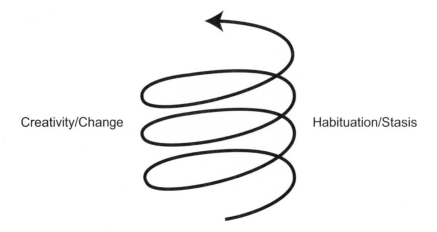

Creativity/Change   Habituation/Stasis

FIGURE 1.5. Upward spiral of the relationship between creative actions and habituation.

Multitasking

The process of multitasking, with which we are all familiar, may sound as if it is unique to modern times. In the contemporary context, the word often is used to convey unwanted pressures on production and a corresponding lack of time to accomplish tasks in a simple sequential or linear fashion. Archaeologists have utilized the idea of multitasking to convey similar ideas about the premodern era, in which multitasking is often regarded as the undesired but inevitable result of technological shifts or changes in sociopolitical organization. Interestingly, archaeologists studying gender were the first to utilize the concept of multitasking, viewing it as a survival strategy for women, who were disproportionately placed under time pressures by the addition of new production systems after the adoption of agriculture (e.g., Atalay and Hastorf 2006:315) or after the development of the state (Brumfiel 1995:113).

As a long-standing component of the human cognitive repertoire, however, multitasking can be viewed as a powerful explanatory concept for the development of economic strategies over time. Multitasking has two aspects: the ability to do more than one activity at a time, and the ability to adjust the timing and sequence of activities in response to changes brought by external or internal conditions (Burgess et al. 2000;

Salvucci and Taatgen 2008). The first component of multitasking, that of doing more than one thing at a time, is something that is within the cognitive capacity of most species. As a basic survival skill, animals can eat, mate, or fight while simultaneously being aware of their environments, and they have the capacity to start and stop activities when thresholds of risk and/or reward are perceived. The second component of task adjustment is the one that requires significant additional cognitive processes of memory and planning. Multitasking encompasses the ability to adjust to unplanned or unpredictable external inputs that interrupt the original task flow, requiring reprioritization, rescheduling, and the capacity to remember and reintegrate delayed intentions (Burgess et al. 2000).

Cognitive studies indicate that humans' use of task sequencing (the ability to simultaneously engage in more than one activity and the ability to rapidly switch from one activity to another) has an evolutionary trajectory that long predated the development of agriculture, sedentism, and social complexity. Multitasking would have been highly beneficial in our ancestors' earliest distinct stages when they competed with other species, many of which were better equipped physically for extracting nutrition from the surrounding landscape. Individuals had to calculate risk and reward at every moment of competition, bearing the consequences of error. The ability to remember sequences of events from the past (including those that were narrated as well as those that were directly experienced) and use them to plan actions in the future provided the cognitive edge over other species' superior physical capacities of tooth and claw. These cognitive skills were simultaneously applied to the other tasks that were undertaken only by humans, such as collecting fire, fuel, and raw materials for stone tool working.

Multitasking would have been essential as soon as toolmaking started, because the linear sequence of tool production and use would have been subject to frequent interruptions by unexpected appearances of danger or opportunity. Even the simplest interlinked activities, such as the collection of suitable raw material while in the process of collecting food, would have required the capacity to constantly reprioritize the tasks at hand as the individual moved around the landscape encountering prey, predators, and members of its own species. Multitasking also was an essential component of the dramatic increase in the human object and communication repertoire of the Upper Paleolithic beginning forty thousand to fifty thousand years ago. Ritual activities in the form of art, burials, and ornamentation would have constituted forms of energy expenditure that were added to daily and seasonal pursuits of food and shelter. Investments in the intangible arts such as storytelling, sacred knowledge, and music were likely to have emerged at this time as well, providing many more potential activities in which people could be engaged.

Even greater amounts of multitasking would have been demanded at the time of sedentism and agriculture, when the material record of human societies increased exponentially, starting ten thousand to twelve thousand years ago. The diverse archaeological record of storage facilities, processing tools, and landscape modifications associated with sedentism would have required not only increased attention to the learning and memory of tasks but also the ability to recover from an increasingly diverse array of potential interruptions to an individual's task flow. Larger numbers of people within a community necessarily resulted in an increasing frequency of disruptions at different time scales. Long-term processes were interrupted by births and deaths, while annual processes had seasonal fluctuations. Daily activities were subject to repeated, numerous small changes of venue, participants, technologies, ingredients, and purpose. In larger populations and under circumstances of increased communal activity, additional external factors included the need to sequence tasks around predictable events such as festivals and ritual events and unpredictable events such as warfare and natural disasters. The presence of leaders, who had an increasing role after the transition to social complexity, added another layer of activities into which individuals had to integrate their preexisting task strategies.

The addition of leadership was, however, merely the last stage of an extremely long process of increasing varieties of expression by individuals in the physical world. Social complexity, in the form of cities, states, and empires, adds different *amounts* of work but not different *types* of activity. In other words, a leader might extract tribute in the form of goods that were already being produced (such as textiles or grain) or work in the form of energy expenditure that was already familiar to individuals (such as lifting stones and dirt or making ornaments and tools). Individual actions through multitasking also were maintained even after the development of institutionalized political hierarchies. From those preexisting levels of individual cognitive capacity, elites were able to achieve large-scale outcomes through the appropriation of *some* food, the control of *some* goods, and the co-option of *some* work.

Assessing Individual Autonomy

Individual autonomous cognitive capacity is evident in the deep past of our species. For each person, the act of living left material traces that we can identify through the categories of health, identity, memory, kinship, time/temporality, space/spatiality, landscape, language, ritual, and the use of fire. Within each category, humans utilized a multitasking strategy to incorporate information, assess results, and identify the next course of action on the basis of prior experiences. Each of these categories identifies the way in which individual actions encompassed memory and planning, interspersed creativity and habituation, and addressed individual perceptions and anticipations of short-term, medium-term, and long-term outcomes.

Health and Illness

Human perceptions of health and well-being are a significant avenue through which to discuss the prehistory of ordinary people. Only the individual is capable of feeling pain, hunger, or intestinal distress from parasites or digestive ailments. Only the individual knows how much discomfort is being felt and how much knowledge of a condition to transmit to others: how much to complain, when, and to whom?

There are two ways that we can know about health in the past: archaeological remains and textual sources. Through skeletal studies, we know that people in the past suffered from a variety of ailments, including many long-term conditions such as arthritis and other degenerative diseases that leave their mark in human bones. Soft tissues and human waste, preserved under unusually dry conditions such as deserts or in exceptionally wet conditions such as bogs, inform us about intestinal diseases, respiratory ailments, and wounds. Analysis of such remains shows that ancient people took steps to alleviate their aches and consumed many substances that have demonstrated medicinal effects against parasites and other afflictions (e.g., Capasso 1998; Kliks 1975).

Food and medicine are both things that are taken in, and the conflation of food-as-medicine and medicine-as-food illustrates the continuum of things that are "eaten" as part of maintaining the body (e.g., Etkin 2006; Etkin and Ross 1982). The ingestion of food was part of a larger bodily relationship with the environment, in which "[d]iet was a synonym for a system of life. It included the practice of eating correctly, of choosing the best places for staying healthy and lengthening one's life, of bathing and washing correctly, of sleeping and staying awake, of expelling useless substances from one's body and of dealing with the ups and downs of the spirit" (Salas-Salvadó et al. 2006, citing Cruz 1997). The interrelated concepts of daily action and health would have been cognized by ancient individuals, materialized into actions as simple as snuggling into a warm garment against a perception of cold or as complicated as the creation and ingestion of elaborate concoctions to cure illness or achieve euphoria.

One sign of the preoccupation of ancient people with matters of health is that when writing was invented, medical subjects were one of the first things written about. Although we often view texts as the words of eminent past scholars who were educated enough to make pronouncements about health, it may be that we should think quite differently about the way in which knowledge made its way into the written word. As R. L. Miller (1991) has suggested for New Kingdom Egypt, texts about medical practices may be the record of folk knowledge and home remedies that were simply streamlined and codified by literate medical practitioners. Health, illness, and medical knowledge were actively cognized by individuals, even those at low levels of medical skill, who would make use of folk traditions to address maladies, injuries, and chronic ailments. People had much to discern about their bodies in the course of treatment; not only did they have to identify the ailment, they also had to assess the rationale for its causality and the relationship between that perceived causality and the recommended cure. Early texts from China, Mesopotamia, and Egypt indicate that there were two recognized, and often competing, systems of medicine: the magical/religious approach and the scientific/practical approach (e.g., Arnott 2002). A patient's treatment could therefore be influenced by the perceived source of the ailment, whether the ailment was thought to have a physical or spiritual origin, and whether the ailment was new or chronic.

Observations of medical behavior in the modern world provide surprising insights about how individuals cognize and mediate illnesses in ways that may have had a long evolutionary trajectory. As Lois Magner (1992:9) has observed, people today "may vacillate between alternative systems of medicine . . . perhaps relying on modern medicine for a broken arm and traditional medicine for arthritis." Within any treatment system, whether religious or practical, there are many potential prescriptions and various types of advice about the use of those prescriptions. This provides the patient with yet another range of decisions to make about the timing, quantity, strength, and frequency of applying the prescribed remedy. Every act of ingestion or application can be a moment of reflexive and deliberate acceptance, a factor seen in modern contexts when patients fail to take medicines at the prescribed dosages and times. Studies of patient behavior have shown that people often selectively adhere to prescriptive regimes as a way of expressing autonomy and that they act idiosyncratically to alter their drug regimes to avoid the acknowledgement of illness and dependency or to space dosages out around other activities (Benson and Britten 2002; Miller 1997).

Individuals' perceptions of health and illness are associated with their perceptions of the physical self and its changes. Some physical changes, such as the growth of a young child or the first subtle signs of arthritis, are incremental and barely noticed from day to day. Other processes of change, such as pregnancy and cycles of gastrointestinal illness, have a predictable duration whose progress could be discerned by both the individual and the surrounding group. The perception of what is appropriate for a given medical condition also changes as the person grows older: "Just as a child is not the same as a small adult, pharmacologically speaking, an elderly person is not just an older young adult" (Brody 2007: D9). As a result, the treatment for an ailment may vary depending on the age of the patient; young children are particularly susceptible to certain communicable diseases, but if they survive, they may carry lifetime immunity. Medicine's palliative effect in that case is to keep the patient comfortable and nourished until the disease takes its course. For adults in the prime of life, medical interventions may mostly consist of remedies for injury (for both sexes) and childbirth (for females). As individuals age past their prime years, they are subject to different kinds of ailments and chronic conditions, such as repetitive-motion injuries and the cumulative effects of smoky indoor environments on the lungs. In the contemporary world, elderly individuals tend to take a relatively high proportion of both prescription and over-the-counter remedies (Hayes et al. 2007), a phenomenon that we should factor in for the aging populations of the ancient world as well.

Identity

Identity is the result of reflexive realization, "an internal process by which one defines and integrates various aspects of the self" (Deaux 2000:222). Because the subject of identity in the social sciences has been treated with many different definitions, Margarita Díaz-Andreu and Sam Lucy urge scholars to focus on what identity does, rather than what it is. In their view, identity is performative, generative, and "inextricably linked to the sense of belonging" (Díaz-Andreu and Lucy 2005:1). Their use of adjectives such as *strategic, positional,* and *contingent* to describe the process of crafting and displaying identity further emphasizes the idea that identity is a process rather than a static condition.

Internally generated identity can be contrasted with the notion of social roles, which are publicly displayed and publicly enacted performances (Kleine, Kleine, and Kernan 1993). Whether or not one regards identity as indivisible, each individual does have multiple social roles (e.g., farmer, healer, mother, grandmother, basket weaver). Material goods are an essential component of both the performance and the symbolism of social roles. Objects can be picked up, gestured with, put on, taken off, gifted, and discarded, serving to facilitate the projection of roles undertaken by the individual in the course of a day, a year, or a lifetime. Roles are often simultaneously enacted (such as mother and teacher, or doctor and group leader), meaning that the multitasking component of cognition is applied to the performative aspects of identity in which different aspects of the social role are highlighted from one moment to the next.

Because the expression of identity is heavily dependent on material objects, archaeologists increasingly have focused on identity as a means of understanding the motivations and actions of ancient people. As Terence Turner (1980) has eloquently argued in "The Social Skin," the use of the physical world to create and display identity is as important in small groups as in larger ones. That observation allows us to reconcile identity formation as a social process with the archaeological record. In the premodern period, individuals could establish and demonstrate their

FIGURE 1.6. Even within small groups, individuals mark their identity through distinctions in hairstyle, ornaments, and the way of fastening clothes on the body.

identity only through the use of distinguishing marks or the possession of certain goods (fig. 1.6). Some of these marks of identity could be painful or costly: tattooing or taking up rigorous and time-consuming forms of ritual that demonstrated one's legitimate rights of participation in a group (Sosis 2003). The possession of markers of identity, particularly after the beginning of the Upper Paleolithic period, is demonstrated through the frequent recovery of ornaments and other distinctive physical objects that would have been worn by individuals.

The expression of identity can involve both distinctive and mundane goods, as we continue to experience today. Identity in the modern world is materialized through a great variety of means, including personalized documents of standard form such as a driver's license or a student identification card. Through these talismans, an individual today can demonstrate a right to entitlements without having a personal relationship with each and every institutional representative. In other words, a means of identification such as a driver's license, passport, or library card can serve to validate an individual's desire to operate a vehicle, cross a border, or borrow a book. Note, however, that materiality is still paramount, as the physical documents are required to demonstrate one's right to be in a certain place or to do certain things.

Identity making also is encompassed in everyday actions with ordinary goods, in which privately created and displayed expressions of self are part of the process of creating a "reflexive identity" (Smith 2007a:413). In private, material culture is used to craft expressions of self by the individual prior to the projection of that identity in public. In the contemporary world, objects that are generally utilized away from public display include underwear, hygiene products, and pharmaceuticals (Smith 2007a). The use of common, often disposable, goods as a component of reflexive identity further indicates the way in which material culture, thought, action, and cognition are interwoven in human daily activities.

Kinship

In addition to physical growth and development, each individual experiences social growth and development. Human babies cannot raise themselves; as a result, people grow up with some semblance of association with others. Throughout historical time, the family unit has been observed to be configured in a variety of ways, from households of extended kin in which all males are addressed as "father" to the extended family concept in which a household consists of siblings and their offspring to the nuclear family that is familiar in most Western contexts today. In every circumstance, individuals have an experience of those who raise them that results in a perception of intergenerational links. Although the creation of human offspring encompasses the universal reality of one male and one female, social interpretations can result in a reworking of what are otherwise recognized as the objective biological "facts" of reproduction. In a provocative article, Mary Weismantel (2004) asks the question "what is a reproductive act?" after citing the case of a Melanesian man who claimed parentage of a newborn even after years of physical separation from his wife. Weismantel's observations show that notions of kinship and beliefs in the supernatural often are culturally held to be more powerful explanations of human relationships than are physical acts.

Kinship (and the incorporation of individuals into a family network) is not merely the result of a concept of "belonging" but has significant material correlates. When a person dies, his or her material goods must be disposed of, a process through which descendants and other kin often claim a share. Humans also have developed mechanisms that augment or circumvent inheritance through kinship. Childless households that are socially challenged to identify their heirs may adopt individuals to serve in that capacity. In those cases, inheritance is not merely a matter of acquiring the goods of the deceased person but often has strong ritual connections as well—for example, in cultures where rituals for the dead were to be undertaken by the offspring. The adopted individual was responsible not only for his immediate beneficiary but also for the beneficiary's whole lineage: "[T]hrough one son the adopter rescues many ancestors" (Goody 1969:63). Adoption, like many other acts related to domestic life, is an intensely personal event that dramatically changes the involved individuals' perceptions of self, creating new reflexive identities as well as new social roles.

Time/Temporality

Long before the development of formal calendars and clocks, our species had expectations about the passage of time. Day and night were oscillations not only of light but also of warmth and danger. The moon provided monthly illumination available for nighttime hunting, movement, and storytelling. The seasons provided changes in weather that were accompanied by new food opportunities, with the predictable ripening of fruit, the migration of animals and birds, the laying of eggs, and the birth of vulnerable prey. Natural cycles enabled people to recognize changes over the course of a day, a year, or a lifetime, but those natural events still required some cognitive response. Moonlit nights stretch visibility on a few days a month, but the changes start and end at a different time each night. Cycles of climate would be perceived on the basis of past memories, preparing people for the reality that a series of mild winters would eventually be interspersed with a harsh one or that well-watered years eventually would be followed by a drought.

Closely tied to time is the concept of periodicity, the regularity of biological actions that are enveloped in culture. Sleep, like food intake and the elimination of bodily waste, is a biological imperative whose configuration is culturally constructed: the timing and surroundings of sleep are different from place to place, and some past adaptations today strike us as uncomfortable and awkward, such as the wooden pedestal headrests of ancient Egypt or the medieval European custom of sleeping in a half-seated position. Yet these fashions of sleep also constitute the relationship between habituated and creative actions, such that people can both adopt the prevailing cultural pattern and also affirm it with each daily action of slumber. Sleep closes the daily cycle of activities, whether the individual sleeps during the night (as is relatively natural for a diurnal species) or sleeps during the day as a consequence of work requirements or activity preferences that alter individual schedules.

People experience time on a variety of scales simultaneously: daily life, the individual life span, and the perception of the "supra-individual" time scale of social institutions (Giddens 1984:xxv; see also Gamble and Porr 2005:11). All time scales are internalized in acts of energy expenditure; moreover, people also know the difference between predictable and unpredictable time expenditures. Individuals use their memory and planning capacities to project the time needed for acts of predictable duration, such as the time needed to gather roots from a known source and afterwards pound, cook, and eat them. Acts of predictable duration also include the time needed to walk to a distant ridge to gather flint for toolmaking or the time needed to tell a long or a short version of a story. Acts of unpredictable duration such as hunting encompass a notion of time that is elastic, as the actions related to hunting come to a conclusion only when the desired prey has been captured or when the hunt has been called off. Humans can estimate time and predict events based on prior experience, such as the time that it should take for a wound to heal or how long it will take for a particular grove of trees to yield ripe fruit.

The implications of assessing time increased greatly with the development of sedentism and agriculture, when humans' material culture repertoire became more elaborate. The production of food through growing grain or tending animals certainly depended on the individual's capacity to recognize and work around the predictable seasonality of weather and the resultant rain, frost, heat, and cycles of insect life. The production of some craft items, such as pottery, requires attention to certain seasons of the year even when the raw materials, such as clay, are abundantly available year-round (Peacock 1982). In other cases, seasonality affected the timing of work such as the production of stone tools, whose raw materials were easily available but the collection of which might depend on cycles of other seasonally dictated work, such as hunting, herding, or fishing (as Kardulias [1992, 2003] has examined for the continued use of stone in the Bronze Age of Greece). Individual perceptions of seasonality and weather thus conditioned how individuals acted to supply basic needs, interact with others, and direct their energies to short-term, medium-term, and long-term outcomes.

Closely related to the concept of time is the process of aging. Numerous physical modifications accompany the transition from youth to old age, including the increase of strength in the juvenile phase and the waning of strength as adults mature. In the absence of mirrors, people may not have recognized the cumulative changes in their own bodies, but the appearance of new children and the death of the elderly would have reinforced a notion of a generational passage of time. Aging does more than change one's physical capacity; it can also bring changes in worldview, as Laura Ahearn's (2001b) ethnographic research in Nepal has suggested. She noted that young people were more likely to be optimistic about individual capacity to craft a particular course in life, while older people were more likely to view fate as the primary determinant of consequences. These shifts included changes in experience, which would have included experiences of gain (in property, skill, social standing, age grade) and well as experiences of loss (death of family members, loss of prized possessions) that culminate in a significantly different worldview as a component of aging.

Space/Spatiality

The human use of space can be divided into two realms: the "inside" and the "outside." The inside refers to the interior of structures and enclosures used as dwellings, while the outside refers to the area outside the hearth and sleeping place, expanding in its boundaries to the farthest horizon. The development of a sense of place as a gradation of "inside" to "outside" indicates the extent to which individuals use their surroundings both as a conscious engagement of the cognitive process and as the subconscious habituation of behavioral patterns.

The space of the "inside," although most closely associated in the present day with constructed houses and other buildings, probably had long-ago manifestations in the human ancestral repertoire. Inside spaces provide opportunities for individuals to shelter themselves from public view, a notion of privacy that reinforces bonds of kinship and inclusion through sex, nurturing, and sharing food. An inside space also enables individuals to decide what possessions and activities will be shown to others, giving visual control over mundane actions such as the storage, cooking, and serving of food as well as the selective display of distinctive objects and features. Objects in interior spaces also can be moved and rearranged to create new configurations that provide the setting for identity construction and social interactions (Garvey 2001; Schiffer and Miller 1999:23–25).

Lynn Meskell (1998:237) observes that while archaeologists may perceive social settings as static, "individuals' actions are highly variable, despite being in a spatial setting which presents only one clear scenario. For example, a domestic context may be the site of industry and manufacture, the housing of farm animals, or preparation of the dead, and may be the stage for all of these activities over a period of time." The longevity of archaeological sites, many of which were occupied for hundreds of years or more, shows the extent to which memory and meaning were invested into settlements from one generation to the next. This notion of continuity was encoded into the built environment when people first started constructing shelters starting around fifteen thousand years ago. Conscious attempts to link one generation to another are evident in the incorporation of selected burials (usually of children under house floors) or the reuse of building materials (e.g., Bradley 2005). Human investments in settlement continuity would be periodically balanced by the drama of abandonment and loss, whether through fire, raiding, or the fissioning of social groups.

Individuals also make assessments of continuity and change in both interior and exterior spaces. Routine and predictable phenomena such as seasonal changes are met with habituated responses, while novel events are treated with cognitive creativity when circumstances change. With the local surroundings being the source of daily provisions, our most ancient ancestors would have perceived the landscape with considerable sophistication, learning its seasons and products with minute interest. Over time, their use of the landscape included manipulations to increase the quantity and quality of particularly desired items, at first through small-scale processes such as diverting streams or selective control through fire and later through the planting of crops and husbanding of animals. The active manipulation of the environment had a strong cognitive impact, such that in "consuming the cultivated or wild products of the land people assert their control over a space through their direct embodiment of it" (Lewis 2007:208). In recent centuries, we have developed very powerful means of controlling our surroundings, but this does not mean that we "know" the landscape any better than our ancestors of a million years ago knew it.

In addition to using distinctive natural features as landmarks for navigation and resource collection, humans would have added physical markers as well as social markers such as place-names. Physical markers could be relatively subtle, ephemeral, and visible only at close range: for example, a branch cut by a sharp tool or a pile of stones made by a human hand. Other physical markers—such as handholds and stairsteps up steep cliffs or rope assists tied along a riverbank—incorporated practical elements along with encoded memory. Markers also could include rapid, singular events that leave a long-term imprint on the landscape, such as a burnt patch of forest transformed over the span of a lifetime from a stand of charred stumps to a meadow of vibrant wildflowers and new tree growth. As evidence of human activity, these markers would have been just as visible and meaningful to local inhabitants as the more labor-intensive constructions that we often think of as "monuments." Indeed, the value of tombs, mounds, and other architecture would have emanated from a long-term human propensity to notice and encode landscape features with information and meaning. Habituation in a particular landscape, along with creative assessments and modifications of that landscape, was part of the cognitive apparatus of individuals who selectively saw, talked about, and modified their surroundings.

Gender

The realities of male and female physiology would have been readily perceived by our most ancient ancestors. Especially prior to the development of constructed shelters and clothing, there would have been few mysteries about the physical changes related to puberty, pregnancy, and sex-related aging processes. The biological components of human life appear, however, to have profound cultural consequences, in which human cognition is applied to biological realities resulting in perceptions of identity, roles, and behavior. The construction of gender is the result of the way in which biology is expressed in social terms, the "constitutive element of social relationships based on perceived differences between the sexes . . . and a primary way of signifying relationships of power" (Scott 1986:1067).

The relationship between women and men in deep prehistory is difficult to discern, but we do know that there were changes in male and female physiology over time. Our earliest preancestors the australopithecines had significant sexual dimorphism, with males being about twice the body size of females (Toth and Schick 2005:57). By the time of early *Homo* around 1.8 million years ago, the body sizes of males and females were much closer to being the same (Klein 2009). The evidence for significant improvements in tool-making capacity and other forms of cultural investment at this same time suggests that this might have been the era when "gender" began to be expressed in social configurations. As Marshall Sahlins observed in his influential *Stone Age Economics* (1972:79), the most basic economic unit consists of a man and woman who contribute differential types of energy transfer to the support of offspring and to the creation of a household that can perform all of the customary social functions. This "economic Adam and Eve" was the basis for both cognized and habituated responses in which each generation articulated for itself the most appropriate way to run a household and perform tasks.

The idea of gender as a social construct provides parameters for behavior that go well beyond simple economic activities. Ethnographic studies show that males and females often operate within different social realms and that gender configurations affect how individuals perceive even "objective" aspects such as their physical surroundings. From her work in the coastal Chiapas area of Mexico, anthropologist Janine Gasco has observed that women and men tend to have different knowledge of the surrounding environment based primarily on the extent to which they travel outside the home. Even in the twenty-first century, there are many village women who live only a few miles from the coast and yet have never seen the ocean (J. Gasco, pers. comm. 2005). This may seem incredible in terms of the relative facility of visiting a natural phenomenon that is literally within walking distance, but it also tells us something about the effects of gendered knowledge domains that may have had a long evolutionary trajectory.

Although patterns of gender appear to be static within cultures, both the creation and the habituation of such patterns are activated through individual actions. Historical documents show how gender relationships can change over time, in which individuals take up new roles within stereotyped expectations. Both males and females can make use of social mechanisms that facilitate the individual's ability to affirm, negate, or step out of their gender roles, whether permanently or temporarily. Environmental factors are one component of these social mechanisms, such as when a spouse dies in a traditional society, leaving a man to raise children or a woman to become the principal farmer or wage earner. Idiosyncratic family situations also provide circumstances in which expected gender roles are reversed, as seen in observations of traditional Inuit lifeways in the Canadian north, in which women would hunt and men would cook and sew under circumstances in which families were either temporarily or permanently deprived of the opposite sex (Billson and Mancini 2007:43–46). Still other forms of gender reversal—such as shamanism and trance-related religious activity in which the individual takes on the persona of the opposite gender for a limited time—are situational and reversible.

Language

Language is made of words organized through grammar. Words are rendered meaningful through mutual understanding, and grammar is the socially recognized structure of interaction through utterance and interpretation. Yet the individual is the one who chooses exactly how and when to say the words that constitute a speech event. Every act of communication either reinforces the "rules" of grammar or constitutes an experiment by an individual speaker to bend the rules towards new realms of understanding. Acts of speech also can introduce new words, which become part of the social vocabulary when individuals use the new word.

Historical attempts to constrain language illustrate the extent to which language use is not a matter of exclusive elite dictates but is created and sustained from the "bottom up." In her perceptive article "Language and Agency," Laura Ahearn (2001a) has discussed the way in which language does not simply reinforce the existence of a certain social structure but actually creates it through the deliberate utterances of individuals. Arguing for a "practice theory of meaning constraint," she voices the strong statement that individuals "construct and constrain—rather than passively receive—interpretations" (Ahearn 2001a:112). Even in very authoritarian modern regimes, languages are virtually impossible to eradicate because they are practiced at the level of the individual; examples of failed attempts to regulate language can be found in the British suppression of Gaelic in Ireland and restrictions on the Tibetan language within the boundaries of modern-day China. Prescriptions about language usually fare no better than prohibitions; for example, the Academie Française attempts to control developments in the French language by proposing francophone alternatives to technical terms from other languages. One speaker at a time, however, the choice is made, rendering the use of imported words such as *e-mail* universal and the academy's proposed neologism *courriel* instantly obsolete.

As in the French example, the social parameters of acceptability are both formulated and changed in the course of many individual actions. In twentieth-century America, very public norms of speech have been codified for groups such as film and television audiences, but the configuration of what constitutes "polite conversation" has been continually redefined. Although one could not say "damn" on television fifty years ago, that phrase—and much more!—is widely heard in today's broadcasts (Kaye and Sapolsky 2001). As those authors observe, what used to be considered "off-color" language has become increasingly common in everyday speech (Kaye and Sapolsky 2001:305). The mismatch between official language and language in practice was addressed not by prohibitions on ordinary speech but by changing the codification of officially recognized discourse to more closely approximate the boundaries of socially accepted use.

Incremental acts of speech define the communication process. Todd Jones (2005) has examined the way that language speakers utilize individual utterances to create perspectives of shared understanding. His article, affectionately titled "How Many New Yorkers Need to Like Bagels Before You Can Say 'New Yorkers Like Bagels?'" examines how the collective effect of individual statements results in generally accepted understandings of the world, even when the phenomenon in question is rarely observed by either the speaker or the listener. Listeners as well as speakers

actively participate in conversations by evaluating, and sometimes object-
ing to, blanket statements. Listeners tolerate deviation and exaggeration
when speakers generalize with words such as *some* or *all*, with both the
speaker and the listener understanding that a projection is taking place
beyond the observed or remembered event.

Jones also notes that individual utterances change the perception of
the world through the way that items are named and talked about. As an
example, he notes that when people talk about a Band-Aid, they colloquially mean a bandage and not necessarily the Johnson & Johnson branded
product. The collective effect of talking this way, however, brings new
linguistic conventions into place because the use of a word such as *Band-
Aid* as a shortcut for comprehension becomes reinforced each time a
speaker utilizes the term: "Hearing few corrections, people come to
believe that listeners have become *completely* tolerant of speakers using
words or phrases to describe situations other than ones that prior convention dictates these phrases refer to. At this point, a new convention has
developed and these phrases now have new meanings in addition [to] (or
aside from) their original ones" (Jones 2005:290, emphasis in original).
In language, therefore, individual utterances both provide the dynamic
interaction of a particular speech event and contribute to the collective
mode of expression and parameters of understood intent.

The frequency of speech events means that language is "embedded in
the concrete activities of day-to-day life" (Giddens 1984:xvi). In reflecting
language as a component of daily existence and the interactions with the
physical environment as well as with other people, the individual chooses
how and what to say, how loudly, and in what context. The role of context
is very powerful in conditioning what can be said, as anyone will recognize who has told a story about the same event to a child, to a spouse, or to
an elderly relative. Language capacity also is internalized by individuals:
unvoiced internal communications enable individuals to craft identity in
the reflexive private realm of meaning and memory. Things unsaid also
permit individuals to contemplate and plan future actions.

Technology

The control of even the simplest technologies is a way in which we see how
individuals as autonomous cognitive entities make quotidian decisions to

selectively modify the world around them. Fire is a particularly good example of the type of technology that any individual can master competently, with results on a variety of spatial and temporal scales. Fire represents a one-way transformation of physical materials whose effects can be readily understood by all: food cannot be uncooked, pottery cannot be unfired, fire-treated stone cannot be turned back into its preheated state. Fire first became controlled by humans perhaps as early as four hundred thousand years ago, although we do not know how much control was exhibited or when our ancestors could reliably produce their own fire instead of scavenging burning materials from natural sources such as lightning-induced fires (Weiner et al. 1998). The resultant control of fire is a marker of human modification of the environment, whether captured in the friendly confines of the hearth or unleashed on a swath of wilderness.

Fire represents a powerful means of transforming the natural and cultural worlds. In Madagascar today, young rural children wander the hillsides and set fires at their whim in a manner that is socially sanctioned and fully in keeping with the way that landscapes have been modified for centuries. Fire was an important component of many anthropogenic landscapes in the past and is credited with forming what we now think of as "natural" landscapes in many regions of the world, most notably Australia (Bowman 1998; for the Indian subcontinent, see Possehl 2002:43). In addition to serving as a routine means of landscape modification, fire is a highly democratic mode of transformation and can be a way for physically disadvantaged or weak persons to control a mechanism of considerable destruction.

Fire in the archaeological record is an unambiguous scene of intentional destruction—a cheap, effective, and dramatic way of waging war. Fire is less risky to the perpetrator than is hand-to-hand combat, and it often cannot be fought by even the best-organized enemy, who instead has to acquiesce to the phenomenon. A fire can quickly ruin cropland, stored grains, houses, corrals, textiles, baskets, and other products of human energy investment and often leads to the loss of human and animal life as well. The aftermath of fire is long lasting, providing thick lenses of ash and charcoal in the archaeological record that lead us to imagine the scenes of destruction and lamentation that occurred. We can see in the burned archaeological record of major sites such as Hazor in Israel, Pylos in Greece, Ebla in Syria, Fishborne in Britain, and Kot

Diji in Pakistan that massive fires were often a prelude to the abandonment of previously thriving places.

The irreversibility and power of fire as a practical and symbolic tool were within the reach of each individual and provided a significant potential for transformation. Richard Bradley (2005:69) notes that some European Neolithic structures were destroyed through fire, often prior to their rebuilding on the same ground plan. The "New Fire" ceremonies of ethnohistorically documented societies in Mexico and the American Southwest similarly record the process of cleansing and renewal symbolized in periodic episodes of burning (James 2000). On a more mundane level, fire and its associated heat can materialize human acts of planning for the future, whether in the form of smoked meats and fish preserved for later consumption or as part of the process of mummification and preservation of the human corpse to activate concepts of an afterlife (e.g., Pretty and Calder 1980:195; Zimmerman 1980:127).

Memory

Individuals hold memories that are unique to their experience of the world and surroundings, even when events are attended by many others. Memories held by individuals are selectively activated in the practice of both routine actions and singular moments of ritual that serve to modify surroundings one person and one action at a time. The dynamic aspect of memory selection and revival means that the "past as memory does not just exist as it was. The past has to be recalled: memory is the act of recalling from the viewpoint of a subsequent time" in which the future is also implicated (Shanks 1997:88). What we might colloquially identify as "collective memory" or the history of communal events is actually the articulation of many individual memories that are shared through language and communication.

Memory is closely linked to learning, as accumulated knowledge can be capitalized on only through the use of memory. The manufacture of tools, for example, is a process that makes use of a variety of learned aspects, including the location of raw materials, the methods by which the raw materials will be worked by human hands, and the uses to which the tool will be put. C. Karlin and M. Julien (1994:152) have described the process of making tools as one that involves a combination of memory, medium-term retention of information, and the presence of a suitable material on which energy will be expended. Repeated applications of energy investment also result in increased skill, so that memory is not only a component of making an object but also a dynamic part of the creation experience in which "practice makes perfect" (see Flood, Scott, and Ewy 1984).

Memory activation involves different time scales in a elaborate process that incorporates aspects of multitasking such as flexibility and choosing among options within task sequences that include both linear processing steps and steps that are inserted idiosyncratically. As Michael Hasselmo and Chantal Stern (2006) have discussed, humans have multiple memory systems, which include short-term "working memory" as well as long-term recollection. Working memory is further divided into two types: that which focuses on novel circumstances and a slightly different kind of process that is activated when familiar circumstances are encountered. These two forms of working memory eventually feed into systems of long-term memory, with the novel-circumstance aspect perhaps the more important of the two; in other words, human active short-term memory filters and facilitates the creation of long-term memory.

We can take the selective activation and dismissal of memory as another proxy for the relationship between habituation and cognition. Memories can (for the most part) be dormant until activated; we cannot simultaneously entertain all past memories. While some dramatic memories (such as extreme physical or mental duress) are difficult to suppress and remain in the forefront of cognition, most memories, even distinct ones, are not actively recalled as a continual focus of day-to-day life. Significant life events can be recounted in detail, whether they are programmed events and rites of passage, such as marriage and graduation, or the novel and unpredicted circumstances of extreme surprise, anger, injury, or delight. Even those clear memories, however, require particular circumstances to be activated. The same is true of habituated actions, whose cognitive effect is kept in the subconscious until activated by a specific thought process or physical event.

Because memory making and memory recall often involve physical objects, archaeologists have become increasingly focused on memory as an emotion that can be elicited from the material record. Ethnographic and historical studies show that memory is encoded not only in special-purpose mnemonic devices (such as writing and rock art) but also in the everyday and ordinary objects used by individuals. In handling those objects, individuals recall specific episodes of acquisition, prior use, and possession. The creation and activation of these memories are flexible and situational, with individuals determining which objects will be handled and which will be put away to avoid the trigger of memory, an active process in which objects such as heirlooms are "defined better by what they do, rather than by what they are" (Lillios 1999:244; see also Van Dyke and Alcock 2003). Memory making also is an exercise that bridges the idiosyncratic elements of individual recall with the social realm in which those memories are activated (A. Jones 2007:41).

Ritual

Ritual activities are another means by which individuals engage in autonomous cognitive actions. Ritual is a "culturally constructed system of symbolic communication . . . constituted of patterned and ordered sequences of words and acts, often expressed by multiple media" (such as song along with dance; Tambiah 1985:128). Douglas Marshall (2002:360) adds that "[t]he practice of ritual produces two primary outcomes—Belief and Belonging." Both belief and belonging are embodied by the participating individual, who engages in both cognized and habituated actions through the use of material culture and language. Each of these aspects requires deliberate action by people who consciously select the objects and words that will be used at any particular moment. Although ritual events often are performed within a community, the memories of the event are held at the individual level, resulting in variability in the experience of even "shared" ritual traditions (Inomata and Coben 2006:23–25).

Ritual need not be religious in its configuration, as ritual is a performative act of belief with secular as well as sacred connotations. As Richard Bradley (2005) has observed, our modern distinction between ritual and domestic life is a relatively recent analytical construct. He advocates the concept of "ritualization" as a process by which the continual performance of symbolic activities becomes part of everyday life (Bradley 2005:33). Viewed in this way, secular rituals enacted upon material culture can be defined as the process undertaken to secure a successful outcome for a subsequent activity. Thus, hunting rituals may involve knowledge about magical or spiritual properties of animals, as well as specific knowledge about animal behavior and situational knowledge about prey location and weather conditions. Cooking involves a literal recipe that combines linear steps of processing with nonlinear idiosyncratic actions to achieve a desired result. But both hunting and cooking can be further ritualized by the use of nonphysical elements such as song, gestures, incantations, and even simple utterances. Small threshold events in the course of a lifetime are all potentially the targets of ritualization as well, even something as simple as trying a new food, experimenting with a new hairstyle, or adopting a new technology.

Ritual and memory are strongly intertwined, but the relationship of memory to ritual is not always prescriptive and linear. Individual responses to surroundings or events can include a refusal to engage in ritual behavior, or a temporary or permanent recategorization of place for other activities; as Lynn Meskell (1998:238) notes, "even ritualized space may have been the site of varied and often mundane activities." For example, a grand room might be the seat of power for a royal authority, a venue of deference for a courtier, and a venue of redress for a petitioner but only a big space to clean from the perspective of a servant. Even "being there" can have different meanings depending on the time of day or the season of the year, with the implications and intent understood by the individual who moves her feet to be present. Such actions can be difficult to see in the archaeological record but may be discerned when special-purpose areas contain domestic debris or selectively fall into disrepair (see, e.g., Kemp 1989:143).

When presented with an external stimulus, individuals use memory to identify the correct response, which may include a ritual or symbolic component. Individuals' memories are further drawn upon in the selection of the steps of the ritual, the specific place and time for its enactment, and the objects to be obtained and utilized in the performance of the ritual. Memory also solidifies the importance of an event as individuals remember their participation over the course of a lifetime. A person may undergo a particular ritual only once, but by being in the vicinity of the ritual enacted by others, individuals encode their own performance as having both a past and a future. They anticipate the ritual on the basis of the memory of others' actions and communication, and they remember the event long after their own personal experience of the ritual is over.

Ritual activities are strongly encoded with spatiality, as they can transform ordinary places and actions into sacred ones. Pilgrimage as a form of energy expenditure usually involves arduous treks across long distances for symbolic effect. But the actions taken at the final destination can often be mundane and reminiscent of ordinary domestic processes. Circumambulation or bathing, undertaken at the destination of pilgrimage, take on a ritual quality not because of the action but because of the surroundings. Studies of historically documented ancient societies such as the Mayas, Greeks, and Romans indicate the extent to which landscape peculiarities, such as caves and other anomalies, were the focus of attention in a landscape that could be simultaneously economic, social, political, and ritual in scope (e.g., Brady 1997; Brady and Ashmore 1999; Brady and Prufer 1999). Pilgrims can even make a spiritual place out of an otherwise indistinct location, in which "the act of encircling the sacred goal ritually defines a sacred space as well as marking the fact that the pilgrim has arrived there" (Coleman and Elsner 1995:29c; see also Fogelin 2004; Mack 2004).

Pilgrimage and other landscape rituals often entail the use of material goods that are deposited at or collected from specific points in the landscape. Each of these acts of energy expenditure, focused on particular objects, requires the active participation of a person who internalizes the meaning of each act of collection or placement. Although pilgrims can travel as a group, the decision to embark on a long and difficult journey far from home is one that is endured by each individual differently and with a different sense of purpose and reward. Pilgrimages involve food, goods, and work but in a manner that makes them different from the quotidian experience, often encompassing privations and exertion as part of the transformative experience. Writer Hilaire Belloc (1902:22–23) reflected on the pilgrim's departure as a moment in which the present and the future achieve a poignant duality: "So far I had been at home, and I was now poring upon the last familiar thing before I ventured into the high woods and began my experience."

Value and Worth

The simplest economic interaction is the exchange of objects from one person to another. Value and worth in common everyday transactions (particularly in the days before standardized currency and fixed prices) required people to calculate the worth of goods or services at a specific time or place and then persuade others to act upon those calculations. What was the relative value of expending the energy to make a hand ax instead of simply striking a blow to a stone to make a sharp edge? What was the "worth" in exchange value of a projectile point made of locally available stone compared to a similar point made from sources a thousand kilometers away? What was the "value" of a painted pot compared to an unpainted one? How much "payment" was due to a healer if the ailing person died? Under what circumstances were two small deer haunches equivalent to, or even better than, one large deer haunch from a hunt?

Closely linked to the concept of value and worth is the perception of wrong and redress. Established systems of behavior and expectations are exhibited by many nonhuman mammals, with consequences that can be predicted by all of the agents in a transaction, such as when a low-ranking individual attempts to take over a food resource. Our human ancestors' cognitive systems of expectations, combined with memory and the capacity for future planning, enabled them to establish hierarchy and rank even in small groups. The early use of writing to express protective and punitive curses indicates that language was probably used for these types of individually directed actions long before the advent of literacy. And it was the individual who materialized these specific requests by wearing charms and amulets, with the possibility of removing them instantly upon cure or vindication.

The study of technological change enables us to investigate how ancient people estimated value and worth as a material analog to the idea of language tolerance outlined above by Todd Jones. Michael Brian Schiffer's (2005) "invention cascade" model of technological change points to the ways in which the adoption of new technologies is not simply a matter of the invention of an objectively "better" apparatus, in the sense of a product or object that can accomplish a task more efficiently. Utilizing the abundant historical record of modern material culture such as radios, electric cars, and lighthouses, Schiffer examines the many incremental steps of development and invention and shows that each step involves factors of unexpected as well as intentional consequences. By carefully unpacking the many decisions and inputs that move an item from invention to adoption, he dismantles the idea of a simple functionalist "advance" in human

FIGURE 1.7. The relationships among food, goods, and work.

technologies. Schiffer's work demonstrates that adoption occurs not only on the autonomous cognitive level one individual at a time but also on a continuum of stepwise development in which many individuals' actions contribute to the long-term and nonlinear trajectory of technological change.

The Material Signatures of Autonomous Cognition

Humans express their autonomous cognitive capacities through the use of memory, language, and notions of worth and value. These capacities, along with specific skill sets such as the control of fire, enable individuals to effect changes on the landscape and within social groups. Through creative approaches alternating with habituation, people interact with each other, extract desired resources from their physical surroundings, and define and modify social parameters. These interactions result in large-scale patterns but have individual decision making as their point of origination. In the remainder of this book, I utilize three basic components of daily life—food, goods, and work—to examine and demonstrate how individuals make use of autonomous cognitive processes that leave their trace in the material record (fig. 1.7).

Individuals experience and interact with food as a vital part of being alive. Food is the essential source of human energy, and human bodies need food on a regular basis. Our species is physiologically adapted to be omnivores and to eat a wide variety of potential foodstuffs. However, people consume a smaller range of things that are biologically edible, enabling us to examine how the concept of food is placed within shared cultural understandings of what is "good to eat." Food preferences are further modified by other actions, such as the types of preparation that are thought best and the relative suitability of a particular food at any given time for persons of a particular sex, age, state of health, or level of social experience. Wholly within the individual's control, however, is the mode of consumption itself: how big a bite, whether to finish all of a portion of food, and indeed whether to eat at all.

Beverages provide a good example of the way in which individual actions constitute the basis of large-scale cultural patterns. In the past five hundred years, the world of beverages has been revolutionized by the widespread availability of a variety of mild stimulants in the form of caffeinated beverages such as coffee, tea, and cola drinks. Our understanding of the impact of this phenomenon is calculated at the global scale in terms of the acquisition of raw materials and the distribution of finished products (e.g., Standage 2005). However, we should remember that tea and coffee and cola are drunk not by systems but by individuals who elect to acquire a particular drink and consume it, one cup at a time.

Objects constitute another realm in which individuals engage in autonomous decision making in a process that involves both active cognition and conscious habituation. As early as 2.5 million years ago, our ancestors were not content with the natural configuration of stones but undertook careful steps of preparation to create artifacts from suitable materials. The process of modifying the portable natural realm was intimately linked with the development of an increasingly sophisticated human cognitive repertoire. A single object can have a variety of meanings depending on the context in which it is used, in which the value of the object is enhanced both by energy expenditure (for example, through decoration) and through language, which is used to convey sentiments of propriety, ownership, memory, and prescriptions for use. People actively seek to acquire goods through the expenditure of energy (either directly from the natural environment or indirectly through gifts and exchange); they then utilize those goods selectively within social parameters that are reinforced through the acts of acquisition, use, display, and discard.

Finally, individuals expend energy when they interact with the physical world to procure the food and goods that fulfill daily needs for social and biological survival. Although we tend to think of "work" colloquially as something that is directed and controlled (or at least coordinated) by others, in this book I use a broad definition of work as the transfer of energy and time. In this way, "work" is not just the fact of energy expenditure directed by others but also includes activities that are self-directed. Individuals engage in work towards a number of outcomes, including the application of energy to raw materials for direct use, such as the preparation of food for eating. Work also is the expenditure of energy to the physical environment in the acquisition, use, display, and discard of goods to achieve some desired physical or psychological effect. In expending energy, the individual engages in the spiral of both cognized and habituated actions. These actions are not merely the result of a linear process of cause and effect within the natural world; the individual also weighs the potential effects on various time scales in a process of multitasking that is a distinct characteristic of our species.

Summary

The long trajectory of human social experience has underwritten the remarkable transition to the modern world: in the past six thousand years, humans have moved from a universal experience of simple societies to one in which complex societies have increasingly dominated the landscape. This transition was not accompanied by any change in human cognitive or physiological capacities. Instead, the shared common denominator of both simple and complex societies is autonomous cognitive capacity on the part of individuals.

Archaeological evidence gives us numerous opportunities to examine the individual in a dynamic mode at every level of sociopolitical complexity, from the earliest hunter-gatherers to the most extensive states and empires. The accidental deaths of people such as the ones we have named Ötzi, the Huldremose Woman, and Kwäday Dän Ts'ìnchí permit us to have an unvarnished glimpse of ordinary people conducting their daily business. By expanding our view to include the ways in which each person in the past acted deliberately, we can provide several important contributions to archaeological theory and to the understanding of our human developmental trajectory. First, both change and stasis were deliberately undertaken by individuals acting upon the landscape. They created, used, exchanged, and discarded material goods that had both practical and symbolic components. Second, the development of individual decision-making capacities at the cognitive level was brought into existence by dynamic human-human and human-environmental interactions. Although human and animal groups have a definite "leader" for some components of activity, most interactions are actualized by the individual in accordance with predictive capacities that do not rely on elite dictates. Finally, the individual capacity for action and decision making predated, and was the necessary underpinning for, the development of social complexity. Under conditions of increasing population size and its frequent corollary—the development of chiefdoms, states, and empires—individuals augmented their multitasking to accommodate additional configurations such as taxation, labor tribute, and new rules of behavior.

CHAPTER 2

Individuals and Food

YOU AND I AND THE other six billion inhabitants of the planet seek to eat daily, because food is the essential generator of the energy that humans expend on any subsequent type of activity. Most food items are prepared in some manner prior to their consumption, resulting in repeated deliberate decisions about the amount of time and work that will be expended. The protocols of cooking, serving, and eating are actively generated and reaffirmed with each act of consumption, with implications for both small-scale household economies and the largest global transactions of food.

Individuals are the ones who make decisions about the components and performance of any meal: what animal to hunt that day, what field to plant and with what crop, what plants to weed and sow, how much of a stored food to retrieve for preparation, which pot to use to cook or brew the food, which serving dish to place the food in, and whom to serve first. In this decision-making process, there is a close connection between food preparation and the household repertoire of goods. Using ordinary tools and familiar household routines, the provider of food purposefully integrates raw materials, objects, and energy expenditure for the production of a meal.

Food is a particularly rich realm for understanding the relationship between creativity and habituation as activities that are interwoven through the process of multitasking. Food preparation requires a reference to memory (of how to prepare the food) and planning (the ingredients at hand and how this particular meal will be prepared). Multitasking in food processing is necessitated by the potential for constant shifts in the availability of ingredients, fuel, and storage capacity for raw and prepared food. Shifts in the availability of some ingredients can be compensated for by the availability of others, and changes in fuel can be substituted by adopting different strategies of preparation.

Cognitive scientists frequently use the phenomenon of cooking to show how the concept of multitasking involves both individually generated actions and external factors that are only partially predictable. In their ·

article analyzing the mental processes sustained in multitasking, David Salvucci and Niels Taatgen (2008) provide the illustration of a meal of fish, pasta, and cake as a process that integrates different types of foods and different precooking tasks but with the use of the same culinary equipment. While some operations can proceed in parallel (for example, boiling the pasta and baking the cake), other activities must be sequenced (the cook cannot simultaneously open the oven and stir the cake batter). The need for sequencing also is affected by external inputs of predictable duration such as the time required for the oven to heat as well as external inputs of unpredictable timing and duration such as new orders coming into the kitchen (or, in a domestic scenario, the demands of others in the household). These shifts can be undertaken from one meal to the next, but the processes of multitasking often characterize each meal-in-the-making, as emphasized by Sonya Atalay and Christine Hastorf (2006).

Aspects of time and temporality also are a component of the multitasking of food preparation. Unlike toolmaking or other activities, food preparation is not an event that can be indefinitely postponed. People need to eat daily, and some individuals, particularly children, thrive on frequent meals. Different types of food preparation, such as baking, stewing, fermenting, and roasting, can make use of the same suite of ingredients but require different levels of energy input, different types of preparation equipment and features, and different degrees of attention in the course of the preparation process. Some types of food (such as stews) can be easily interrupted and restarted, but other types of preparation (such as baking and roasting) require precise monitoring and a linear sequence of production.

Changes in food preparation strategies have implications for all other components of individual and household activities. For example, the simple decision to make grain into beer, bread, or porridge sets into motion a sequence of activities that have varying levels of time and energy expenditure. Bread can be made relatively quickly but has high fuel and labor costs in grinding and baking. Beer can be made with little energy expenditure by putting grain and water in a pot to ferment, but it requires time to become a consumable product. Porridge is perhaps the least labor-intensive mode of preparation, but it requires the infrastructure of cooking vessels, fuel, and a hearth. Once ingredients and fuel are secured, the timeline of food preparation has a relative degree of certainty and predictability. Food preparation can be rapid and can provide almost immediate gratification to the preparer and to the eater, but it can also be a lengthy process that requires the acknowledgment of delayed gratification by both the preparer and the consumer of food.

The need to plan and to compensate for unplanned circumstances is necessitated by shifts in resource availability. Raw ingredients have a seasonality experienced by both hunters and agriculturalists, who must tailor their acquisition of migratory animals, agricultural produce, flowering plants, and nut-bearing trees according to the time of year in which these are available. Even items that may not intuitively seem "seasonal," such as shellfish that are available year-round, have components that lend themselves to a seasonality paradigm based on aspects such as the reproductive cycle of the animal. For example, Cheryl Claassen (1986:34) and Jon Erlandson (1988:103) suggest that there is seasonality in the consumption of shellfish (paralleling the protein and carbohydrate levels of shellfish that varied from season to season), meaning that information about even "perpetual" resources would have perceived by early foragers.

For both foragers and agriculturalists, obtaining ingredients involves a degree of uncertainty (will the hunt be successful? will this harvest be abundant? will the stored food be edible?). Once obtained, the process of preparation encompasses many sights and sounds of the anticipated meal: the crackling of wood in a kitchen fire, the dry sliding of grain around and around as it is picked through to clean it, the sizzle of oil in a frying pan, and the deep, dull sound of a knife chopping meat. Aromas are quickly released, too: the green, fresh smell of crushed herbs, the damp and earthy scent of tubers, the lingering dry-grass smell of grain. For the preparer, there is a visual and tactile component, with texture and color constantly assessed in the process of mixing ingredients.

Storage constitutes another aspect of food preparation. For foragers, food is collected and consumed fairly directly, with a limited range of techniques for preparation that involve pounding, leaching, or roasting the collected product. Some foods such as fruits can be collected and eaten directly without any further processing, while others such as meat and tubers require practice and skill in extraction and preparation. When groups begin to cache or store food, new factors of planning and strategy are called into play. Calculations are made each time a stored resource is tapped, as removal of food steadily reduces the remaining stockpile. Even when human actions are tightly controlled, stocks can still be unexpectedly destroyed by vermin, seepage, or spoilage. As a result, some maintenance is needed even for untouched foodstocks, and these stored foods often are imbued with ritual significance that reflect their importance as a source of household and communal stability (e.g., Bradley 2005:5).

The creativity with which food has been approached by people at different times and places affirms the autonomy of human cognition. For early humans, communal gatherings were probably rare and seasonal, and the manufacture of tools and ornaments something that was done on an irregular basis. By contrast, the creativity and innovation applied to food, the transformation of the natural into the cultural through the use of minds and hands, was an everyday exercise of the cognitive process applied to the natural range of edible materials. After the advent of sedentism and agriculture, the range of potential foods increased, as did the range of energy inputs required to produce, prepare, serve, and consume food. By about ten thousand years ago, food was probably second only to language as a form of regularly expressed autonomous creativity.

Studying Food

As one of the basic requirements of human survival, food has probably inspired more scholarly prose than any other subject has. While sex, power, and warfare are equally popular topics in the social sciences, they are episodic in their occurrence, and sometimes whole decades go by without substantial new insights. But, just as one cannot go without food, social scientists cannot go without talking about food. Wherever researchers have gone, they have watched people eat and have often shared meals with them as well. Observations about what people eat, where they eat, when they eat and with whom help us to understand individually generated actions and their resultant impact on large-scale patterns of economics, politics, and technology.

Discussion and analysis about food has preoccupied the most famous names in anthropology, including Mary Douglas, Jack Goody, Marvin Harris, and Claude Lévi-Strauss. The title alone of Lévi-Strauss's classic work *The Raw and the Cooked* (1964) tells us about the perceived importance of the cultural transformation of the natural world from outside to inside spaces. Projecting these patterns back into the past enables us

to identify when and why humans became the species with a particular fondness and skill for the manipulation of food. Using the material
remains of the past, the idea of cooking as a transformative experience
has been explored by many archaeologists, who see in the "hearth" the
means by which nature is literally domesticated through the act of cooking (e.g., Crown 2001:227; M. Jones 2007).

One of the most basic ways of understanding the evolution of
human food patterns is to evaluate what there was for our ancestors to
eat. Although we may just now be realizing it on a large scale for our-
selves, global climate change has in the past provided dramatic parameters for human action. The earliest significant environmental event for
our ancestors was the emergence of grasslands in the African continent
starting around 2.5 million years ago (Reed 1997). With the opening up
of the landscape, a species that could travel longer distances and make
use of a diverse series of food resources had an environmental edge over
others. Our human ancestors' habitual bipedalism, unique among the
primate species, is viewed as an adaptive strategy for climate diversity
through space and climate change over time (Bobe and Behrensmeyer
2004; Klein 2009). Scholars also propose that climate change ushered in
the right conditions for the natural growth of species such as tubers, the
collection of which would have required certain skills in digging, yank-
ing, and cutting up these large, nutritious foods (O'Connell, Hawkes,
and Blurton Jones 1999).

Climate change continued to affect our ancestors' use of the landscape after the migrations out of the African homeland. In Europe, where
human ancestors first appeared around 600,000–800,000 years ago, glacial conditions dramatically affected the types of prey that would have
been available to early hunters (Klein 2009; McBrearty and Brooks 2000).
Even small changes in temperature can increase the geographic range
of certain plants that support particular species of insects and rodents,
which in turn are followed by larger predators that extend or contract
their range according to food availability. The cave paintings of today's
temperate France and Spain depict many animals that no longer live in
the region, including penguins, aurochs, and other cold-weather beasts.
Changes in global temperature routinely made some places accessible
and others closed, as seen for North America by the consolidation of
ice, which lowered sea levels and revealed a strip of solid land between

Alaska and Russia along the Bering Strait, and for Australia by the periodic attachment of Tasmania to the mainland.

The Holocene, starting ten thousand years ago, is a particularly dramatic geologic era, as it is the time in which humans made the transition from hunting and gathering to deliberate planting and cultivation of the food supply. The intimate relationship of climate stability to the beginnings of agriculture was addressed by Peter J. Richerson and his colleagues (2001) when they asked "Was Agriculture Impossible during the Pleistocene but Mandatory during the Holocene?" For the authors, the answer is yes, because the climate fluctuations of the Pleistocene (the geologic era from 1.8 million years ago to ten thousand years ago) would have precluded long-term successful adoption of agriculture. It was only the relatively warm and stable period of the Holocene that sufficiently rewarded experimentation with plant reproduction and control.

In addition to studying the environment, archaeologists also examine artifacts made by humans for extracting and preparing food. Some of the first deliberately made human artifacts include stone tools such as hand axes, cleavers, and choppers from as early as 1.6 million years ago (Mithen 2003; Klein 2009). Replication studies have illustrated how they might have been used for processing food, such as the hand ax that has been called the "Swiss army knife" of ancient technology—suitable for crushing roots, chopping meat off the bone, and other food-related tasks (e.g., Ihde 2006; Klein 2009:95). For later periods when agriculture became prominent, there are numerous types of equipment that are depicted in art and leave archaeological traces, including digging sticks, plows, fragments of animal harness, sickles, knives, and grinding stones (fig. 2.1). Pottery vessels, first made around twelve thousand years ago, give us a particularly direct way of understanding food consumption. Many types of foods, particularly oily or fatty ones, leave traces on porous clay vessels that can be chemically analyzed. When pots are used for cooking, they have different types of scorch or burn marks that can reveal the types of preparation process, ranging from placement over direct heat to the use of heated stones. Pots that are used for fermenting often develop distinctive pockmarks from the chemical effects of the fermenting process (Arthur 2003).

Pottery vessels are durable, and the clay used to make them could easily be shaped in a variety of forms useful for storing, preparing, and transporting food. Large storage jars could be used for liquids, of course, but

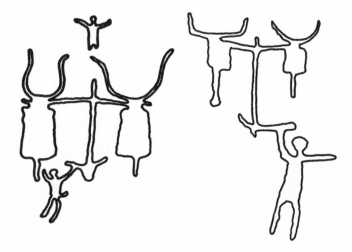

FIGURE 2.1. Early European images of plowing show the different configurations of animals, people, and equipment needed for the use of new agricultural technology.

also were good for protecting grain from nibbling rodents and damp storage conditions. Serving vessels also tell us about food practices. Although many perishable objects such as wood, bamboo, broad leaves, coconut shells, gourds, and other natural containers would have been used for serving food, the advent of pottery was quickly accompanied by the production of cups, bowls, and beakers as well as cooking and storage vessels. The use of specific shapes for specific foods is demonstrated when texts preserve consumer intent, as with the Roman-era drinking vessels from Britain that have written on them "Don't be thirsty" and "Serve wine unmixed [with water]" (Cool 2006:148).

Fixed-place installations such as storage areas, hearths, and animal pens also are indicators of what was being prepared and eaten (fig. 2.2). Their size and placement in the landscape inform us about the relative importance of different types of food in the social realm of ancient people, as well as how much work would have been required to construct and use the features. Sometimes these storage areas are built-in, such as underground pits, and in other cases baskets and wooden bins indicate the extent to which people worked to keep food secure from insects, vermin, damp, fire, and theft by other people. Some other uses for pits include

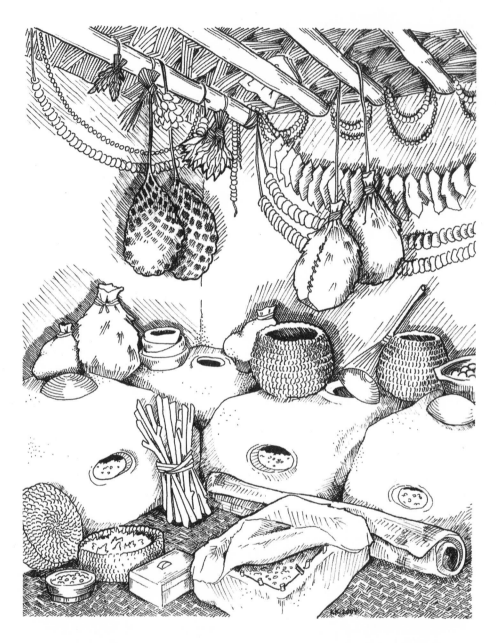

FIGURE 2.2. Food storage has implications for architecture, living space, and the subsequent preparation of meals. This artist's re-creation of a food storage area from the Turkish Neolithic site of Çatalhöyük shows the variety of food storage used in an early agricultural village.

fermentation, not only of alcoholic beverages such as wine and beer but also of other liquids, such as the Roman *garum* (fish sauce). Some types of preparation tools are semiportable, such as querns and other large-scale grinding equipment for grain, but they were probably not often moved and constituted a fixed feature of a household or community.

Another type of feature from which archaeologists can extract information is the midden. A "midden" is a nice archaeological term for something that was a relatively messy, smelly slump of trash that often is found quite close to ancient habitations. Middens are places of deliberate discard that usually involve considerable quantities of food waste, such as vegetal matter, shells, bones, and other inedible parts that are thrown out in the food preparation process (e.g., Beck and Hill 2004). As outdoor spaces that are the venue of discard, middens are a structural afterthought; rarely were they given purposeful boundaries by ancient inhabitants. At the same time, they were regular features of the landscape in which people repeatedly discarded food and other forms of waste in patterns that lasted for generations. Discard in itself was not necessarily unidirectional, however; as Tim Ingold has observed, "Among some hunters and gatherers, materials initially dumped as waste may be reprocessed for consumption as emergency food, in the event that all other sources fail, so that the dump comes to function as a kind of store" (Ingold 1987:201).

Burials and their associated funerary rituals constitute another source of archaeological evidence about foodways. With our durable skeletons, each of us is a walking record of the individual food quest. Mineralogical signatures in bones and teeth can be linked to specific geographic areas, meaning that the plants and animal matter from different places consumed during youth are still found in the signatures of the skeleton in old age. Teeth are particularly valuable as a source of information, as they are among the hardest part of the human skeleton and can survive even in conditions where bones decompose. We also can use teeth to examine social distinctions in diet and the negative results of agriculture starting around ten thousand years ago. At the beginning of this transition, two things adversely affected teeth: grinding-stone grit in the diet, which caused teeth to wear down quickly; and the high quantity of starchy carbohydrates, which precipitated a high rate of tooth decay (e.g., Lukacs 1996).

The placement of objects in the intense, short-term process of burial ceremonies can include food, preparation tools, and serving vessels.

Funerary collections of food often included the presentation of animal foods, such as selective meaty portions of a kill (Cool 2006; Welch 1991). There were also prepared foods such as bread and other grain products interred with the deceased. At the time of funerals, alcoholic beverages often were served to the mourners and poured out as libations to the dead, as seen by the frequent remains of beverage containers suggesting heavy consumption of alcoholic beverages and other stimulants associated with funerals. Food is such an essential component of being "alive" that the placement of these items with the deceased probably signals some belief or hope in an afterlife (regardless of whether the dead were viewed as helpful or malevolent, in which case the food might be an attempt to placate the deceased and keep them from returning to take up the foodstocks of the living).

In rare cases, exceptional conditions result in preserved human stomachs, intestines, and other organs that provide information about food consumption. The purposeful creation of mummies starts in the archaeological record around eight thousand years ago with the very elaborate eviscerations and wrappings of the Chinchorro people of Peru (Browman, Fritz, and Watson 2005:338–39). Detailed attention to the body is perhaps best known from Egypt, where animals as well as people were subjected to bodily preservation (Peck 1980). Natural processes of desiccation also have resulted in mummies from the American Southwest (El-Najjar and Mulinski 1980) and from Japan (Sakurai and Ogata 1980). High-altitude environments can produce naturally "freeze-dried" bodies, as is the case in Nepal (Alt et al. 2003) and Andean South America (Vreeland 1998). And frozen environments also have preserved bodies, as seen in the cases of Ötzi and Kwäday Dän Ts'ìnchí.

Finally, there is the study of human coprolites. A "coprolite" has an elegant and clean-sounding scientific name, but it refers to preserved human waste. While many components of food are digestible and provide nutrients, some fiber, seeds, and other waste products pass through the body and leave their traces in excrement. Coprolites can be preserved in exceptionally dry conditions such as caves and salt mines, and aggregate human waste can be excavated from latrines and cesspits. Nicole Boenke's (2007) study of Iron Age coprolites from the Dürrnberg salt mine in Austria provides a particularly good example of how this type of artifact can be used to reconstruct dietary patterns of both individuals and groups. Working in dark, unpleasant conditions, the mine workers probably had a relatively low social status; nonetheless, the coprolites proved that they enjoyed a varied diet, including grains, fruits, legumes, and high-status foods such as meat. The proportions of different foods in the coprolites varied, an indication that different "recipes" were used by different households or in different seasons.

The Evolution of Human Food Habits

We as a species have bodies that are adapted for a diverse diet. The generalized dentition pattern of humans is an inheritance from our long-ago primate ancestors: incisors for biting, canines for slicing, and molars for grinding (Teaford and Ungar 2000). Consider how this is different from animals with narrow diet niches: cows have flattened molars for grinding vegetal matter and no upper incisors at all, while cats' sharp canines and molars are ideal only for shearing and chewing meat. Today's primates eat a variety of foods in the wild; for example, chimpanzees in Uganda are recorded as consuming 117 species (Wrangham's data, reported in Krief, Hladik, and Haxaire 2005:3). This same pattern of behavior was probably evident in long-ago hominids as well, but perhaps as early as 2.5 million years ago, our human ancestors began to acquire a larger proportion of the diet in the form of meat (summarized in Shea 2006). Although some of this meat was hunted, some of it also was scavenged from the meals of other carnivores, as indicated by the presence of animal toothmarks that are overlain by human scrapings (Shipman 1986:30).

Humans steadily increased their capacity to hunt and kill for themselves, primarily through the improvement of hunting weapons. Lacking the speed and natural killing equipment of teeth and claws possessed by other predators, our ancestors utilized cultural adaptations to acquire meat resources, involving both archaeologically recoverable tools and communication skills utilized in group hunting. Most of the evidence that we have for hunting and capture involves weapons such as stone projectile points. Other techniques, such as snares made of cordage, pits covered with vegetation, and game drives over cliffs were means by which human ancestors probably captured their prey as well, though the archaeological evidence for this type of hunting is scanty. However, these cultural adaptations were not limited to the production of specific tools; they also included a change in the notion of prey. As Mary Stiner (1994) has discussed, humans are the only species that regularly targets prime animals, unlike other carnivores, which concentrate their attention on the weakest members of the herd. Her research in central Italy shows that around 55,000 years ago, there was a shift in prey procurement from a scavenging mode to a hunting one in which people began to selectively prefer prime adults. Although she suggests that hunters may have been selecting for higher-fat animals at a time of decreasing temperatures (Stiner 1994:308), it is also likely that these prime animals were socially valued as an indicator of hunting prowess. Hunting also provided social status through the potential to give and receive shares of the hunt. As there was no way to preserve meat, "storage" would have consisted of mutual obligations to share meat whenever a hunter or hunting party achieved success.

Another important cultural amendment to hunting was the use of fire to cook food. Cooking requires more than just a change in the technique of processing; it also reflects changes in ideas because people must accept a delay between the time of acquiring food and the time of consuming it (Wrangham et al. 1999). Cooking also requires skill in fire making and an investment in time spent to gather and safeguard suitable fuel. Direct evidence for the first cooking is, however, difficult to find in the archaeological record. Open fires leave little permanent evidence, and the earliest cooking—which was done long before pottery was invented—would have been done with the food wrapped in leaves or propped up on a wooden spit, an arrangement that similarly leaves few archaeological traces. As with many other questions of early human behavior for which hard evidence is rare, the resolution of the earliest human control of fire has prompted creative approaches to proxy evidence. For example, Wrangham and his colleagues (1999) have suggested that we can look at changes in dental morphology to see when cultural skills such as cooking began to supplant strictly biological adaptations to the surrounding environment.

In addition to hunted mammals, our earliest ancestors collected, prepared, and ate many other types of foods. Fruits are particularly favored by our primate relatives and would have been an important resource for early humans too. With their strong scent and bright colors, ripe fruits are particularly easy to detect in the environment; among contemporary foragers, these are the first foods that children learn to collect (e.g., Kaplan et al. 2000:168; O'Connell, Hawkes, and Blurton Jones 1999:466). Fruits also are attractive because they can be eaten without further processing, in contrast to items such as nuts or tubers that must be soaked, roasted, or otherwise processed to remove toxins and alkalis. Along coastal and riverine areas, shellfish and seashore creatures such as crabs would have been a good source of protein. Marine foods would have been processed through cooking, whether simply on an open flame or baked in leaves over coals. Roots and tubers were another important source of calories start-ing with the very beginning of a distinct human species. J. F. O'Connell, F. Hawkes, and N. G. Blurton Jones (1999) emphasize the way in which tubers probably developed in prominence in the natural environment of eastern Africa by about 1.8 million years ago, coincident with the emer-gence of *Homo erectus* and also with the development of pigs, which would have competed with hominids for this resource.

The example of tubers reminds us that early humans were not the only species looking for sustenance, and our ancestors would have con-tested with every kind of animal for food: pigs for tubers, predators for meat, birds and small mammals for nuts, and other primates for fruit. Speed, agility, persistence, and the ability to work with others as a group were all key aspects of early hominid food success. Each individual would have benefited from the possession of these skills, such that autonomous cognitive capacity and multitasking in the face of variable resources enhanced the biological propensity for omnivory. Rather than waiting for direction from a leader, people individually learned how to hunt and gather suitable foods, remembered the location of stone sources suitable for making tools, managed the sequence of collection tasks that would bring them back to a home base where other group members were pres-ent, and negotiated successfully with others to manage "social storage" through sharing. The constant process of multitasking informed each individual's actions with food acquisition, preparation, consumption, and waste discard on a variety of temporal scales.

These individually held skills became further accentuated when early humans moved beyond their original East African homeland to very diverse parts of the planet in which new resources were found. By the time that *Homo sapiens* migrated to Australia (about forty thousand years ago) and North America (about eighteen thousand years ago), they were highly skilled hunters who targeted, and rendered extinct, many species

of slow-moving prey. Cultural adaptations in the form of new composite tools such as grinding stones and hafted blades enabled people to
more efficiently extract food from the environment but also let them
be choosier about the foods that they elected to consume. The environment of the time also fluctuated considerably; although these changes
were not something that an individual would have been able to discern
in a lifetime, the relatively rapid warming and cooling cycles of the late
Pleistocene meant that behavioral innovations that made use of variable
environments were more effective than rigid, unchanging adaptations.
The net result was that people were making use of a much wider variety
of foods, including large and small mammals, birds, fish, and wild plants
(Kuhn and Stiner 2006).

Human population growth, along with migrations, eventually resulted
in concentrations of people in the most favorable environments. Starting
around ten thousand years ago, natural conditions also shifted, as rapid
and dramatic fluctuations of climate at the beginning of the Holocene
shrank the margins of those favorable areas. Faced with the increasing
potential for competition and conflict, humans took an approach that
was highly labor intensive but resulted in the potential for resource abundance. For populations reaching the limits of sustainability in gathered
resources, the solution was "Stay Put and Grow Food."

Randi Haaland (2007) has discussed the incremental stages of this
transition, in which the first important step is cultivation as a process that
enhances the growth of wild foods. Full domestication came later, and
only for a subset of the species that humans tended in their landscapes.
Domestication adds a significant amount of human energy investment
to the process of cultivation because it involves human control over
plant and animal reproduction (B. Smith 2001). Human control focused
primarily on docile and multipurpose "meat packages" such as cattle,
sheep, and goats and on grain resources such as starchy carbohydrates
in the form of tubers (yams, potatoes) and grains (rice, corn, wheat,
barley, amaranth, and others). Why did foods such as these, rather than
fruits or nuts, become the predominant plant staples? At first glance, the
use of grains in particular seems to be a significant departure from the
plant resources used by foragers. Grains are small, slippery, and seasonal
and are found on plants that tend to disperse their seeds easily through
wind or touch, making them particularly difficult for humans to harvest.

Recent work by George Perry and colleagues (2007:1259) suggests that one explanation for a focus on grains was a human genetic predisposition to digest starch, which is evident in the long evolutionary adaptation to the consumption of tubers.

The multitasking skills that already were part of the human cognitive repertoire were essential to the adoption of cultivation, domestication, and sedentism. People used their perceptions of time and space to make use of landscapes that reflected increasing quantities of human energy investment. Memory, planning, and task management were material- ized in the archaeological record through the remains of substantial resi- dences that replaced mobile forager camps, storage facilities that trans- formed seasonal harvests into daily points of access, and processing tools such as grinding stones that are required to turn grains into food. Com- munication, identity, and memory were the social components that were implicated in cultivation, as manifested in issues of property investment, land tenure, inheritance, and access to stored resources.

Cultivation also required the acceptance of delayed rewards. For plant foods, this includes tasks such as preparing the soil, planting, watering, weeding, and fertilizing, all of which are energy-intensive activities for which there is no immediate payoff other than a sore back and callused hands. Cultivation requires daily investments with the expectation that there will be future rewards. For animals, investments are represented by the time that it takes to rear an animal until it is old enough to be used for milk, wool, or traction. Economists describe these types of incremen- tal investments as "sunk costs," with the practical effect that a repeated application of investment is required to achieve a deferred reward. The ability to understand and capitalize on these delayed rewards was made possible by the use of the same capacities of memory and planning inher- ited from our most ancient human ancestors.

Animal herding presents a particularly interesting calculation of rewards, as there is the potential at any given moment of acquiring caloric value from a domesticated herd. In economic terms, slaughter and con- sumption result in a net present gain with a complete future loss. Given the lack of refrigeration in the premodern world, these calculations also involved the commitment of additional energy investment in preserva- tion processes (such as salting or drying the meat). Social and economic calculations also affected the choice of the animal to be slaughtered.

In contrast to the ideological preference for prime animals expressed by hunters, the domestication of animals favored selection strategies that mimicked the patterns of nonhuman predators. When our Holocene ancestors domesticated animals, they selectively culled the youngest and the oldest herd members, leaving prime animals to reproduce and to provide renewable products such as milk, hair, wool, dung, and traction. Subadult males were a particular target for culling, as they provided meat while leaving the herd's breeding capacity limited to a few optimal specimens (Zeder and Hesse 2000).

As a result of the domestication process, individuals had many more choices to make about animals on a daily basis. Faced with a young animal, a human caretaker could decide whether to train it for drafting, breed it for wool or milk production, or cull it and transform economic loss into social gain, as even a young animal would provide meat for a larger-than-household-sized group. For animals raised to maturity, additional daily decisions had to be made that impinged on long-term as well as short-term outcomes and labor requirements: would the animal be sent to a nearby pasture, on local daily rounds with a herder, or to a distant range with an expectation of return in weeks or months? Seasons and cycles would affect the production of by-products; for example, breeding an animal would initiate a round of milk production and continuation of the herd but could also affect the quality of both wool and meat production (Paducheva 1956).

The process of cultivation also results in the acceptance and mitigation of many new types of economic risk. For foragers, a diseased wild animal is of little concern, as it does not represent any energy investment. But to herders, a diseased or injured domestic animal represents a lost expenditure of time and energy that cannot be recovered easily. Animals' illnesses and injury are perceived within cultural frameworks as well; while an injured animal could be slaughtered to at least recoup some social capital through the sharing of meat, an ailing animal would be a poor choice for impressing one's kin or for making a ritual offering.

The Concept of Food Preference

There are many more things that are edible than what is consumed by any human group. Food preferences are acted upon not only in the selection of the item to eat but also in the style of its preparation, how much time will be devoted to the preparation, how the prepared item will be served, and who will be given which portions of the meal. Food preferences can be expressed positively (how to choose from among available foods) as well as negatively (in the form of food prohibitions and taboos).

The tenacity of food preference by modern people even under very adverse conditions shows why the consideration of food preference for prehistoric populations is essential. One example is provided by the circumstance of refugee groups who utilize food preferences to demonstrate autonomy, retaining identity through daily actions even when their circumstances are dire. Stories abound of recipient nations' difficulties with food aid that emanates from Western surpluses of culturally inappropriate foods, including the shipment of pork to Muslim nations, cheese and milk to non-dairy-consuming populations, and wheat or corn to rice-eating peoples (Singer, Wood, and Jennings 1987). Even when the provided foods are of the right type, cultural preferences can still affect acceptability, as Singer and his colleagues (1987) have noted with the sub-Saharan preferences for white sorghum and white corn against the dominant varieties of red sorghum and yellow corn from donor nations such as the United States. As a result, food preference has been evaluated by applied anthropologists seeking to mitigate cultural losses and alienation as well as working to improve the success of food relief and international aid programs (Agency for International Development 1985; Pottier 1999:11–22). The Committee on Economic, Social and Cultural Rights of the United Nations has specified that the fundamental human right to food is in part defined by the "availability of food in a quantity and quality sufficient to satisfy the dietary needs of individuals, free from adverse substances, and acceptable within a given culture" (Eide 2000:329).

The development of African and African American foodways in the Americas constitutes another example of the phenomenon of cultural identity expressed through foodways by an otherwise disenfranchised group. Slaves in the New World had distinct consumption patterns that developed from both involuntary sources (the provisions given to them by owners) and voluntary sources (foods whose production or acquisition they directly controlled). The creation and maintenance of slaves' foodways was a conscious component of labor management, in which owners allowed slaves to hunt and to keep kitchen gardens as well as small livestock under their own control (McKee 1995). However, the move to allow slaves to provision themselves through gardens or hunting was not merely an economic calculation on the part of slave owners eager to shift the burden of provisioning. The use of particular foods appears to have been tacitly acknowledged and encouraged by plantation overseers who "encouraged Africans to maintain a degree of behavioral autonomy that highlighted perceived differences . . . upon which the institution of slavery was based" (Armstrong and Kelly 2000:379).

Another historically documented case of the tenacity of food preference comes from Australia, where early European settlers included a significant number of British convicts who were transported there as laborers. They were to be fed by their overseers according to a prescribed set of rations, particularly for meat. Although the free settlers consumed a wide variety of domestic and game animals, the acceptable repertoire of convict food was more restricted. As Bruce Hindmarsh (2002:139) notes, "Convicts were rigid in the items that they would accept from their employers as rations, and . . . commonly refused to accept kangaroo or other bush animals in their ration, recognising that such food cost their masters little if anything." Convicts also cooked their rations for themselves, transforming the raw ingredients into meals that were quite basic but nonetheless formed a component of "convict culture" (Hindmarsh 2002:143).

How far back in human history can the notion of food preference be traced? If we take energy expenditure and the willingness to undertake risks as proxy measures, the observation of early hunters' disproportionate taking of prime animals was perhaps the first use of costly, energy-intensive strategies to acquire preferred foods by around fifty-five thousand years ago. Research on hunter-gatherer sites of the Mesolithic period in Europe has led Preston Miracle (2002) to suggest that notions of culinary preference and cuisine are evident in subsequent eras as well. His research at the site of Pupicina, Croatia, shows shifts in the proportions of ungulates and molluscs over time. Although the site was occupied before the development of pottery and therefore lacks the containers usually identified with food storage and preparation, the presence of accumulated mollusc shell and a high proportion of meaty ungulate bones signal a preference for such foods. At Pupicina, culinary changes, such as baking or steaming molluscs, were incorporated into the cyclical occupation of the site. As Miracle (2002:84) concludes, "It is not surprising that the transformation of the 'raw' into the 'cooked' become[s] more complex from the Meso-lithic to the Neolithic."

Although sedentism and the domestication of both plants and animals tend to happen at the same time, it would be interesting to use a more finely delineated chronology to learn whether plants or animals were domesticated first in a particular locale. It may be that animals were first kept by people and had a long period of commensality before animals began to display the distinct physiological characteristics that we can track through the study of animal bones. The more immediate potential payoff of herding, which might have been practiced for many generations before the transition to crop production, might also account for the curi-ous phenomenon of the "Pre-pottery Neolithic," a time period (particu-larly in the Near East and South Asia) in which there is sedentism but without the pottery that would seem to be otherwise a requisite feature in plant storage and preparation (see Haaland 2007; Jarrige 1995:60).

Food preference is expressed in preparation styles as well as in the ingredients. As Paul Halstead, Ian Hodder, and Glynis Jones note (1978), an animal can be butchered in various ways, producing distinctions in slaughter waste, kitchen waste, and waste at the point of consumption (elaborated in Hill 1995:25; see fig. 2.3). A change over time in the prefer-ence for certain cuts of meat might mean the elaboration of particular culinary practices that allow for the more effective use of certain body parts; for example, the advent of stew-type cooking would highlight the recovery of bony parts of the carcass because nutritional and taste value could be extracted through boiling (as B. A. Chase [2005] has noted in his ethnoarchaeological study of contemporary South Asian butchery practices). Similarly, the mode of plant use might indicate both relative availability of a food and ideas of preference in cuisine; for example, a lot of grain is required to produce a serving of bread and a bit less to provide a serving of porridge, but only a small amount of grain is needed to make a soup or beverage. The ratio of raw materials to water in the case of soup and beverages indicates the way a perception of a large volume of food could be elicited from a relatively small amount of solid ingredients in a way that suited the preference of the eaters or the wealth of the cooks.

How are food preferences acquired? We know that infants have a predisposition for sweetness, which is linked to the slightly sweet taste of mother's milk. Other tastes are acquired in the course of a lifetime

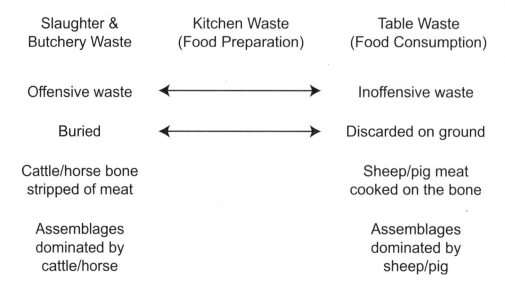

Slaughter & Butchery Waste	Kitchen Waste (Food Preparation)	Table Waste (Food Consumption)
Offensive waste	←——————————→	Inoffensive waste
Buried	←——————————→	Discarded on ground
Cattle/horse bone stripped of meat		Sheep/pig meat cooked on the bone
Assemblages dominated by cattle/horse		Assemblages dominated by sheep/pig

FIGURE 2.3. Types of waste. Within the general social parameters that result in patterns that can be archaeologically discerned, individual acts of discard are each a conscious choice, particularly in the creative realm of food preparation.

or through the experience of eating different substances. Humans can acquire a desire for foods that are unpalatable at first taste, a characteristic of eating that makes us quite distinctive among species. As Amy Bentley (2004:212) has observed, humans learn not only to experiment with and tolerate unpalatable foods but also to actually crave them. In my university course on food and culture, the students are invited to construct a "sushi index" describing the typical ladder of taste acquisition: first the vegetable rolls and cooked seafood, then the fatty raw fishes such as tuna and salmon, and, after more experience, the more unusual tastes and textures such as squid, octopus, and eel. Another index involves remembering how they learned to drink coffee: first with heavy doses of cream and sugar, then lessening amounts of each until a day in the future when they agree that they will probably take it black. Similar trajectories of preference from sweet to strong or bitter tastes can be tracked for fermented foods such as chocolate, cheese, and alcohol.

These examples illustrate that the development of food preferences is one in which the individual consciously engages in expanding a personal repertoire through a process of both creativity and habituation. Food choices can be affected both through the social milieu in which the acceptance of new preferences signals status-yielding connoisseurship, and through the temporality of the palate over the individual life span that leads to seeking out unusual, distinct, or strong tastes. The modern example of sushi indicates the extent to which the selection of unpalatable foods and acquiring a taste for the novel are enveloped in social terms, in which the expertise or appreciation for a strong taste marks the individual as having achieved a certain (usually adult) status. Such foods are a signal of sophistication in a social setting, but it is still the individual who has to come to terms with the taste and texture of the food item.

Even for our earliest hominid ancestors, omnivory was accompanied by the tolerance for unusual tastes such as bitter greens, fermented fruit, and gamy meats. Textures could prove unpleasant, too, ranging from stringy bark and teeth-sticking starches to the cold and slimy innards of freshwater clams and marine mussels. Some inclinations towards otherwise challenging foods may have been overwritten by considerations for their nutritional or medicinal value; as Sabrina Krief, Claude Marcel Hladik, and Claudie Haxaire (2005:11) note, bitterness may be an indicator of bioactive compounds that have pharmaceutical effects, leading to a positive inclination to experiment with or habitually ingest bitter-tasting substances. Deliberate modes of preparation also would have been an acquired taste. When foods were first prepared with fire, the texture and taste of cooked meat may have seemed very odd and unpleasant. Cooked foods also would have required the development of a sense of timing that is driven partly by biology (foods that are too hot can burn the tongue and lips) and partly by idiosyncratic preference in which each person may have a slightly different idea of the ideal temperature of a food (what we could call the "Goldilocks principle"). Even the geography of the culinary act could be a locus for expressing preference, as in the case of ancient Mesopotamian householders who complained of having to eat "bought bread" instead of being able to make their own at home (Keith 2003:69).

When containers became available, they could be used to mix foods together in new ways that were very different from the one-taste-at-a-time methods of roasting or eating food raw. The use of containers enabled other experiments, such as the soaking and leaching of toxins from nuts and other wild foods to produce an edible product. By about ten thousand years ago, newly acquired tastes included bitter fermented beverages such as beer and wine, as well as other fermented products such as cheese, pickled vegetables, and fish sauce. Domestication produced foods that may not initially have been very palatable, such as small, bland, and slippery grass seeds that required tedious methods of collection and preparation. Other domesticated products such as tobacco required the development of new skills in the application of fire to activate desired properties. Dairy products may have triggered allergic reactions in adult humans, who widely lack the capacity to absorb the lactose found in cow's milk (Bersaglieri et al. 2004). Dairy products also required overcoming aversions to the novel taste of cheese and yogurt through fermentation or buttermilk through churning (butter itself, being similar to long-desired fatty meats, may have been more easily adopted as a food).

How much does an individual decide to eat, and what is a standard food portion? While we cannot evaluate what the cultural expectations of a "serving" of bread or meat might have been in ancient times, we can examine the archaeological record of eating vessels to have an idea of an expected serving size of fermented beverages, stews, and porridges. Studies of modern food consumption indicate that there is a cognitive link between the size of a vessel and the sense of appropriate portion size, a concept identified as "unit bias" (Geier et al. 2006). Using the "unit bias" idea, we can expect that a serving size was somewhere in the range of 75–95 percent of an eating vessel's contents (allowing for some air space to avoid spillage of contents). Individuals can compare the contents of bowls more easily than they can discern the division of a yam, a pile of nuts, or handfuls of fresh meat from a kill. Measuring the capacity of bowls over time should provide data by which we can see how the cultural expectation of comestibles, individually perceived and actualized, is manifested in the durable material record.

Preference Deferred: Famines, Taboos, and Fasting

Nutritional stress is biologically the hallmark of our ancient ancestors and politically the hallmark of our contemporary world; we should not assume that everyone has access to a nice meal whenever they want it. Food shortage conditions the way in which people conceptualize the landscape and utilize their resources on a daily basis, and food shortages were likely to have been a powerful motivator in both the biological and the social expression of food preference. As discussed by Greg Laden and Richard Wrangham (2005), many species besides humans have developed evolutionary responses to food shortages that result in morphological or behavioral adaptations focused on the most dependable rather than the most preferred foods. They propose that for humans, these fallback foods are actually a more important driver of biological and cultural adaptations than are preferred foods. The capacity to use fallback foods, and adapt to new fallback foods, was a critical element in enabling our human ancestors to successfully compete in a variety of surroundings, including the new environments encountered in migration.

The cognitive factors of memory and planning exhibited through multitasking enable individuals to address circumstances of shortfall through a variety of approaches. Although periods of resource stress can result in physical and social damage, they also can be viewed as an opportunity for creativity within new parameters. In many parts of the world, the adoption of sedentism and agriculture was accompanied by periods of severe nutritional stress, as seen in bones and teeth preserved in burials. Skeletal analyses show that people lived through these periods of nutritional stress, probably by adopting practices that would enable them to survive shortfalls. The *Sirupanattrupadai*, a South Indian poem of the early centuries BC/AD, paints the scenario of "the wife of the drummer with a lean and slender waist and bangled wrists whom cruel hunger gnawed did saltless cook the herb her sharp nails plucked from refuse heaps, and made a meal of it with poor relations, having closed the door ashamed to be so seen by prying folk" (lines 180–86; Chelliah 1985:155). Mark Stiger provides an analogous archaeological case for the premodern American Southwest, where the diversity of food consumption increased over time as measured by the range of comestible residue in coprolites (Stiger 1977, reported in Crown 2001:237). Changes in diet included an increase in the range of foods eaten to include insects and grass seeds of a weedy type, which the investigator interpreted as the result of stress brought on by population pressure and environmental disruptions.

Agriculturalists generally practice various mechanisms, such as storage, that help to mitigate lean seasons and crop failures, and the knowledge of wild resources can be an important supplement in times of food shortage (fig. 2.4). Responses that may initially have been generated by

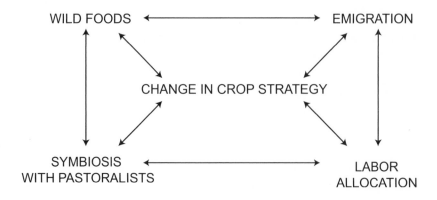

FIGURE 2.4. Decision-making parameters of how agriculturalists interweave their decisions about food with landscape knowledge and modifications of energy investment into direct (wild goods) and indirect (production of tradable surplus) modes of subsistence.

strained circumstances may even take on significance as the new norm for household and communal identity. Ethnographic observations of farmers in the twentieth century show how agriculturalists even in modern nations such as Italy, Spain, and India retain a knowledge of the natural environment and supplement their diets through hunting, fishing, and the use of wild plants as herbs, flavorings, and medicine (e.g., Pieroni 1999; Smith 2006a; Tardío, Pascual, and Morales 2005). Social mechanisms called into action at times of food stress also are deliberately enacted at the level of the individual and the household. In an examination of the Greek rural communities of the Methana region, H. Forbes (1989) utilized interviews and observations to show how people are cognizant of the meaning of any given response to food shortages and simultaneously consider various short-term and long-term solutions. Local villagers reported "having survived serious food shortages in the past by breaking the normal social rules: begging for food; getting rid of excess dependents by forcing them into unwanted marriages; eating foods outside the culturally acceptable range" (Forbes 1989:90).

The Greek example shows that circumstances of stress can result in several different responses, each enacted on the individual level: the reaffirmation of parameters through retained but increasingly costly practice; the reaffirmation of parameters through a temporary intent to step outside of them; and the reconfiguration of parameters through a permanent intent of modification. Through each act of food preparation and eating, individuals acknowledge both habituated social norms and the historical trajectory of the circumstances that have led them to craft new norms at any given moment. Just as in the case of language use in which words, grammar, and acceptable contexts can be modified through the sheer frequency of individual utterances, new patterns of food consumption can transform previously marginal foods into newly acceptable, even desirable, targets of consumption (in our society, recent entrants into the mainstream of consumption include foods such as ribs and fajitas, which were dishes originally developed to make use of low-value meat cuts [see, e.g., Bentley 2004]). We can easily apply the same reasoning process to the introduction of new foods at any time in the human culinary repertoire, from the resources encountered by our earliest migrating *Homo sapiens* ancestors to the adoption of a grain-heavy diet in the earliest agricultural period ten thousand years ago.

Even when provisions are abundant, however, there are almost as many ways that people avoid food as ways that they consume it. Modes of food deferral by the individual include food taboos and fasts, both of which are undertaken as conscious decisions about what *not* to eat. Food taboos mean that individuals choose to avoid foods that are otherwise palatable but are culturally defined as "inedible," either for the group as a whole or for particular individuals. Nearly every major religious tradition encompasses some form of food restriction on a cyclical or permanent basis, such as abstention from meat (by Buddhist practitioners), from root crops (by Jains), and from beans (by the Pythagoreans of ancient Greece). The religious traditions of Islam, Judaism, and Christianity similarly encode food taboos as part of the individualization of faith.

Prehistoric food taboos are suggested in the archaeological record of earlier eras as well. Research on the precontact period of Hawaii by Patrick Kirch and Sharyn O'Day, for example, indicates that there were considerable numbers of gender-related food taboos. Although pork was considered a luxury food, it was forbidden for women, along with coconuts, sea turtles, sharks, some kinds of fish, and most kinds of bananas (Kirch and O'Day 2003:487). Gender-specific prohibitions included preparation and serving as well: food for women and for men was supposed to be cooked in separate earth ovens and consumed in separate eating houses.

For their adherents, religious dietary restrictions and practices provide an important component of quotidian identity and group solidarity. However, these food restrictions are negotiated and reevaluated when new circumstances arise. One example is seen in the dietary prohibitions (meat versus fish) of Catholic Europe in the late medieval and early modern period. When French Catholics came to the Americas, they encountered new animals for which official decisions had to be made as to their dietary suitability. In the 1600s, the Church classified New World animals such as beavers and muskrats as "fish" (because they spent most of their time in the water) and therefore permissible on fast days, a factor that Elizabeth Scott (2007:249) credits for the relative abundance of beaver in the midden deposits of French Canadian archaeological sites.

As seen in the example above, the relationship between individual food preferences and institutional approval is a complex and dynamic one. In the modern context, the provision of food aid from one country to another sometimes results in the introduction of foods that become desired even when they are not part of the traditional culinary repertoire. In many poor nations, white bread is a status symbol even though it has relatively low nutritional qualities; the same conditions apply to infant formula, which can displace local practices of infant nutrition. As a result, donor nations of wheat are exhorted to consider food aid's potential for "creating new and unsustainable eating habits" (Singer, Wood, and Jennings 1987:104). The observation that people deliberately seek unhealthy foods in industrialized nations today also indicates the extent to which food preferences, actualized on the individual level, create and sustain large-scale cycles of production, distribution, and consumption of items such as "junk food" even when those patterns of consumption are officially discouraged.

At the opposite end of the spectrum is the individual denial of permitted foods in the form of personal fasting meant to achieve a particular spiritual or aesthetic result. Although anorexia is viewed as a uniquely modern ailment, the historical record of self-starvation suggests that this was a popular form of female devotional activity starting as early as the thirteenth century AD in Europe (Gooldin 2003). Buddhist monks in Japan and elsewhere have been recorded to have practiced slow starvation that eventually rendered their bodies into a virtually mummified state even prior to death (Sakurai and Ogata 1980). Even further back in the archaeological record come other suggestions that starvation and dehydration were used as a powerful stimulant for hallucinations of the kind that may have inspired Paleolithic rock art (Lewis-Williams and Dowson 1988). Just as food could be utilized as a means of satisfaction and identity, so too is denial a form of autonomy. Eating and not eating are self-governed options, put into practice at the level of the individual.

Cuisine and Culture

Contemporary and historical records of culture contact and culture change are particularly rich in examples of how social identities are negated, negotiated, and reinforced through food preparation. Anthropologists such as Arjun Appadurai (1981) and Brad Weiss (1997:167) have reminded us that everyday acts of food preparation and consumption are a powerful affirmation of social ties and identity. Everyday foods take on special social roles precisely because they can be repeated into habituation, which is re-cognized whenever staple foods either fall into short supply or become superabundant (e.g., Diner 2001).

The sharing of food can be accomplished at a variety of temporal and spatial scales, from the intimate meals of the household to larger communal feasts. At every scale, these events address both nutritional need and symbolic intent through performances of preparation and consumption that reinforce feelings of kinship, identity, and internalized well-being. Ritual activities also accompany many food-related events, from the blessing of routine meals to the special presentation of foods associated with rites of passage such as weddings, funerals, and celebrations. Not every communal event invokes significant ritual, however; Mike Parker Pearson (2000:222) reminds us that in many cases, we can consider events as "festive but not ritual moments" in the social calendar.

The technologies associated with food also changed over time. As people started to cultivate domesticated plants and animals, the notion of what to do with them changed from the previous processing of wild plants and animals. Whereas fruits can be eaten directly from the tree and meat requires only simple roasting to make it edible, grains need more-significant treatment. They are a good source of carbohydrates and sugars but were a particularly labor-intensive choice for intensification because they cannot be consumed by people without further processing.

The harvesting of individual grain seeds was facilitated by selective breeding to favor characteristics such as larger seed size, more seeds per head of grain, and changes in plant morphology. Plants naturally reproduce when seeds are dispersed, often through wind or other movements that favor quick release from the stem. Humans, however, favored plants with a tough stem; after all, a seed that stuck to the plant long enough to be harvested and carried to a place of processing was much more useful to humans than a plant that spontaneously shed its seeds when touched.

Once harvested, grains require special treatment with a variety of tools for both storage and processing into food. Seeds must be released from the stem through threshing, an action that can be accomplished through simple actions such as beating the heads of grain with sticks or trampling by animals to release the seeds. The grain must then be swept up and winnowed to remove the remainder of the chaff, and some grains such as rice must also be dehusked to remove the inedible seed coating. The storage of the grain also entails significant amounts of work. Commensal nibblers such as mice, rats, and insects target humans' stored resources worldwide, meaning that time must be devoted to the construction and maintenance of sturdy facilities such as tightly sealed storage pits and jars.

After a long chain of decisions about storage comes another set of decisions about preparation: how should the food be cooked and served? For the preparation of grain, the three simplest options are boiling, baking, and fermenting, each of which engenders a significantly different time span for preparation and different culinary equipment. Fermentation is a relatively simple process but takes more time than either boiling or baking. By contrast, boiled grain can be rendered edible within a short time and with basic equipment such as a cooking pot, but it requires the input of fuel. Baked goods require still more processing time because the grain must first be turned into flour, mixed (often with a time interval for resting the dough), and then baked. Although baked goods require more equipment in the form of grinding equipment and the construction of ovens, baked goods have the advantage of having greater storability, a factor that can have significant effects on labor investment elsewhere. In a study of Aztec household economies, Elizabeth Brumfiel (1991:241) has suggested that the culinary transition from boiled foods to reheatable tortillas may have marked a significant shift in household economies, because by making tortillas women would have been able to reallocate time otherwise spent on constant cooking towards making other types of crafts.

Modern examples of food as a cultural marker show how we can build more-sophisticated models of food interaction for the past. In a study of Italian immigrant foodways at the turn of the twentieth century, Hasia Diner (2001) has observed how newcomers transformed their cuisine with the addition of ingredients that were more abundant in their new surroundings, essentially inventing new dishes such as spaghetti with meatballs and pizzas with abundant meat toppings that defined their ethnicity in ways that were uniquely American yet still made them seem distinct from the meat preparations of other groups. Amy Bentley's (2004) engaging insights about modern southwestern cuisine shows how food associated with immigrants—such as barbecue, chiles, and tortillas—serves both to unite Spanish-speaking communities and to provide a sense of identity to Euro-Americans who appropriate the visual and sensory aspects of these same foods as a part of regional identity. The hasty remarketing of Middle Eastern cuisine as "Mediterranean food" in the United States after September 11, 2001, further illustrates the extent to which ethnic groups are most immediately and widely represented through their foodways. Because food preparation and consumption are quotidian activities that are perceived in the public sphere through sight and smell as well as taste, foodways have the potential to change more rapidly than any other cultural marker.

The archaeological record of culinary tools, storage facilities, and food waste tells a similar story of adaptation and change. Using such remains, Kent Lightfoot, Antoinette Martinez, and Ann Schiff (1998:212) were able to evaluate the interactions of the multiethnic community constructed by Russian whalers, Kashaya Pomo women, and Alaskan whalemen in early California. Lightfoot and his colleagues describe the "new menu" that was developed through an amalgam of traditional techniques and previously unfamiliar foods: new comestibles included mutton and beef, but they were cooked Pomo style, using hot rocks; although Alaskan-preferred marine mammals were also added to the diet, they too were prepared in the Pomo way rather than in the Alaskan fashion. Lightfoot and his colleagues (1998) also note that patterns of food consumption among the non-Russians at the site indicated that new foods were adopted by all of the inhabitants and that the new bonds of shared identity were overlain onto retained identities that resulted from natal affiliation, gender, and occupation. Similar accommodations to new foodways have been documented for the colonial Spanish inhabitants of the North American Southwest, who adopted Native foods such as quelite and goosefoot at the same time that Native peoples adopted European foods including watermelon and wheat (Trigg 2005:127, 142).

Culinary traditions through migration would have greatly affected our ancestors at many different periods and in many different regions. When people first entered the New World as hunters and gatherers, new species such as mammoths were available for consumption. In Madagascar, Malayo-Polynesian speakers encountered—and quickly rendered extinct—the pygmy hippo, while in New Zealand the first human inhabitants encountered the moa, a large flightless bird that met a similar fate in the cooking pot. Polynesian migrants would have met with a great diversity of animals, plants, and birds as they expanded throughout the Pacific.

Contact affected the development of early complex societies as well. When the Romans encountered the Celts in the area that is now France, we know that Celtic groups had already imported wine as a marker of political authority and social sophistication (Dietler 2007). How did the Romans change their culinary practices as a result of the encounter? Might we be able to discern frontier cuisine as a component of the rapidly expanding Roman state, changing as military supply caravans encountered local culinary traditions not only in continental Europe but also in North Africa, Greece, and the Near East? Although we often think of changes in foodways through migration as the result of economic opportunities and rational agent models of energy inputs and caloric yield, the actual processes of preparation and consumption were the result of individual, daily decisions about selecting and processing food for the consumption and presentation to the self and others.

The World of Beverages and Stews

When archaeologists talk about "food," we usually take this to mean solid food, in the form of Egyptian bread or Mississippian deer haunches. Thinking about "liquid food" enables us to expand our understanding of ancient consumption patterns and the way in which boiling and fermenting

FIGURE 2.5. Bowls, jars, and cups are the most common forms of vessels worldwide and indicate the high frequency of liquid foods in the diet after the invention of pottery starting around ten thousand years ago.

broadened the culinary repertoire. These simple but sophisticated ways of preparing food had a significant effect both on individual consumption patterns and on the organization of household work. Liquid foods such as stews and brews are "scalable," meaning that they can be prepared even by households that possess only one pot and a small hearth (see Rolle and Satin 2002). The development of pottery suggests that many early forms of cuisine consisted of liquid meals, with many archaeologically known cultures having just two basic forms of clay vessel: the bowl and the jar (fig. 2.5). Jars often are round-bottomed for cooking and can be balanced over a fire using three rocks or other props. Bowls are a highly versatile form of serving vessel, shaped to be held by one person at a time. In the earliest domestic repertoires, few other tools were necessary beyond (perhaps) a spoon or scoop for eating.

Soups, stews, beer, and other liquid foods are relatively efficient modes of production and consumption that can be interwoven into other task sequences and were highly suited to the multitasking environments of early food producers. Beverages can be kept in jars for long periods of time, enabling both cooks and eaters to integrate consumption with other activities. A stew can be kept on the fire or even removed and reheated without affecting the final product (in many cases, reheating actually enhances the flavors of the cooked meal). Soups and stews also can make use of a very wide variety of inputs and additions, from staple domesticates to wild herbs, mushrooms, and other types of "found" foods. For the cook, another advantage of the stew is that any number of raw materials can be utilized, usually in any order. Items can be added to the pot by the cook throughout the course of cooking, and some overcooking can be tolerated by the ingredients (in contrast to roasting, in which overcooking can drastically alter food value and palatability). This is unlike the linear and precisely timed steps of the baking process, in which ingredients such as yeast must be added at exact intervals and steps such as rising and baking must be undertaken in a relatively careful sequence.

Even minor changes in foodways imply significant shifts in technology similar to the steps described in Schiffer's invention cascade model. The simple repertoire of bowls and jars could only be replaced by other forms when ancillary technologies of preparation and presentation were adopted as well. Plates and platters, which we associate with our principal Western meals, are a very late addition to the material repertoire. Plates are suited only for relatively dry foods, such as roasted meat or baked goods, and usually require other utensils and settings (such as knives, tables, and chairs) for effective use. Oven-baked foods in turn require more processing and time investment for the transformation of raw ingredients, including the time spent in grinding grain and overseeing the rising of food such as bread. Ovens are special-purpose constructions that enclose the food being cooked, requiring large amounts of space and a steady supply of fuel. Ovens also have an economy of scale for use, such that a single household might not be able to effectively heat or use an oven on a regular basis, particularly for cooking small amounts of food. In Mesopotamia and in Rome, for example, ovens were a neighborhood installation (Keith 2003:69–70). The use of communal ovens was experienced until relatively recently even in the early modern period, where individuals would take their meats for roasting in the ovens of off-duty bakers.

From the perspective of the consumer as well as the cook, a stew provides advantages over other forms of cuisine. The stew eater can dip into the pot at any time, because once the ingredients are cooked the meal can be kept ready. Our contemporary idea of "mealtime" as an occasion in which all foods are prepared for simultaneous consumption in a group may be a far cry from the practice of earlier people, who ate as and when other tasks allowed. Another advantage to the consumption of food in the form of stews is that the water in which the materials are cooked is sterilized in the process of boiling the other ingredients. Waterborne illnesses were a particular danger for early village-dwelling residents, who had yet to perfect systems of drainage and sanitation (in comparison to their mobile hunter-gatherer predecessors, who simply shifted camp and moved away from their biohazards). The presence of liquid in soups and stews would have reduced the amount of raw water consumed by individuals. The watery nature of liquid cuisine also meant that raw ingredients could be "stretched" to satisfy more people. Stews may even have redistributed nutrients among a household group in a more equitable fashion by enabling some of the nutrient value of scarce meat to be present in every serving even if each person did not get an actual piece of meat in his or her bowl (Crown 2001:255).

Another important liquid food is in the form of beer, wine, ale, and other fermented beverages. As in the case of stews, fermented products provide sterilized, storable, and ready-to-eat products for the consumer. Fermentation changes the nutritional quality of foods as well as their taste, renders some inedible substances suitable for human consumption, and is a method of food preservation (Rolle and Satin 2002). Fermented beverages require an investment of time but may not have been otherwise difficult to prepare; recipes for early Egyptian and Mesopotamian brews seem to have involved very little energy on the part of the maker, as the grain was not even husked prior to fermentation and the beer was simply strained or drunk through straws (Sherratt 1987:94). As Sherratt also observed, fermented beverages have an effect that is far more than a matter of calories prepared in a hygienic and energy-efficient manner. Fermented beverages are an ideal way to create social bonds beyond the household: to reward the work party, to enhance the camaraderie of a communal meal, to cement ties of friendship among fictive kin and strangers in the course of exchange transactions, and to provide a mechanism for strangers to interact (Arthur 2003; Dietler 1995; M. Jones 2007).

Medicine as a Form of Cuisine

Cooking to address hunger is what we often think of when we consider the artful mixing of edible ingredients. But another important type of cuisine consists of the mixing up of substances to make medicine. Ancient people had much shorter life expectancies than we do, and they faced a greater range of injuries and illnesses. They probably escaped many of the age-related illnesses that we face, such as cancer (Halperin 2004). But our premodern counterparts had a much higher incidence of ailments that were uncomfortable if not completely debilitating, including intestinal parasites, lung ailments from living in smoky dwellings, minor injuries and infections, dental distress, and skin conditions. Illnesses and injuries, with their elements of unpredictability, constituted a significant potential for interrupting task flows. As a result, multitasking was not merely a matter of capitalizing on opportunity but also a means of maintaining outcomes in the face of unexpected hindrances.

Other species have been observed to selectively ingest plants that are known to have medicinal properties (Krief, Hladic, and Haxaire 2005). But humans face a wider range of biological and social challenges than do other species, which would have increased the impetus to cognize the surrounding landscape for multiple means of alleviating distress. We have unique biological risks in childbirth, given the evolutionary trade-off between large infant brain size and upright bipedalism, a factor that causes humans to have higher rates of childbirth-related distress and death than are exhibited by any other species (see Rosenberg and Trevathan 2002). In other ways as well, the human body is a fragile entity that is taxed by the ability of our brains to plan challenges that are executed at or beyond our physical capacities. Humans not only experience the range of injuries and illnesses faced by other mammals but also creatively and deliberately engage in risky behaviors such as hunting prime animals, exploiting raw materials in precarious locations, undertaking ritual pilgrimages to distant destinations, and experimenting with new and potentially poisonous foodstuffs.

FIGURE 2.6. A statuette of a woman grinding grain, Old Kingdom Egypt. The development of agriculture brought with it increased types of work that also resulted in physical stresses on all parts of the body.

Humans' cultural adaptations bring other species-specific injuries such as stresses resulting from energy investments in grinding, pounding, and toolmaking; the muscle strain of transporting heavy loads; burns from cooking and production fires; and smoke inhalation from the use of hearths enclosed in small living spaces. Skeletal evidence from the initial development of food production between ten thousand and twelve thousand years ago shows that people were living longer but suffered many new ailments, such as arthritis and repetitive-motion injuries from agricultural activities such as weeding and grinding grain (fig. 2.6). This means that attention to health and wellness was not, as it is for most of us today, a matter of unconsciously maintaining a general state of healthiness but instead was a constant monitoring and mitigation of various levels of discomfort.

The intimate portrait of human health seen in well-preserved bodies shows that even high-status people in the past were often unhealthy. The Marquise of Tai was an elderly woman who lived in China during the

Western Han dynasty about 2,100 years ago. By the time of her death, she had endured a variety of bodily stresses:

> [A] gallstone about the size of a bean completely obstructed the lower end of the common bile duct, and this must have caused excruciating pain. . . . There was evidence of tuberculosis infection, indicated by calcified tuberculosis foci in the upper lobe of the left lung; blood fluke (*Schistosoma japonicum*) ova were found in the connective tissue of the liver and the walls of the rectum; ova of whipworms (*Trichuris trichiura*) and pinworms (*Enterobius vermicularis*) were present in the intestines; the fourth intervertebral space was narrowed and had a bony outgrowth that could have caused severe back and leg pains. . . . Her right forearm was deformed as the result of a fracture that had not been properly treated. Altogether, the autopsy shows a picture of an elderly lady suffering from the traumas and hazards of her age and time." (Ascenzi, Cockburn, and Kleiss 1980:234)

Twentieth-century ethnographic studies, often undertaken in the quest for pharmacological information, have permitted researchers to understand the concept in traditional societies of "food as medicine and medicine as food" (Etkin and Ross 1982). Ancient texts similarly indicate that there was not a great dichotomy between the concepts of medicine and food, and that many foods had medicinal qualities in and of themselves. Thus, a prescription for healing might involve either a specifically prepared substance or the use of a common food in a specific way. For example, ancient Sumerian texts encapsulated a wide-ranging view of what could be ingested for health and well-being, with "about 250 vegetable and 120 mineral drugs, as well as alcoholic beverages, fats and oils, parts and products of animals, honey, wax, and various kinds of milk thought to have medical virtues" (Magner 1992:19). The *Brihadaranyaka Upanisad*, a South Asian text of the early centuries BC/AD, proposes that to conceive a daughter "who would be a scholar and attain a full term of life," a couple should have rice cooked with sesamum and served with clarified butter; to conceive a son with these qualities, they should have rice cooked in milk (Swami Madhavananda 1965:935–37). In other cases, recipes blended common foods with uncommon ones for pharmaceutical effect. The ancient Egyptian text known as the Papyrus Ebers, dating to 1550 BC, tells of a recipe "to allay itching": take "Cyperus-from-the-Meadow, Onion-meal, Incense, Wild Date-juice, Make into one and apply to the scurvy place" (Anderson 2007:28).

In addition to outright ailments, recipes also address cosmetic issues and social concerns. The Egyptian document known as the Edwin Smith papyrus dates to the seventeenth century BC but contains traditions that are probably much older, perhaps as early as the beginning of the Old Kingdom around 3000 BC. It contains a "Recipe for Transforming an Old Man into a Youth" that is quite elaborate:

> Let there be brought a large quantity of hemayet-fruit, about two *khar*. It should be bruised and placed in the sun. Then when it is entirely dry let it be [husked] as grain is [husked], and it should be winnowed until (only) the fruit thereof remains. Everything that comest therefrom shall be measured, (and) let it be sifted after the manner of the [threshing floor] with the sieve. Measure likewise everything that comest from these fruits and make them into two portions. . . . Let it be set aside, mixed with water. Make into a soft mass and let it be placed in a new jar over the fire (and) cooked very thoroughly, making sure that they boil, evaporating the juice thereof and drying them. . . . Now when it is cool, let it be put into (another) jar in order to wash it in the river. Let it be washed thoroughly, making sure that they are washed by tasting the taste of this water that is in the jar (until) there is no bitterness at all therein. It should be placed in the sun, spread out on launderer's linen. Now when it is dry, it should be ground upon a grinding mill-stone. (Brested 1930:495)

The modes of preparation described in this passage indicate the cognitive proximity of medicine to food, with the same types of words and tools used to describe the cooking, winnowing, and grinding of the medicinal product. The desire to change one's appearance through something edible is very akin to our modern consumption of similar preparations, ranging from gingko biloba to sports beverages and energy drinks, and suggests that the human propensity to link ingested substances with strength, prowess, and sexual potency has a very long history.

In ingesting medicine, just as in ingesting food, individuals determine the timing and context of consumption as well as whether they will follow the prescriptions for use. Medicinal treatments might often have been unpleasant or dangerous; ancient practices also included things that tasted bad, such as excrements, foul-smelling plants, and rancid fats in a process that Lois Magner (1992:12) has called a "dreckapothecary," designed to drive out an illness or bodily invader. Medicine also includes concoctions meant to enhance self-perception through stimulants, hallucinogens, and sedatives that were disproportionately appealing. Honey, perhaps one of the earliest stimulants known to our ancestors, has a surprising number of affiliated medical as well as nutritional qualities. In addition to its use as a sweetener, honey can be used to treat infections, burns, and gastrointestinal ailments, and its effectiveness for this purpose has been replicated in modern medical studies (e.g., Cooper, Molan, and Harding 2002; Sato and Miyata 2000; Vardi et al. 1998). The use of fire and smoke probably assisted in honey collection and made it a more predictable resource to acquire, starting perhaps as early as four hundred thousand years ago (when the first suggestion of human-controlled fire appears in the archaeological record). Because there were very few sources of sweetening prior to the cultivation of sugarcane, the ingestion of even a modest quantity of honey in ancient times would have been enough to send an individual into a sugar shock. Other forms of natural substances that alter states include those with effects ranging from mild (such as fermented fruit) to hallucinogenic (such as mushrooms and certain plants).

The adoption of agriculture—with its supporting technologies of pottery, grinding tools, and storage jars—meant a great expansion of the repertoire and availability of mind-altering substances. Some agriculture involved the cultivation of plants with stimulant properties, such as cacao in Mesoamerica, with its caffeinelike alkaloid theobromine (Bletter and Daly 2006). In many ways, the agricultural revolution should be characterized as an alcoholic revolution because the elaborate processing systems developed for growing, storing, and parching grain could, with additional labor and time, also produce fermented beverages (Haaland 2007; Sherratt 1987). The types of foods that were domesticated were primarily starchy grains that were not abundant prior to human cultivation: from corn in the New World to rice, wheat, and barley in Eurasia and Africa. Once developed, fermented beverages played a considerable role in social life as well as in nutrition.

Culinary knowledge has another formulation related to the practice of medicine: poisons. Some plants that are nutritious and edible nonetheless have poisonous elements (such as the noxious leaf of the rhubarb), and some plants (such as acorns and tubers, which can have high levels of toxins and tannins) require sophisticated treatments before they can be utilized for human consumption. Early textual sources indicate that people used these ingredients even when they recognized the potential for distress. Medieval Spanish texts note that "[t]he poor even made bread from roots, wild plants or acorns, even though they realized that these ingredients could be poisonous and that doctors recommended that they should not be eaten under any circumstances" (Salas-Salvadó et al. 2006: S103). But purposefully created poisons also were part of the cultural landscape, whether as part of routine health care (such as abortifacients) or as components of political control. The same early texts that codify medicinal treatments also record the use of poisons, and one of the earliest recorded practitioners of the art of poisoning is Menes, the first Egyptian pharaoh (Cilliers and Retief 2000). The development of poisons also brought a lively business in antidotes. L. Cilliers and F. P. Retief (2000) discuss the range of known antidotes in the early days of the Roman Empire, a time when political poisoning was commonly reported.

As comestibles, food and medicine are at two ends of a continuum. Their preparation encompasses the same cognitive processes of memory and planning through the consideration of time and energy expenditure. Many of the same tools and techniques—including fermentation, boiling, and grinding—were applied to both medicine and food. Specialized knowledge about modes of storage that enabled food to be kept free of harmful bacteria, vermin, and other forms of spoilage would also have been applied to medicine. Food and medicine also are at two ends of the philosophical spectrum; one needs to eat to stay alive, so that idea of food that is "good for you" in addition to being filling is a logical extension of the quest to alleviate hunger.

Food and the Development of Social Complexity

There are four significant ways that foodways are affected by the development of social complexity, and all of them build on earlier adaptations at the individual level: the enhancement of communal food events such as feasting, the investment of energy into increased production, the acceleration of food stress into conditions of famine, and the expansion of networks of trust and social interactions in the provision of food.

Human groups have a propensity for feasting that dates well back into the ancient past, as seen from archaeological investigations of large middens that show collective food waste and the butchery patterns of large animals that would have provided food for groups of people larger than

FIGURE 2.7. In complex societies, the production, distribution, and consumption of food become a focus of political activity.

a single household. Feasts often are inferred from unusual quantities or types of foods that are recovered from trash middens, or from large quantities of lightly used serving vessels such as cups or bowls. Feasting also can be signaled indirectly through the presence of very large serving or cooking vessels that would have been larger than a normal household's quantity of daily food (e.g., Marshall and Maas 1997). The context of finds, including exotic ingredients or signs of labor-intensive preparation, is important to the consideration of whether the interpretation of feasting can be supported. The distinction of feasts is that unlike ordinary meals, feasts are provided to large numbers of people and take place on selected occasions rather than every day, requiring coordination that may become incorporated into permanent social and political distinctions.

In complex societies, the function of feasting is augmented when the power to provide food becomes the means by which some individuals establish and maintain control over others (fig. 2.7). As W. H. Wills and Patricia Crown (2004) have noted, food constitutes a significant component of research on status differentiation in prehistory. For the most recent time periods, this scholarly development follows on seminal work by Bryan Hayden (1990), who proposed that the development of agriculture was not a result of necessity as human groups outgrew their environments' capacity to provide food but instead was the result of the desire for status among aggrandizing individuals. Hayden's work subsequently has focused on the phenomenon of feasting as a social activity that binds leaders and followers together in mutual cycles of obligation (e.g., Hayden 1996, 2001, 2009). Other scholars have followed in this mode of inquiry in different parts of the ancient world, including Barbara Mills for the premodern American Southwest (2004), Michael Dietler for France in the Roman period (1995, 1996, 2007), and Lisa LeCount for the Maya region (2001).

Although archaeologists discuss feasts as though they were always successful in achieving the goals of aggrandizement and the enticement of followers, a closer look at the feasting process shows that there were challenges as well as rewards for leaders who engaged in food presentations. Food for feasts had to be accumulated, transported, and prepared in sufficient quantities and at the expected time; managers of all of the different components of the preparation process had to plan carefully and multitask to avoid the risk of "feast failure." Feasts also are successful only when they are attended; if the food was meant as an enticement for obligations that were greater than individuals were willing to pledge, they could elect not to attend the feast and thereby avoid the pressure to reciprocate through work.

The notion of food preference enables us to look at other aspects of the relationship of leaders to followers in the development of complex societies. While labor-intensive projects sponsored or guided by political authorities often are analyzed either as despotic undertakings by a predatory or manipulative leadership or as the impersonal result of economic systems' movements towards efficiency, we might instead evaluate these projects as something that builds on shared cultural understandings of what is "good to eat." Leaders' goals of aggrandizement were most likely to be achieved when framed in terms of prevailing social norms, as indicated in the archaeological record. For example, investigations at the Giza Plateau in Egypt show that large groups of people contributed labor for the construction of the pyramids under a rubric of shared values in which there were also substantial rewards in the form of abundant food and drink (Hawass and Lehner 1997). Widespread items of consumption signal that there was a common repertoire of daily caloric intake, a basic larder upon which social divisions were subsequently added through aspects of cuisine, relative abundance of the preferred food, or the addition of rare or unusual ingredients.

The Indian subcontinent provides another example of the way in which political authorities facilitated the development of agricultural systems by calling upon shared cultural ideals of food preference (Smith 2006b). Starting in the earliest literate period of the first millennium BC, textual sources show how rice was a particularly celebrated food that had medicinal and ritual value in addition to being the most sought-after source of daily meals. Later texts offer lyrical praise of rice as the ideal food for both humans and gods, complete with recipes for how to prepare rice for occasions ranging from the cure of ailments to the greeting of the sun deity. These texts precede the development of large-scale agricultural systems designed to grow rice in large quantities, indicating that shared cultural value systems were already in place. Rice was a familiar trope that underlay the organization of labor for production systems that benefited both central authorities and ordinary people, a process engaged in both by nascent political authorities (Smith 2006a) and by Buddhist religious organizations (Shaw et al. 2007). New research by others working on complex societies shows the promise of looking at the impact of daily food choices in the articulation of large-scale food production and distribution for other regions as well (e.g., Janusek and Kolata 2004 for ancient Tiwanaku; Twiss 2007 for the Levant; van der Veen 2003, 2007 for Iron Age Britain).

The investments by political authorities can, however, be countered by administrative failures that exacerbate the food stresses that are a natural part of the environment. Famines are distinct from periodic food stress because they occur when sociopolitical factors propel environmental fluctuation into catastrophe. These factors include political extraction of agricultural products for taxation; heavy dependence on monoculture crops that are susceptible to disease or sudden environmental degradation; the use of food supply routes and transportation devices for war materiel or other political purposes; and the inability of people to access available food supplies (D'Souza 1988; Sen 1981). When one or more of these conditions are present and when there is also a precipitating natural event (such as insect invasion, drought, or flood), a famine can result. Given humans' omnivorous tendencies and the documented strategies (including "famine foods") that mitigate against lean times, it seems unlikely that famine as a widespread cause of demographic collapse occurred in prehistory, because the political conditions of supracommunity agricultural decision making did not then exist.

The stream of provisioning in complex societies includes a high level of individual participation in the networks of distribution. Greater populations and the development of hierarchical social and economic networks provide additional mechanisms for food access beyond the self-provisioning seen in simple societies. These new mechanisms include working for others; the incorporation into institutions such as the military, religious institutions, and leader-sponsored workshops; and slavery. The capacity of individuals to suspend their disbelief in the attenuation of their food supply is replaced by a complicated calculus of entitlement, privilege, and reliance on a highly interdependent mechanism of provisioning. We have inherited these mechanisms in our own society: we may not know where our next meal is coming from, but we trust that the place that has our food (a store, restaurant, or dorm cafeteria) will have what we need. In turn, the managers of those establishments may not know exactly where the actual food is coming from, but they trust in the supplier to be able to deliver the needed goods in time for preparation.

Studies of historically known disenfranchised and marginal groups indicate that people retain the capacity to manipulate food consumption practices, with implications for their selective input in the production process. The development of specialized economies means that although elites and non-elites participate equally in the desire for certain foods, they participate differentially in the increased production of staple domesticates. For elites, the incentive to provide capital and coordination lies in the production of sufficient surplus for elite consumption (in the form of tribute or taxes) that can be used to support specialists, sponsor feasts, feed armies, or feed themselves (D'Altroy and Earle 1985; see also Billman 2002; Earle 1997). Non-elites must provide the labor utilized in the production process, but they benefit when capital-intensive and managerial inputs coordinated by elites result in greater quantities of food. However, the choices of *what* foods to manipulate are heavily influenced by social factors and actualized at the level of lived, daily experience one person at a time. Moreover, the preparation and serving of these foods, as well as their specific acts of consumption, are based on individual autonomous decisions at the household level whose cognitive antecedents long predate social complexity.

Summary

As a highly social species, we have an approach to hunger that has both physiological and social implications. In his book *Feasts*, Martin Jones (2007:19) asks two provocative questions: "Why should one of the most basic biological functions, eating, develop into an elaborate costume drama of manners and gestures?" and "What do such social dramas contribute to the food quest, and indeed, how has the food quest found itself at the heart of social life?" One potential answer to these questions is that the preparation, eating, and discussion of food constitute a social realm in which every individual can participate. Dealing with food gives each of our big, social, human brains something to do on a regular basis. The daily process of food preparation means that there is an ongoing opportunity for dynamic social relationships to be expressed, renegotiated, and reconstituted (Jones 2002:136). Just as people cannot live biologically without food, they cannot live socially without the regular performance of food events. Food makes use of many of the components of individual cognitive autonomy, including memory, if-then logic, future planning, and the recognition of social networks through language and ritual. Food events are enacted in the present but also are encompassed in the memory of past events and the projection of future events. Food enables the sustaining of health and has a spatiality of acquisition, processing, and consumption. It also has a temporality of consumption, fulfilling regular bodily requirements that affect nearly all other uses of the landscape.

Each day, individuals engage in a dynamic interplay of decisions that incorporate both creativity and habituation for each act of food preparation, distribution, and consumption. Food, goods, and work are closely intertwined at the level of action, and individuals engage in multitasking to assess the potential range of foods, the time needed for acquisition and preparation of foods, the range of tools required for rendering natural substances into edible portions, and the physical and social contexts of consumption. Increased trade and economic networks brought more people and more foodways together. While contemporary experience suggests that these culinary encounters often resulted in syncretic cuisine and cross-group adaptations, there also were foods that served as distinguishing markers of ethnicity and geographic origin. The capacity of food to serve as the focus of individual decision making is highlighted by the expressions of cultural autonomy by refugee groups, slaves, prisoners, and children in institutional settings.

The increased attention to food consumption by both elites and non-elites in complex societies illustrates that shared behavior is the basis upon which subsequent social distinctions are made. The multitasking capacity of humans related to food increases, rather than decreases, with the development of social complexity. Whereas in a small-scale society even elites partake of food prepared by basic cooking techniques, we can observe that the concept of "cuisine" developed in complex societies at all levels of the social hierarchy. Cultural standards are invoked in basic subsistence activities such as food preference and styles of food preparation, but individual and household choices are always paramount: no coercion can be found in the way in which food is prepared by even the poorest household! Nor are society-wide changes in food preparation predicated on the availability of increasingly exotic ingredients; in most cases, preparation style (often involving increased time in preparation) is what renders a food culturally appropriate from the perspective of the individual who is eating it.

CHAPTER 3

Individuals and Goods

FROM THE FIRST MOMENT of morning consciousness, our daily actions involve objects. We awaken from a resting place that was fashioned by human hands to be a comfortable place for sleep. We make our first meal from a kitchen repertoire that involves at least one container or utensil or food wrapper. We prepare for the day's activities through the application of a toothbrush, a razor, a comb, some soap. We put on clothing in anticipation of what we will be doing that day, with some consideration of anticipated weather, work, and social engagements. We move from the inside space of the household to the outside landscape of the community, from dwellings to open areas and neighborhoods. Throughout the day, we use objects to perform tasks, communicate with others, engage in social relations, and give others an idea of who we are.

Most objects are designed to be utilized by one person at a time, indicating the extent to which the human-made world is at its essence an individualized one. Prior to large-scale industrial processes, most objects also were fashioned by one person at a time, and usually from start to finish by the same person. Each person had a sense of how to make and utilize basic goods, often intertwining the production of such goods into a multitasking strategy that sequentially allocated energy to short-term, medium-term, and long-term outcomes.

Human-modified natural objects can be discerned as early as 2.5 million years ago, in the form of bashed-up stones characterized as Oldowan choppers. By 1.6 million years ago, our ancestors' ability to modify natural materials was greatly elaborated in the development of the Acheulean hand ax (fig. 3.1). The hand ax is a particularly noteworthy creation both because of its aesthetics and because this same form was made for more than a million years (Mithen 2003). However, these distinctive and multipurpose tools should not be the only measure of the earliest human cognitive development. The variability of stone tools that were *not* hand axes indicates that both stasis and creativity were evident in the creation of durable items. We also should envision that active processes of stasis

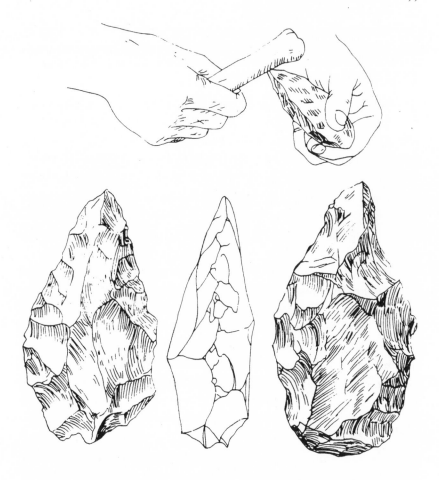

FIGURE 3.1. The Acheulean hand ax is the most elaborate early form of human stone tool. Evident in archaeological sites in Africa, Europe, Asia, and the Near East starting as early as 1.6 million years ago, the hand ax would have required considerable skill in the choice of materials as well as the incremental reduction of a piece of stone to a desired teardrop shape.

and creative change were manifested in the types of materials that rarely survive in the archaeological record, such as wood, grass, gourds, leaves, skins, and other natural items upon which individuals would have exercised their creativity in toolmaking and tool use.

By about a quarter-million years ago, we can discern in the fossil record the emergence of anatomically modern *Homo sapiens* along with the material signatures of modern human behavior. New techniques of stone blade production starting in Africa as early as 250,000 years ago are suggestive of a more sophisticated understanding of energy efficiency in stone tool production and use (McBrearty and Brooks 2000:495). The acceleration of new material expressions is particularly marked during the Upper Paleolithic of Europe and the Levant some 40,000 years ago, with a discernable abundance of ornaments, painting, and figural representations indicative of highly developed symbolic behavior (Bar-Yosef 2002; Kuhn et al. 2001). As summarized by E. J. Lowe (1998:90), the emergence of symbolic activity at this evolutionary juncture is perceived by many scholars as having "freed human memory (both working memory and long-term memory) from the severe limitations imposed by the biology of the brain, as an information-processing system." This view of material objects serving as place markers for cognitive activity recalls the discussion of memory by Michael Hasselmo and Chantal Stern (2006), who discerned between short-term "working memory" and longer-term memory. With objects serving as memory storage that was always activated in the present tense, individuals could remove even more types of memories to long-term status, enabling them to devote a greater proportion of cognitive energy to multitasking in the present moment.

Consumption and the Individual

From the moment of birth, all humans are consumers. But why are so many different types of objects sought, acquired, and used? Why do nonlocal objects appear when local raw materials are physically adequate for a given task? And why do styles of objects change when their utilitarian function appears to stay the same? These components of artifact shape and style indicate the relationship between creativity and habituation in the crafting, selection, and use of material goods. Far from being the unique result of large-scale manufacturing processes developed in the Industrial Revolution, the conscious selection and use of physical objects has a long evolutionary trajectory and is a fundamental component of what it means to be human.

Archaeologists have traditionally studied production rather than consumption, for both practical and philosophical reasons. On the practical level, the physical locations of production activity are relatively easy to discern in an archaeological landscape (Costin 1991). Production areas tend to be distinct, marked by features such as kilns or pits and by concentrations of debris such as stone flakes or metal slag. Production areas also can be predicted through the study of geological maps that show the location of likely raw material sources, such as ores, stones, and clay.

Archaeologists' focus on the production process also stems from our approach to the evolutionary development of human societies. We can identify the distinct stages of increasing technological sophistication through materials analysis, calculation of production efficiencies, and the relative increase in the quantity of goods produced. We can analyze how humans developed their technical skills through time, first bashing rocks to make a crude chopping tool and eventually becoming the species that can craft a corkscrew, a rocket ship, or a Fabergé egg. This stairstep approach of increasing complexity fits well with our understanding of cultural evolution as a development of hierarchies in political, social, and technological terms. Political and economic control becomes intertwined when political figures support those specialized craftsmakers while defining who shall have access to labor-intensive goods (e.g., Brumfiel 1987; Earle 1990; Helms 1979; Wright 1984).

Production is thus viewed as the prerogative of the powerful, another factor that enables archaeologists to link production with elites as the perceived drivers of social complexity. Aidan Southall (1998:9) provides a view of the relationship between production and consumption that illustrates the passive implications for the latter: in his view, production is related to matters of religious, political, and economic activity as well as kinship, while consumption bears only the stamp of "recreation." Power is tied to the "articulated combination of forces and relations of production, where the forces of production consist *essentially* of the mode of appropriation of nature by men and women, the relations of production being the system whereby the surplus product is extracted and distributed, consisting of property relations and the class order upholding and enforcing them" (Southall 1998:12, emphasis in original).

Archaeologists' longstanding view of production connected to power reinforces the idea that by studying elites, production, or both, we will capture the essential elements of how socioeconomic systems come into existence. Richard Blanton and his colleagues (1996:3), in their evaluation of the way that authority is expressed in newly emerging state systems, note that sources of power include "wealth and factors of production." The relationship between these state systems and their surrounding hinterlands is similarly expressed in terms of production; Michael Smith and Frances Berdan (2000:285) have proposed that political manipulations of the hinterland through core-periphery relationships can be more precisely delineated by substituting the idea of a "core" with the notion of an "affluent production zone." These production strategies usually involve elite goods that are afterwards distributed and acquired as part of political activities.

Archaeologists' focus on production enables them to skirt a significant moral issue as well. Like other social scientists who are disapproving of humans' wasteful tendencies, archaeologists have mixed feelings about consumption as a process that results in a rapid rate of goods acquisition and discard over time. In our contemporary world, the study of consumption is guided by the juxtaposition of a desire for economic growth (how people can be induced to consume more) with a moral debate (how people can be induced to consume less). On the economic side, there is a push for greater amounts of consumption because sustained, or even accelerated, demand is now eyed by economists as a fundamental component of economic prosperity (e.g., Prahalad 2005; Witt 2001). This function as an economic growth engine is, however, counterbalanced by an injunction against using too many goods. Consumption, with its accompanying implications of wastefulness and reliance on nonrenewable resources, is often portrayed as *over*consumption, with deleterious moral, social, and environmental effects including the erosion of traditional culture (Miller 1995:156). This perception of consumption as wastefulness is hardly limited to the twentieth century; as Neil McKendrick (1982) has observed, philosophers and social theorists of the early seventeenth century decried excess spending as morally suspect, at the very moment when large quantities of low-cost goods were being made available to the consuming public (the furor eventually was transformed by those who extolled the benefits of consumption as a significant component of state-level economic health, as exemplified by Adam Smith's *Wealth of Nations* in 1776).

Scholars sometimes propose that large-scale consumption of goods by ordinary people was only made possible in the modern era, a perspective summed up by Steven Miles and Ronan Paddison (1998:817):

"[C]onsumption has traditionally been the preserve of the higher éche-
lons of society. From this point of view, it is only in the aftermath of the
Second World War that access to consumption, or at least the prospect
of consumption, has become a prime focus for the aspirational working
classes." In the same way that social theorists view "individuality" as the
unique privilege of the modern Westerner, they also portray consumption as a very recent development in which "[t]he rise of a consumer society did not come into its own, as such, until the onset of industrialisation.
As production for subsistence came to be replaced by wage labor, people
inevitably became consumers as well as producers" (Miles and Paddison
1998:818). Consumption and individuality are explicitly tied together by
Julie Bettie (2000:14): "The expression of self through one's relationship
to and creative use of commodities (both artifacts and the discourses of
popular culture) is a central practice in capitalist society," with the implication that premodern people neither desired to consume nor had the
means to do so.

Archaeological evidence, however, shows that people in the past
did utilize goods on a massive scale whenever possible. At the twenty-
thousand-year-old site of Kutikina in Tasmania, there were "over 75,000
stone flakes and tools recovered from a less than 1 percent sample of the
site" (Feder 2004:259); at this rate, the hunter-gatherers living at the site
would have made and used 7.5 million tools. Similar rates of discard can
be seen in sites of the early agricultural period; in the Sudan, a Khar-
toum Neolithic settlement yielded 30,000 fragments of grinding stone
in an excavation of just a small portion of the site (Haaland 2007:172).
Premodern cities, with their vast waste dumps and large-scale manufacturing areas, further indicate that production and consumption were
undertaken on a considerable scale long before the invention of steam
engines and modern factories.

Ancient texts on taxation, market exchange, and currency conversion
rates also indicate the scale of transactions in daily-use goods at the beginning of complex societies. Although some of these goods were useful
tools imported from long distances, other goods were desired in large part
precisely because of their exotic origins. For the Roman world, we are
fortunate in having documents such as the first-century AD merchant's
handbook known as the *Periplus of the Erythrean Sea*, which remarks on
good supplies of tortoise shell from the islands off Western Arabia, large

quantities of dates from Oman, and "a considerable amount of cloth of ordinary quality" from India (Casson 1989:71, 73, 81).

What are the parameters affecting the individual's acquisition and use of objects? Although the technology and raw materials of production can be controlled through the selective processes of apprenticeship or the guarding of natural resource zones, consumption is controlled only haphazardly. Control of consumption is usually attempted through largely ineffective moral calls to action or through sumptuary rules that specify what people *must not* do, rather than the considerably greater range of what they *may* do. Preserved in texts, these sumptuary rules may be efficient from the point of view of rulers, but they also inflate our historical and archaeological expectations of the impact of political will on non-elites.

Comparison of archaeological assemblages with documentary records illustrates that even when sumptuary rules exist, they are only one factor influencing consumption practices. Practical effects such as variability in resource availability, as well as desires to demonstrate links between groups, also affect the use and display of goods. Diana DiPaolo Loren (2001) has looked at Spanish colonial sites for the effects of elaborate sumptuary rules imposed by the Spanish government in an attempt to preserve distinct *castas*, or racial/status hierarchies. Although the sumptuary rules were clear about clothing, food, and other items that were to be used in each social level, actual practices appear to have been quite flexible, especially at frontier posts, where supplies of appropriate goods from Mexico City were infrequent. Thus, both high-status and low-status individuals appear to have displayed mixed styles of dress as well as making use of a variety of local foods and vessels that would otherwise have been deemed inappropriate for their social station (Loren 2001:68–72). The ineffectiveness of sumptuary laws in the colonial period, in which elite power was reinforced by advanced weaponry and punitive religious codes, illustrates that for more-ancient periods, with their weaker enforcement mechanisms, prescriptions on consumption should be interpreted as suggestions rather than facts.

The development of sumptuary laws was paralleled by other ancient commentaries on the idea of consumption as a "conspicuous" act that proclaims social status. The Indian king Asoka, writing in the third century BC, complained about women who carried out "trivial and useless" rituals that would have included specific types of objects (Thapar

1997:254). The Romans, who also were astute observers of cultural fashions and consumer taste, frequently commented on the cost of items in economic terms that encompassed a moral overtone (one of the best known of these critics was the first-century AD historian Pliny the Elder [1980:101, 1949:41]). Excessive consumption as a mode of social advancement by the nouveaux riches was famously parodied in *The Satyricon*, written by the Roman Petronius but with a resonance that would not be out of place in the celebrity magazines of today (Arrowsmith 1959). In the modern period, the idea of conspicuous consumption was articulated by Thorstein Veblen in *The Theory of the Leisure Class* in 1899, followed by other important works such as Pierre Bourdieu's *Distinction* (1984) and Mary Douglas and Baron Isherwood's *World of Goods* (1996).

In both modern and ancient cases, social commentators have observed how the acquisition and display of the "right" material culture enable individuals to project their social rank. Individuals of high social classes retain their visible superiority through the constant pursuit of distinctive or rare objects. Objects can be classified as rare if they exist in nature in only small quantities (such as large diamonds), if they require special expertise in acquisition and maintenance (such as exotic animals), or if they represent large amounts of labor investment in terms of time and skill (such as finely woven shawls or intricate carvings). Often, there is a link between labor investment and exotic materials, adding extra prestige when rare materials are graced with skilled artisanry. Archaeologists theorize a link between political power and the control of exotic materials in the past as well, in which leaders built alliances through the conspicuous donation and placement of exotic or labor-intensive goods (e.g., DeMarrais, Castillo, and Earle 1996; Helms 1993).

The production and consumption of goods engage the human cognitive capacity for multitasking through memory, planning, and the addressing of contingencies (such as what to do when a production process fails or a consumption event produces an unexpected effect). Some actions of production and consumption are so intertwined as to be unclear about whether the intent is one of production or consumption. For example, the decision of how much herb to put in a stew or how large a stone to start with for a stone tool involves choices and acts that are simultaneously consumptive of raw materials and productive of a finished product.

To describe this interlinked relationship, researchers have utilized a variety of terms, such as "productive consumption" (Patterson 2005:378) and "consumptive production" (Paynter 2000:176). Alison Bell (1999) and Tristan Carter (2007) have both utilized the concept of "conspicuous production" to describe the way in which production can involve extralarge supplies of raw materials or prominently displayed tools to achieve a performative effect through the manufacturing process.

One principal difference does remain between production and consumption: production is a one-time event, while consumption is a process in which the same object can be used and reused, displayed and transferred, mended and modified, and transformed and recontextualized in a variety of ways. Studies of individual artifacts also show that while production constitutes a linear sequence of events, consumption often is a nonlinear process of utilizing food, goods, and energy expenditure in a process of constant feedback between the objects used, their user, and the social context of that use (Steedman 2001:32). Consumption through the handling of material objects thus becomes the quintessential forum for multitasking in which cognitive processes become materialized through an individual's physical surroundings.

Temporality also plays an important role in the multitasking aspects of consumption, as explored in Ian Steedman's stimulating *Consumption Takes Time* (2001). Work time (production time) cannot occupy all of a worker's twenty-four hours, as some fraction of time is necessarily allocated to the acquisition and use of goods. Applying the concept of temporality to the notion of consumption as a matter of both tangible goods and intangible space and services, we can see how the principle of consumption is integral to every act of time allocation. The implications for archaeology are significant, because each person constantly makes decisions about production relative to perceptions of available time. In matters related to food, for example, we can see how time allocations are involved not merely in the daily consumption of food but in all of the events leading to that consumption, including the way that the individual structures the day around meals, snacks, and beverages. Feasts have temporal requirements as well, as time is needed for gathering resources, preparing food, and distributing it to eaters. Feasts also require time allocations by eaters, both to physically consume the feast and in the form of projected time allocation for reciprocation.

Material Goods and Human Cognition

Symbolic activity, conscious toolmaking, and language all appear to have developed as complementary cognitive processes in the evolution of *Homo sapiens*. Recent studies utilizing brain-scanning technology show that humans store information about objects in a sorting sequence that places data about different properties (e.g., color, size, form) in different physical parts of the brain. This processing mechanism, in which knowledge about objects is stored as segmented "packets" of information, allows for more-efficient processing of newly encountered objects because they are likely to share some aspects of previously known entities (Martin 1998:72; see also Schiffer and Miller 1999:78). Moreover, the neural structure related to human-made objects (as opposed to naturally occurring entities such as animals) appears to have an added dimension of elaboration. Abstract aspects of tools such as name and form are stored in the same neural region that is active in the use of tools (Martin 1998:79–82). The evolutionary implications for created objects as part of human cognitive and linguistic capacities are significant: the growth of cognitive processes including memory, future planning, and conditional thinking appears to have taken place coincident with, and dependent on, the manufacture and use of objects.

A complementary model of the evolutionary link between human cognition and objects can be developed through the study of infants, children, and the physical world. The sense of self that is brought into being and projected through basic modifications and daily-use goods is itself an outgrowth of an even deeper capacity to articulate the self as an independent physical and psychological entity. The ability of children to recognize themselves in mirrors signals the presence of a self-concept that is activated through material means. Although mirrors are a modern invention, our most distant ancestors would have been able to gaze at themselves by looking down into still water. These visual assessments of the self would have been supplemented by other sensory distinctions, such as the perception of one's own voice, the sensation of touching one's own body compared to touching another's, the recollection of distinct memories of an event that might be different from another person's, and the sensations of illness and injury that individuals perceive as being wholly within their own bodies.

The use of created or natural objects to actualize the self is seen in the phenomenon of another basic psychological activity observable in children: the "transitional objects" that are the first things utilized by an infant to mediate between the self and the surrounding world. D. W. Winnicott's (1971:2) seminal work on this topic defines "transitional" objects as those materials that "are not part of the infant's body yet are not fully recognized as belonging to external reality." In the modern realm, these transitional objects include toys and blankets, although Winnicott suggests that any external reality, including a parent, can serve in this role. Long before an infant can locomote or even feed itself, there is an interaction with objects that appears to be a precursor to reality-testing (Winnicott 1971:9).

If Winnicott is correct, then interaction with objects is a necessary precursor to subsequent engagement with the world and with other individuals. As Michael Tomasello (1999:513) notes, infants often interact with an adult and an object in ways that promote distinctly human developmental processes of gaze-following and social referencing, as well as "joint attention," in which adult and child are engaged with the same object. The subsequent contextualization of an object, including its spatial placement and rearrangement, permits both parties to communicate efficiently even prior to language use. Subsequent language-based communication takes place within a realm of shared understandings, in which the specificities of a particular speech interchange are creative yet bounded by rules of meaning and grammar (e.g., Benveniste 1971:223–29; Pinker 1998:118–21). The placement of portable objects and the arrangement of space allow the range of interpretations to be efficiently constrained by the established contexts while allowing for a nearly infinite number of language-based communicative messages to be generated — another important way in which cognitive creativity and the potential for habituation are actualized by the individual.

Children can distinguish between animate and inanimate objects, another factor that indicates the deep interconnection of tool use and cognitive evolution. Marissa Greif and her colleagues (2006) have conducted experiments with preschool children and have shown that even at an early age, children know the difference between the inherent properties of living things and tools. In one experiment, they showed children pictures of unfamiliar objects and unfamiliar animals and prompted the children to ask questions. The researchers noted that children always asked questions that were domain-specific, for example, never asking about eating or reproductive habits of artifacts and never asking about the use or function of animals. In other words, children appear to have a sense of the inherent characteristics of living things and inanimate objects. This ability to consistently separate domains is another indicator of the extent to which the human brain became specialized in artifact identification and use.

The long developmental trajectory of objects in the human repertoire suggests that social investment in material goods was also present from a very early time period. Objects serve as the vehicles for the storage and activation of memory and are the setting for communication and interaction in a social group (Schiffer and Miller 1999). There is a vast archaeological literature on the potential of style to communicate group membership, ethnic identity, and other forms of information transfer (e.g., Conkey and Hastorf 1990; Hill 1985; Miller 1985, 1987; Sackett 1977; Wiessner 1983; Wobst 1977). Moving beyond this literature to consider the effects generated and assessed by individuals requires a somewhat different approach. Although traditional archaeological theorists have evaluated how style generates particular expectations of action, it is also important to consider how individuals can differentially interpret the displays in a way that generates the potential for creative alterations of meaning by both the sender and the recipient of such messages.

Examining the implications of receiver-based communications, Michael Schiffer and Andrea Miller (1999:65) note that "we can register more or less simultaneously the multimodal performances of multiple emitters . . . supply(ing) us with an enormous stream of potentially relevant evidence for fashioning inferences and forecasts, and generating responses." However, the management of this information stream is dependent on hierarchical processing capacities including the ability to discount or downplay some information and the ability to store some information through material proxies. The presence of coherent means of information processing provided by a hierarchically organized brain means that humans could not have become highly intellectual and social creatures *without* having increasing quantities of material goods to store information. Multitasking was thus enhanced through the use of objects not only as tools to apply to the job at hand but also as mnemonic devices to facilitate the restarting of an interrupted work flow.

A corollary to the use of objects as memory-storage is the use of objects to accentuate different components of identity. Although the term *identity* is often utilized to refer to both the private and public perceptions of the self, it is useful to assess the different properties of inner and outer representation. Robert Kleine and his colleagues (1993) thus suggest that we should use the term *identity* to refer to the internalized perception of individual capacities and the term *role* to describe the way in which the individual is perceived in social interactions. Material culture is an important component of both identity and role, but the same goods may not be displayed in both contexts; for example, Kleine and his colleagues cite the ownership of sports equipment that prompts individuals to think of themselves as "athletic" even if they have not used the equipment for years.

The use of material objects enables individuals to demonstrate multiple roles each in their own appropriate context. In our culture, an example might be the person who is a dentist, a soccer coach, and a volunteer at the annual Boy Scout pancake breakfast. For each of these roles, she dresses differently and utilizes different types of objects, and each activity takes place in a spatial setting that is entered but neither created nor modified by the participant. Each of the role enactments also has a temporal component, ranging from daily activities (dentist) to weekly (soccer coach) and even infrequent (volunteer). In each case, the use of objects identifies the person as performing in a particular social role at a particular place and at a particular moment. These defining objects also enable the other participants and observers to more easily identify which social role is being played by which person. The use of material culture as a guide to expectations of behavior probably acts in the same way as segmented memory and networked language, as the potential for conflicting messages is reduced through the use of material objects that prepare people for particular kinds of expected interactions. Setting the stage through material objects continues to condition our behaviors and expectations today (such as the cross-cultural preference for doctors and other professionals to dress in a certain manner, as well as the cross-cultural appreciation of branding as a means of identifying products with specific qualities [e.g., Rehman et al. 2005]).

Although one might expect stage-setting through material objects to be particularly useful in large group settings where individuals encounter many strangers, the use of material culture as a marker is seen even in small-scale societies where people expect to be known to each other. In a brief but illuminating paper on the power of material objects to project social roles, Terence Turner (1980) examined the use of social signaling through material modifications by the Kayapo people of the Amazon rain forest. Although the Kayapo people do not wear clothes as such, their bodily adornment includes age- and sex-separating decorations such as body coloring, ear piercing, and keeping hair shaved or long. Temporality is indicated by modifications in adornment, such that men acquire increasingly larger lip plugs to signify their increasing social status with age. Even the condition of the body without adornment conveys significant social information: cleanliness and the removal of facial and bodily hair carries out the "fundamental principle of transforming the skin from a mere 'natural' envelope of the physical body into a sort of social filter" (Turner 1980:116).

In sum, people utilize material objects as a fundamental component of what it means to be human, on both the cognitive and the social level. The integration of the material world and cognition can be seen in a variety of ways, ranging from the first stages of intellectual growth in infants' and children's perceptions of animate and inanimate objects to the use of goods as social signaling in both small- and large-scale societies. Items can be used singly to represent achieved and ascribed social status, as in the case of the lip plugs worn by Kayapo men, and they can be used sequentially to signal different types of roles, such as the rapidly changeable clothing worn by professionals in different contexts. Multiple items can be used in both habituated and creative combinations to achieve particular physical and social results. We can analyze the use of goods from the perspective of ordinary people through four different perspectives: goods we get (acquisition, gifts, consumption); goods we use (patterns of use, technological capacities and changes); goods we show off (display, style, culture as communication); and goods we discard (through burial, loss, deliberate abandonment).

Goods We Use

People use objects, whether natural or human-made, in nearly every daily activity that they undertake. The first goods utilized by our human ancestors probably were very similar to the lightly modified natural objects, such as stones and sticks, used today by our closest primate relatives. By as early as 2.5 million years ago, the archaeological record of stone tools indicates that humans systematically modified natural objects to enhance their capacity to perform a task. The subsequent relationship between energy expenditure and portable objects was one of increasing elaboration. Objects were designed and made not only to make more effective use of the raw materials' natural properties but also to express individual investment in the production process and social standing in the consumption process. By about 130,000 years ago in Africa and 40,000–50,000 years ago in Europe, we have evidence in the archaeological record for objects that do not appear to have had any "practical" use, such as pendants and other types of ornaments (Kuhn et al. 2001; McBrearty and Brooks 2000). These forms of ornamentation were perhaps accompanied by bodily modifications such as scarification, tattooing, and piercing as permanent markers of rank.

We can utilize examples drawn from the lithic age to illustrate the transportation of finished products and raw materials over long distances. In part, the transfer of materials appears to be attributable to their physical properties, such as ease of knapping or durability of sharp edges. However, some materials appear to have moved around because of their distinctive visual aspects. In eastern Africa by around 100,000 years ago, obsidian (volcanic glass) was found as far as 320 kilometers from the source (McBrearty and Brooks 2000:515). At the Tasmanian site of Kutikina (dated 20,000 years ago), the investigators noted the presence of stone tools made of a meteoritic glass from the Andrew River valley 25 kilometers away (Kiernan, Jones, and Ranson 1983:30). In late glacial Europe (14,000–10,000 years ago), a stone called "chocolate flint" was mined from central Poland but was carried throughout a wide area; it was in such demand that even at a distance of up to 200 kilometers from the source it constitutes 90 percent of the lithic assemblage of some sites (Sulgostowska 2002:13; see also Bratlund 1996).

The example of chocolate flint shows that some distinct items were readily traded across large spaces, and they were desired for their distinctive qualities. Michael Schiffer and James Skibo (1997:30) have discussed how desired "performance characteristics" encompass utilitarian, sensory, and socially generated qualities. Social factors can even override utilitarian considerations, because not all available objects are adopted and used, even if they are "better" in some objective way. An example is provided in the archaeological evidence of trade routes throughout the prehistoric American Southwest that moved marine shells, turquoise, and pottery over long distances. Through these exchange mechanisms, people were able to learn about other types of potential trade items such as food. One of the most important introductions was corn, first domesticated in Mexico and appearing in American Southwestern sites between 2000 BC and 1500 BC (Adams 1994, cited in Crown 2001). The adoption of this new food took place as part of a dynamic process in which new varieties with different cooking properties were introduced; for example, the first corn was a flint/pop variety that was hard to grind, but despite the later appearance of a floury corn that was more tractable, it was adopted in only some parts of the region.

Schiffer's (2005) invention cascade model of the many steps required in the adoption and use of new items is helpful in identifying the patterns of behavior related to new foods and new modes of preparation. Mere availability or objectively "better" qualities are not the only factors that condition adoption and use; there also are personal and social assessments that are implicated in individual decision making. Most food-related activities involve the use of objects, and the variability of the environment over space and time has provided humans with many opportunities to create and use different types of items related to the procurement, preparation, storage, serving, and consumption of food. In fact, most of the artifacts and features that we find in archaeological sites have something to do with food: projectile points, knives, grinding tools, hearths, storage pits, cooking pots, and serving vessels (M. Jones 2007). As seen in chapter 2, these objects reflect individually internalized cultural perceptions of the "right" way to procure, prepare, and serve food.

Material objects also enable people to interact with the supernatural, whether in the form of portable objects, architectural constructions, or even the representations of those physical elements in iconography and text (fig. 3.2). Goods utilized in ritual activities, such as amulets, rosaries, and other portable talismans, often have no "practical" utility but are a ritually invested form of ornamentation. The archaeological remains of human ritual activities are significant, ranging from single burials with a pot or stone tool to more-elaborate forms of architecture

FIGURE 3.2. People make use of goods such as artifacts and architecture to materialize symbolic actions as seen in this rock art panel of a Buddhist stupa from Chilas, Pakistan.

such as pyramids, tombs, and other monuments. Some items devoted to ritual do have practical utility, as is evident in ritual vessels, but their use is possible only in a very restricted context: a chalice and a paper cup can both hold liquid, but they are not interchangeable, whether for picnics or for Mass.

Goods We Get

The transfer of goods among people involves two topics of great anthropological interest: exchange and gifts. Objects in these two modes of acquisition are sometimes characterized as commodities or goods (when exchanged) and gifts (when the transaction is personalized). A brief consideration of these distributional modes highlights how the two forms of transfer are mutually interdependent and the way in which specific individual decision-making processes generate both exchange and gift activity.

Starting with our earliest tool-using human ancestors, many objects were acquired directly by the individual, whether in the form of hunted prey or as gathered resources. Even items that are acquired in a relatively straightforward way are, however, subject to an elaborate decision-making process. Should the acquired item be used for direct consumption, stored for future use, or given away? Each of these decisions in turn encompasses a set of ancillary considerations: if the item is consumed directly, where and with what accompaniments should it be consumed? If stored or cached for future use, how much preparation is required, for how much time can the item be left, and what mnemonic or marker should be used to record its location? If the item is given away, should this be done at the earliest opportunity (important for perishable goods) or should its disposition be the subject of negotiations about the expected return? The giver can demand immediate benefits such as sex with the implications of reproduction (seen in primate exchanges of high-value foods such as meat, and imaginable for our earliest human ancestors as well) or longer-term benefits such as a social obligation to reciprocate.

For each act of exchange, each party involved had to evaluate the risk, benefits, and complications of the transaction, with social implications assessed before, during, and after the exchange process. Exchange may take a different form and encompass different expectations taking into account the social standing and life stage of the individuals conducting the exchange: between a woman and a man, a woman and a woman, a man and a man, an adult and a child, an adult and an elderly person; between kin and non-kin; or between newly met strangers and habitually met acquaintances. Different personal and social expectations affect the decision-making process, but each transaction is between real individuals who calculate value to the best of their ability within the understanding of short-term, medium-term, and long-term outcomes.

Both gifts and exchange can be considered in more detail to examine the social relationships activated at each moment of action. Let us consider gifts first. In our culture, most of the time gifts exchanged among adults are things that people could probably buy for themselves: a nice sweater, a dinner out, a bouquet of flowers. The act of giving serves as a memory of past interactions and as a framing device for the future of the relationship between the giver and the recipient. When the gift consists of something that a person could not otherwise afford or have access to, the exchange becomes overlain with social leverage. The range of relationships revealed in the gifting process is a subject on which Marcel Mauss's volume *The Gift* (1990) stands as the classic anthropological treatment. In this book, Mauss (1990:20) uses ethnographic examples from Polynesia and elsewhere to show how the exchange of gifts takes place at times of emotion such as weddings, in which "[s]ouls are mixed with things; things with souls."

Gifts do not always cement social relationships; they also can be used by the givers to challenge expectations and create new social dynamics. One such scenario is the potlatch, a ceremony conducted by the Native inhabitants of the prehistoric and historic Northwest Coast of North America (Marshall and Maas 1997). This ceremony involved the presentation of large amounts of food and gifts as a sign of the host's political and social strength. The phenomenon of the potlatch became perversely accelerated after contact with Europeans, because the number and diversity of goods increased at the same time that the population decreased, leaving many social "offices" open to contention (Mauss 1990; Marshall and Maas 1997). Another example is provided by C. A. Gregory (1982), who described the upending of social relationships related to gifts and status in Papua New Guinea after young men began to take wage-labor jobs and returned to the community with goods and knowledge that challenged the dominant status of elders. Similarly, L. Frink (2009) writes of the way that access to guns (for men) and iron cooking pots (for women) enabled young people in historical coastal Alaska to bypass their traditional dependence on elders for knowledge and apprenticeship. Older people saw the value of their skills in mentoring traditional hunting techniques and pottery production diminish rapidly when trade routes opened to Russia and other countries, causing alienation and the realignment of power dynamics in the community.

The power of the gift is so great that its effects can even transcend death. Brad Weiss (1997) has discussed the way in which inherited goods serve as a component of enforced memory making, in which the recipients must do something with the physical object that the deceased has bequeathed. Using the ethnographic example of a broken bicycle in Tanzania, he discusses how an object can be "useless" for practical purposes but when it is given as an inheritance it becomes revalued and "an *obligation* to remember which . . . not only preserves the legacy of prior generations, but actually *projects* itself forward in time" (Weiss 1997:167, emphasis in original). The recipient still acts consciously in the handling of the gift, with the result that useless objects can become a physical repository of memory and, conversely, "useful" goods can be shunted aside if their use or display is accompanied by burdensome social obligations or crippling emotional attachments.

Some giftlike exchanges greatly favor takers over givers. One example is theft, which is the appropriation of objects by one party from another, an action that can be interwoven with subtleties, particularly in the small-group settings that would have characterized our earliest ancestors. Nicholas Blurton Jones (1987) has proposed the idea of "tolerated theft" to explain the way in which participants remove resources that are in excess of what the givers can physically utilize or consume at a given moment. He illustrates his argument through the example of large-game hunting, which can result in more fresh meat than can be consumed by the hunters; in such cases, what appears to be altruistic behavior is simply the lack of willingness on the part of the givers to protect their catch. Other long-term relationships of dependence can be encompassed in the idea of "tolerated scrounging" (Isaac 1978:312). Although this term was first coined to explain the behavior of nonhuman primates, the concept encompasses many human relationships as well, particularly when perpetually disadvantaged individuals attach themselves to more-affluent community members. Patron-client relationships as well as relationships of extended kinship might easily devolve into relationships of tolerated scrounging when the recipient's capacity for work declines because of disinclination, infirmity, or old age.

Begging is another form of unequal giftlike behavior, in which the giver receives neither a tangible benefit nor the expectation of such a benefit in the future. Begging takes advantage of well-placed individuals' emotional impulses, such as the desire to avoid the fate of poverty through the talisman of donation, the desire to experience the emotional satisfaction of largesse, or the desire to be publicly acknowledged for that largesse. Charity may be a social investment, but it is not an economic one, as the giver expects that there will be similar requests afterwards over and over again. The status of the beggar is never likely to alter, although the fortunes and inclination of the giver can decline. Thus, theft, begging, and "tolerated scrounging" all leave the power of the relationship in the hands of the recipient, who acquires desired goods with little relative energy expenditure from a giver who may be distinctly uncomfortable with the transaction.

Even in the modern world, the acquisition of goods is overlain by multiple layers of economic investments that also have emotional overtones in the choice of goods and in the choice of where we will acquire them. Although many of the exchange mechanisms experienced by modern people are relegated to large corporate entities, we still have our "favorite" stores from which to purchase, indicating our recognition of perceived social alliances in the process of ostensibly neutral transactions. Initial experiences tend to be particularly memorable, for example, when first encountering a new potential exchange venue; if our initial experiences are positive, we are likely to downplay a subsequent negative experience as anomalous. By contrast, if the initial experience is negative, much convincing is required to give an establishment a second try. When we engage in transactions at an even more intimate, face-to-face scale, such as with the person who delivers the paper or with a vendor at a craft fair or a farmer's market, rarely is the transaction a form of silent exchange with only the economic worth of the object a matter of discussion. We expect that some conversation and some social interaction will be part of the exchange process. The objects themselves may be mundane or even disposable (a newspaper, a tomato, a balloon), but the individuals involved in the transaction retain and build on the social relationships experienced in each act of exchange.

When archaeologists write about ancient exchange, they often characterize the exchange process as one that resulted in economic flows of inert items that have either a practical utility (sharpness, durability) or display value (rarity). We seldom envision the individual, quotidian decision-making processes encoded in those early exchanges, reasoning that the appearance of any novel material was greeted enthusiastically by potential exchange partners, and that favorable terms of exchange were always reached. However, just as we envisioned the feast as an event that could engender mixed feelings by the participants, so too should we imagine that the exchange process contained the potential for failure. Some traders would have been favored over others, and some buyers favored with better terms, even when the same goods were at stake. Itinerant merchants would not always have been welcomed, no matter how desirable a cargo they carried. Today, a person may prefer FoodWorld to SuperGiantMart even if they stock the same items and even if the enaction of preference requires additional costs in terms of item price or transportation time. We should envision how the encoding of material culture in personal identity and social roles similarly affected the exchange process deep in the human past.

Goods We Show Off

People use objects to display both belonging and status. Objects of "belonging" might be as simple as a head covering or as substantial as a house built in the prevailing style. Objects of "status" can be similarly variable: as common as a ring of a type worn by a large number of people that signifies marriage or as rare as a unique possession that signifies the individual to be of a privileged class.

Here it is important to consider how the word *status* is misleading because it covers two very different concepts. *Status* often is taken to mean the role of the individual within a perception of hierarchy, as seen in the terms *social status* and *economic status*, in which there is implied competition between ranks for visibility, deference, and access to goods. The presence of a status hierarchy often results in rapid style change when groups of lower rank begin to adopt particular goods as status markers, leaving higher-ranked groups to continually search out new forms and styles to confirm their own status (e.g., Miller 1985). But *status* also conveys the positionality of an individual with regards to simple presence/absence categorizations, such as "adult/child" or "married/unmarried." Individuals use objects (along with bodily modifications and language use) to convey these forms of status as relatively long-lasting categories.

As a result, people actively utilize material goods to display both forms of status, constantly engaging in an interplay between creativity and stasis in the proclamation of individual identities and social roles. Because goods are actively obtained, used, displayed, and discarded by all people, the relationship between goods and social action is a close one.

People do not even have to actively handle objects as part of the communication process, as the display itself provides the visual context in which a range of communication actions can take place (Schiffer and Miller 1999). A contemporary example would be the way in which a conversation with a friend is conditioned by different contexts. A church, a nightclub, and the friend's house would all have quite different objects in their settings, and the conversing people would likely be wearing different kinds of clothing, ornaments, and even hairstyles in each setting. Although these physical aspects would not be specifically identified or named in the course of the conversation, their presence serves to condition the behavioral expectations of both parties as they talk.

A few archaeological examples allow us to open a window towards the consumption of goods by non-elites as a marker of the recognized value of items for identity formation, communication, and stage-setting. Eric Cline (1999) was one of the first scholars to critically examine the idiosyncrasies of consumption in the ancient world from the perspective of ordinary goods. In his article "Coals to Newcastle, Wallbrackets to Tiryns: Irrationality, Gift Exchange, and Distance Value," Cline (1999:119) considered the Bronze Age phenomenon of very "ordinary, functional Eastern Mediterranean objects of non-exotic and non-precious material which hardly seem to have been worth the cost of transportation, but which somehow and for some reason made their way to Aegean sites." The objects in question are wall brackets made of clay and formed with a scoop to function as a lamp or lamp holder; they are found in a variety of contexts, including funerary, domestic, royal, and nonroyal contexts. Because there were plenty of brackets made of local materials, Cline (1999:123) posits that the fact that these objects were "foreign" is what made them attractive and that "the very nature of these Cypriot wall-brackets (i.e., everyday objects made of non-precious materials and with a very functional nature, yet possessing 'distance value') may have rendered them affordable and desirable to both royal and non-royal inhabitants of Tiryns." H. Wolcott Toll (2001:60) notes a similar phenomenon at Chaco Canyon in the American Southwest; although the importation of utilitarian pottery has usually been explained to be the result of local fuel depletion, the presence of a high number of trade wares even where fuel is abundant suggests that "gray ware exchange must have been based on more than pure need."

The Mediterranean region provides other good examples of the way in which individuals selectively adopted new goods when they were exposed first to Greek and then to Roman customs. In France, people quickly adopted wine as a component of ceremonial activities but did not adopt olive oil or other Mediterranean staples or any other aspects of Greek culture, such as coinage, dress, and writing (Dietler 2007:233). In central Europe, the presence of substantial Roman garrisons boosted the local productive economy at the same time that they became a conduit by which the locals adopted fancy Mediterranean goods such as pottery and glass. Rather than a unilateral colonial imposition of an imperial economy, however, interactions between Romans and indigenous groups should be considered one of "negotiation, interaction, and mutual self-interest" (Wells 1999:96). In England, H. E. M. Cool (2006) has noted that the adoption of Roman foodways, including cooking gear as well as imported foodstuffs, varied according to whether the individuals lived in the country or the city and whether they lived in the northern or southern regions of the British Isles. As these authors emphasize, political fortunes do not always change acquired tastes for certain goods. Foodways and other material practices are modified through many generations of habituation and are likely to be retained long after colonial governments have been dismantled.

The historical archaeology of eras that are more recent provides additional insights about contact-period adoptions of material culture. Working at the Ghanaian city of Elmina, Christopher DeCorse (2001) has shown that long-standing local traditions of trade and materiality were quickly overlain by new types of European goods. Urban residents at this coastal site distinguished themselves both from interior peoples and from foreigners, often using goods that emanated from both source locations in the creation of their material world. In Elmina, the traditional practice of burial under houses was retained, but the burials began to include European pottery. Architectural forms in the city underwent change as local African inhabitants learned European building techniques in stone. Foodways remained largely unchanged in terms of preferred forms of comestibles such as stews, but food began to be served in imported bowls with new types of decorations.

In the Americas, colonial encounters between Native and European people similarly encompassed interactions between more than two groups. In their study of the Fort Ross site in California, Kent Lightfoot, Antoinette Martinez, and Ann Schiff (1998) examined the three-way contact between Russian traders, Aleut men from Alaska, and Native California Pomo women. While some European food imports such as beef were acquired and eaten by local peoples, other aspects of imported European culture such as the use of ceramic and glass tableware were not adopted. Nor did all aspects of the material-culture assemblage indicate that ethnic identity was constructed simply as a reaction against the presence of Russian authorities who were the intermediaries of trade. Concepts of appropriate domestic activity such as artifact use and trash disposal were activated by individuals with reference to a variety of ethnic and gender configurations that alternated dynamically between cognized creativity and the retention of habituated traditions (see also Silliman 2001).

As can be seen in these examples, the notion of "showing off" goods involves many different scales of audience, from the self to the household to the neighborhood to the greater community. The contexts of display involve the social signaling of each person's engagement with the "right" way of doing ordinary tasks such as cooking, eating, and household management, in which the display of objects simultaneously solidifies individual identity and proclaims the variability of the individual's social role at any given moment. Material goods enable individuals to demonstrate both types of status: the hierarchical status of rank and the presence/absence status of belonging in a particular group. Hierarchical status may involve "costly signaling" though exotic, labor-intensive, and rare items that confirm the identity of the individual through material accompaniments (see Sosis 2003). But identity, in the form of group belonging, is maintained through thousands of acts of "cheap signaling" with ordinary domestic goods.

Ordinary goods are made in accordance with prevailing styles and can be part of rapid turnovers of fashion that enable all members of a group to demonstrate belonging through consumption and display (see Miller 1985). We can see this process of rapid turnover as a matter of low "switching costs," meaning that status can be demonstrated through a number of transactions in inexpensive or ephemeral daily-use goods (see Prahalad 2005). When trade and contact bring new potential repertoires of material culture, the actual acquisition and use of goods depend on decisions exercised in the market or trading ground by individuals who choose which goods to seek out and which objects to ignore. A consumption perspective places labor-intensive or nonlocal goods in a holistic interpretive framework, indicating the extent to which "ordinary" households participate in networks of economic activity.

Goods We Discard

There are many ways that individuals cease their association with objects: they give them away, they throw them away, they abandon them, or they place them in burials. All of these means of discard have the same effect because the person no longer claims, controls, or is in physical proximity to a particular object. Getting rid of objects is the necessary corollary to getting them, and the means by which humans get rid of possessions are as highly symbolically charged as their means of acquiring them. We can return to the concept of the gift to evaluate discard in a novel way, that is, the way in which giving objects away can relieve the giver of some unwanted possessions. We may clean out our closets and give the accumulated clothes to a charity in the intent that they be utilized by the less fortunate. But the recipient is just as important as the giver, because an object can only be said to have been given away when there is someone to receive it.

Why do people discard goods? In some cases, they do so because the item has become broken, worn, or damaged and is no longer serviceable. However, practical utility is rarely the only reason for discard, just as it is rarely the only reason for adoption of a particular item or style. Humans clearly have a sense of reuse and recycling; for example, in the lithic period, there is evidence for resharpening of stone tools that indicates a conscious expenditure of energy for maintaining the utility of a stone object. By about 65,000 years ago, composite tools consisted of multiple microliths hafted into a handle, which carried a built-in provision for repair through the continual replacement of the worn pieces (McBrearty and Brooks 2000:500). Broken pottery carries with it the potential for an even greater range of reuse: crushed potsherds can serve as a base

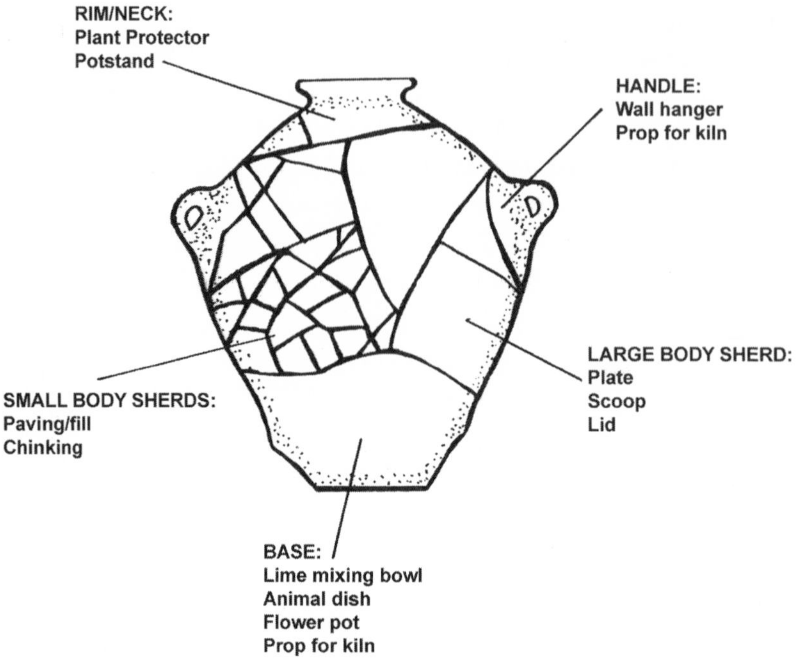

RIM/NECK:
Plant Protector
Potstand

HANDLE:
Wall hanger
Prop for kiln

SMALL BODY SHERDS:
Paving/fill
Chinking

LARGE BODY SHERD:
Plate
Scoop
Lid

BASE:
Lime mixing bowl
Animal dish
Flower pot
Prop for kiln

FIGURE 3.3. Objects can be used for a variety of purposes even after they are "broken" or otherwise discarded, as seen in the way that modern Tzeltal Maya people use pottery fragments.

material for new pots, while larger fragments can be transformed into scoops, covers, animal pens, architectural fill, garden mulch, and many other objects (fig. 3.3).

When objects are not recycled or reused, they may be thrown away altogether. But even the type of "throwing away" tells us about how objects are viewed after their useful life—is an object thrown out into a public trash heap or in an alleyway, where anyone else can salvage the item (or conversely, where it becomes a potential nuisance to others)? As ethnoarchaeologists have observed, all "trash" is not regarded the same way in a community, and refuse disposal is patterned even when trash appears at first sight to randomly cover the landscape (Beck and Hill 2004; Brugge 1983; Hodder 1982). Areas of trash deposition often are quite large; for example, in the relatively remote highland Philippines, midden deposits were found to constitute around 10 percent of the entire residential living area (Beck and Hill 2004:307).

The application of ethnographically derived models of trash deposition to ancient sites is in its infancy. Archaeologists often see little reward in excavating "empty" space of the kind where middens are found, meaning that our understanding of ancient trash usually is limited to the spaces immediately around buildings and the swept-up microdebris that accumulates at the juncture of walls and floors. But "trash" as the discard of material objects has much to offer us in the understanding of the ancient use of goods. The close-in deposition of trash in many ancient societies may not be simply a matter of differential aesthetics about discard but also the use of waste material to affirm status: "I discard, therefore I am." Like the deliberate excess that is an essential component of feasting, the close-in deposit of middens and trash heaps performs a social function long after the discarded materials cease to have any practical use. The accretion of visible trash deposits as a form of identity may strike many of us as odd, given our modernist inclination to have trash carried as far away and as thoroughly as possible. Nevertheless, such an interpretation sheds light on the logic of visible trash that accumulates even in our culture, such as the heaps of old and rusted equipment that often grace otherwise industrious-looking farmyards. In these locales, visible discards serve as a genealogy of past wealth that still yields some social capital in the present.

Examples of front-and-center trash can be seen in the archaeological record as well, such as the Iron Age huts of the site of Wendens Ambo, for which the authors note that the density of potsherds was high at the front of the huts compared to the sides and rear of the structures (Halstead, Hodder, and Jones 1978:128). In the same fashion, large shell middens in coastal archaeological sites may not be just a result of past meals but an incremental monument to abundance and an affirmation of community identity through discard. Shell middens are common at coastal and riverine sites worldwide, indicating the widespread human propensity to create visible piles of food waste. Some of these sites are considerable in size, such as the shell midden at Indian Knoll, Kentucky, that was large enough to accommodate over one thousand human burials (Morey et al. 2002).

The symbolism of trash also can be seen with regard to its contents. As Ian Hodder has described in his ethnographic work *The Present Past* (1982:65), some cultures codify their trash so that different types of waste are thrown in different places; for example, the Mesakin of the central Sudan "discard cattle bones, associated with men and seen as pure, separately from pig bones associated with women." An archaeological example of differential trash deposition is found among the Bronze Age and Iron Age middens examined by Richard Bradley, described in his *Ritual and Domestic Life in Prehistoric Europe* (2005). He notes many cases in which trash deposits are differentiated: for example, with cattle bones in one area of the site and sheep bones in another. These distinctions are viewed as part of the ritualization of domestic activity, similar to the observations made by Hodder for the Sudan.

Similar patterns of differential trash deposition are noted in other regions as well. In their study of the Maya site of Aguateca, Richard Terry and his colleagues (2004) have noted that the chemical signatures show that some middens had high phosphate levels, indicating that they were representative of food debris, and others had mixed chemical signatures that included heavy metals, probably related to manufacturing activities that involved pyrite and pigments. David Brugge's (1983:186) study of Navajo trash deposition in the American Southwest shows how material culture use changed from the prehistoric to the historic period, resulting not only in different kinds of objects being available but also in the placement of the trash: "Most . . . trash in aboriginal times was of minor consequence or naturally degradable and did not cause problems. . . . In recent years, the accumulation of nontraditional trash presented a problem that has been solved by the establishment of formal trash heaps at a much greater distance from the hogan than is the ash heap."

The discard of objects has temporal as well as spatial aspects. Items can be casually dropped in places where they will be frequently seen and trampled prior to disintegration, or they can be violently flung with the intent of removing them from the premises. The removal of objects also can occur on a massive scale associated with social and spiritual cleansing and renewal. The phenomenon known as "spring cleaning" in our culture is not just about removing dust and dirt; it is also an acknowledgment of the cessation of winter and the renewal that is symbolized and materialized in a cleaned-up dwelling. Historical accounts similarly signal a link between discard and renewal in the past; VanDerwarker, Scarry, and Eastman (2007:18) describe the ceremony of the "busk" in the pre-contact American Southeast as one that occurred at harvest time, when "sacred and household fires were extinguished, houses and villages were cleaned, and worn out clothing, cooking pots, and so on were destroyed." Such ceremonies, with the habituated practice of regular action, can also be cognitively reconfigured at times of crisis. At the Saratown site that is the focus of their study, VanDerwarker and her colleagues note that the busk ceremony became intensified after European conquest when drastic increases in mortality due to introduced diseases may have resulted in a perception that "a more drastic means of purification and renewal" was required (VanDerwarker et al. 2007:23, citing Eastman 1996:10).

Items such as figurines and other special-purpose artifacts are often retrieved from what archaeologists describe as "trash" deposits. These finds are usually interpreted as a decommissioning of sacred objects, perhaps associated with renewal ceremonies. Given that trash may have significant symbolism in being highly visible in public spaces, we should consider whether the discard of ritual objects in trash deposits is a way to further sanctify the trash, rather than a way of desanctifying the ritual objects. Another expression of this phenomenon can be found in the formal, deliberate breaking of objects as part of foundation deposits or burials. Even the individual pieces of broken materials that resulted from this process could have symbolic value. At ancient Maya sites, Scott Hutson and Travis Stanton (2007:138) note the odd phenomenon of single potsherds and portions of previously broken vessels carried deep into caves. Because caves were highly symbolic locations, these materials are not likely to have been a routine deposit of ordinary trash but may signal a particular type of partible ritual activity.

Another indication of the social value of trash is seen in the numerous cases in which human burials are found in trash middens. Far from being merely a convenient and easy-to-dig place where bodies could be "discarded," middens as a material record of past events may have been the ideal place for the existential affirmation of people as well as things. Kenneth Ames (2003:28) notes that by the Middle Pacific period in the Northwest Coast (1800 BC to AD 200–500), there are "formal midden cemeteries" indicative of considerable planning related to burial. The presence of midden burials does not mean that all persons in the group were buried that way, however. In the American Midwest by around six thousand years ago, people buried their dead in two different places: the very young, the very old, and the infirm were interred in middens, while able-bodied individuals were buried in bluff-top cemeteries (Charles and Buikstra 2002). This suggests that middens, as close-in areas of activity, had a special symbolism and were perhaps associated with liminal and transitional states of being.

Sometimes objects are discarded in a location from which they cannot physically be extricated, such as a water body. In other cases, goods are disposed of in places from which they cannot psychologically be extricated, such as a human burial. Deliberate burial of the dead with objects is something that characterizes the development of fully human behavior starting with *Homo sapiens* around 120,000 years ago; although the Neanderthals did bury their dead, they did not include burial goods (McBrearty and Brooks 2000:519). Funerary objects are particularly widespread in the archaeological record starting in the Upper Paleolithic period around 40,000 years ago. Although the objects in graves were often the materials that the deceased might have utilized in life, burial traditions of later periods show the ways in which objects for burial might not have a one-to-one correspondence with objects of daily use. For example, Mesopotamian goods came in standard "sets" that were manufactured for burials, a purpose-specific production strategy that can be seen in India as well (Choksi 1998; Simpson 1997). When materials were directly taken from daily use in association with burials, they might be ritually "killed" and included with the deceased (as in the case of Mimbres pots from the American Southwest [Brody 1977:52]) and serving vessels used by mourners and smashed at the gravesite (as seen in Iron Age England [Cool 2006:163]).

Interment with the deceased constitutes discard in the sense that the objects are removed from circulation in a manner that is performative, an act of closure and mourning that reaffirms the social position and standing of those who contribute to the burial rite. In the case of goods buried with the person, which can often include a very lavish display, various economic and social effects can be calculated (e.g., Treherne 1995). Some forms of burial are a projection of ancient ideas of the afterlife as being a continuation of the present world—perhaps most famously encompassed in Egyptian burials that had all of the items that the deceased would need, including food. Another psychological rationale would be to remove the items of the deceased either because they were personal property that could not be legitimately used by another individual or because their presence as physical reminders of the deceased would be too emotionally powerful for the surviving kin to sustain.

While we might think of discards as static entities (perhaps because of our experience of modern landfills, from which materials are almost never re-extracted), ancient trash mounds interspersed around residences were active zones of use in addition to being a silent testament to prosperity. Open-air trash deposits can serve as a zone for recycling, whether as a grazing ground for domestic animals (Beck and Hill 2004), a socially accepted place for scavenging durable goods by those less fortunate, a stockpile of potentially usable goods such as building material that has gradually become "trash" through neglect, or a stockpile of recyclable by-products such as manure (Ingold 1987). Until trash is reused, however, it is ever-present and requires daily deliberate actions on the part of each community member, from those who deposit trash to those pick through it, walk around it, move it, or ignore it.

Goods and the Development of Social Complexity

For at least the past million years, humans have had a cognitive and social reliance on physical objects and have developed a wide range of strategies for acquiring, using, and discarding them. At the simplest end of the continuum, individuals gather raw materials themselves and transform these materials into a finished product. At the most complicated end of the spectrum, the production process involves many steps of specialized energy expenditure through elaborate networks of procurement in which some individuals are devoted to just one component of the process, such as mining raw material, raw material preparation, different stages of manufacture, and transportation of the final product. By 100,000 years ago, individuals began to cognize the relative costs of these multiple strategies for the acquisition of any particular object, as seen in the archaeological distribution of stone raw materials and finished objects. The adoption of sedentism and agriculture starting 10,000–12,000 years ago resulted in a much greater variety of material items required for producing, storing, preparing, and presenting food. When households were no longer mobile, people could accumulate bulky objects and duplicates of goods within settlements. Yet each action with material goods, from acquisition to discard, was still carried out by individuals who created, affirmed, or negated perceptions of utility and social meaning through objects.

By the time of the development of complex societies starting around six thousand years ago, the use of goods as practical objects and material signifiers had begun to accelerate. There are three reasons for this. First, there were increased numbers of people who could potentially receive, encode, and retransmit situational communication symbolized through objects. Second, the opportunities for using objects to signal belonging were increased by the potential for a greater number of identities and roles per person. Igor Kopytoff (1986:89) notes, "In complex societies . . . a person's social identities are not only numerous but often conflicting, and there is no clear hierarchy of loyalties that makes one identity dominant over the others." In larger populations, where there are a greater number of permanent and temporary social roles, the "social skin" becomes inadequate to convey the numerous roles taken on by individuals, a factor that results in the addition of new goods, new styles, and new decorative elements to the material repertoire. Third, complex societies are marked by the emergence of hierarchies of individuals who show their social rank through distinctive possessions (e.g., Wright 1984).

Mintcy Maxham's (2000) study of ancient Mississippian rural households shows how the three components of consumption are interwoven in early complex societies. Social links between individuals and households were exhibited in lateral ties between farmsteads that were also grouped into communities linked by clan ties. These ties facilitated exchange of desired items, including both raw materials and finished objects; at the household level, the presence of these items, as well as pottery types indicative of feasting activities, indicates a shared ethos of kinship. Maxham (2000:350) observes that the implications of this shared ethos were significant for subsequent political expansion: "While central, public space was reorganized in the Moundville I phase to reflect the emergent political hierarchy, the surrounding countryside reflected the maintenance of 'traditional' relationships among people." The successful development of a hierarchy thus relied on a consistent base of shared community ties (see also Smith 1999:130).

Political entities such as states and empires may appear to present the most prescribed and restrictive conditions for the acquisition, use, display, and discard of objects. Yet even under those circumstances, individuals and households selectively interpret dominant paradigms in their choice and use of goods available to them (VanPool and VanPool 1999:38). Each pot, house, and burial shows the selective and conscious acts of people acting as individuals rather than as collective statistics, and each artifact permits the assessment of the parameters of meaning and context. Prevailing social norms of action, seen at the scale of sites and regions, come into existence only when they are deliberately enacted at the individual and domestic scale. Indeed, what we call an archaeological "site" is the result of numerous and often-repeated actions on the individual and household level that have a collective effect.

Urban centers provide a particularly high concentration of people, leading to accelerated consumption by individuals in dense networks of interaction. Studies of modern cities show that urban dwellers add new suites of possessions to their domestic sphere, indicative of new statuses and identities that augment existing displays of household and individual identity (e.g., Abu-Lughod 1969:384; Ntole 1996:139). Similarly, the archaeological record of premodern cities shows accelerated patterns of consumption in which new items are added to previously existing repertoires (e.g., DeCorse 2001; Kenoyer 1998:127–57). Ancient people increased their interactions with material goods not only through production, acquisition, and use but also through the process of disposal as they adjusted their waste streams to cope with new consumption patterns. In the higher-density populations that constituted the earliest villages and towns, all types of waste—including human and animal waste alike—would have been the subject of deliberate decision making, planning, and the multitasking of energy expenditure. Human waste was channeled back into fields in ancient Mesoamerica (Evans 1990:122), and ancient Mesopotamian communities appear to have utilized household garbage to "manure" fields (Wilkinson 1982). Other forms of waste were recycled en masse: pottery-rich deposits were utilized to make structures and bricks in ancient India (Mohanty and Smith 2008) and were reincorporated into adobe bricks in the American Southwest (Crown 1991:292).

Rarely were the cultural shifts seen in quotidian activities the subject of political control. Although rulers might oversee markets for taxation purposes or issue prohibitions about certain kinds of goods, the vast majority of items consumed, along with their styles, decorations, and forms, were crafted by individuals to suit the needs of other individuals.

The presence of similar goods provided a sense of social unity that was the basis upon which the material expressions of social complexity were added for the subsequent differentiation of new forms of political hierarchy (Blanton et al. 1996:2; Kenoyer 1998:143; Smith 1999:130). Subsistence goods always remained a necessary and fundamental component of individual action and household strategies. Roderick McIntosh and Susan McIntosh (2003:106) summarize that for early cities, "The symbiosis characteristic of the urban system emerges out of the circulation of goods and services essential to subsistence." As a result, ancient state leaders—with an eye towards cities' concentrated populations as a source of both support and rage—often coordinated large-scale programs of provisioning, such as Rome's famous grain handouts (e.g., Garnsey 1983).

Studies of consumption that highlight the economic and social self-determination of the non-elite illustrate the mutual interdependence of different sections of society in creating and sustaining a shared cultural ethos. Studies of core-periphery relations, for example, have tended to emphasize the activities and motivations of the expanding, controlling core. When archaeological evidence of the encounter is assessed, however, the interaction is far less straightforward than the mere submission of a periphery. In an insightful treatment of the relationship between an expanding Roman empire and the local societies of northern Europe, Peter Wells sees the provisioning of Roman military camps as a way that local, small-scale producers beyond the boundaries of the empire provided goods such as pottery and metalwork in exchange for desired Roman trade goods. These goods were incorporated into local customs such as burials, and emulation of "Roman" tastes was popular; yet, a few generations later, new local pottery styles were developed that incorporated older pre-Roman elements and provide an expression of indigenous identity. Wells (1999:97) sees the resultant dynamic interactions as archaeologically visible proof that there was "mutual interdependence" and that "interactions [were] maintained to further the interests of all involved."

Summary

In discussing consumption, archaeology integrates its findings with the other social sciences to provide a long-term view of the relationship between humans and material culture. As Lauren Cook, Rebecca Yamin, and John McCarthy (1996:52) have urged, "Consumption, to be understood, must not only be 'linked to specific commodities and population segments' (Henry 1991:4) but must also be linked to individual, intentional, communicative acts." Much of the consumption behavior seen in the archaeological record is the result of the manipulation, use, and disposal of ordinary goods by ordinary people (Smith 1999). A consumption perspective, evaluating the way in which goods are used, allows for a highly diversified, person-centered approach to the archaeological record. Even in chiefdoms and states where the production of some objects is highly centralized, consumption activity is cognitively and socially enacted one person at a time.

A consumption perspective also situates archaeology at the center of a growing focus of study in the social sciences, namely, the relationship between material goods and human social systems. As Ulrich Witt (2001:2) has lamented, "[L]ittle attention has . . . been paid to the empirical facts characterizing what happens on the demand side in the process of economic growth." In an increasingly globalized economy, these "empirical facts" have a tremendous potential impact; understanding the long-term origins of material culture use can help us to mitigate the impact of increasingly diverse consumption possibilities. One way that we can already see the differential messages of sustainability is through the relative popularity of recycling. Although the tripartite mantra of the ecologically minded is "reduce, reuse, recycle," only the last component appears popular. Nor should we be surprised: by recycling, we can still acquire, use, and discard as much as we want, as long as we are mindful of the place where the refuse is discarded.

CHAPTER 4

Individuals and Work

WORK IS THE TRANSFER of energy that produces a change in a person's environment. Work can be as simple as plucking a fruit or as elaborate as building a multistory structure. It can be done by an individual acting alone or by groups of people whose coordination requires many levels of management. It can involve daily, repetitive tasks or preparations for once-in-a-lifetime events. Work can be predicted and planned for, or it can be prompted by opportunity or emergency. Work can take a short amount of time and energy to produce results (such as the application of fire to a stand of undergrowth) or can involve years of rehearsal for a single momentous event (such as the assembly of a trousseau for a wedding).

Work often is a physical act undertaken through the use of muscles and the actions of feet and hands. But work also can be the result of exercising cognitive skills through the performance of rites, the playing of music, and the adjudication of disputes. Even serving simply as a witness to others' performances constitutes a form of work in the expenditure of time and energy. The physical and intellectual manifestations of work have profound social consequences, ranging from the production of objects that can be exchanged and shared to the performance of rituals. Although humans are not the only species that allocates time to social investments (as seen in the grooming behavior of many primate species), we are the only species that has so many different tasks among which to allocate our time.

Although the idea of "work" has been a prime focus of inquiry by social scientists for more than a century, its analysis has largely focused on labor as a form of exploitation. By looking instead at energy expenditure, we locate the impetus for work at the individual level in the same way as we have considered the use of food and goods. Each day, individuals act upon the world around them to address basic needs including the satisfaction of hunger, the avoidance of discomfort, and the sustaining of social ties. Individuals assess the timing, duration, and efficacy of that energy expenditure as they move from one task to the next and orchestrate their energy expenditures in accordance with other activities. In the process of multitasking, individuals also assess the value of their energy expenditures and mitigate the consequences of unplanned opportunities and interruptions. As a result, they often consciously calculate the order in which tasks will be done, what tasks to downplay or avoid, and what tasks can be given shortcuts of investment that will still yield acceptable results.

Humans have sophisticated memory and planning capacities, dense and interconnected social networks, and a long period of juvenile development. These factors combine to enable many configurations of energy expenditure over a lifetime, in which expressions of skill and expertise are not limited to multistage manufacturing processes but involve the potential for sophistication in everyday activities. Think of it this way: for those of you who work in an office, you may notice that the maintenance person can tie the trash sack very tightly to the rim of the trash can. For those of you who eat in restaurants, you may notice that a server can carry five or six full plates of food at once. Delivery persons can manage heavy loads on narrow carts and maneuver easily along pathways and through crowds, and professional gardeners can deftly trim bushes and haul off tree branches and lawn clippings. Are these things that you can do easily? Most likely not, because such tasks require certain skills and expertise born of many episodes of practice which most of us lack.

The recognition of specialized skills in what is traditionally characterized as the "lower end" of the economic spectrum is an important window into the way that ordinary individuals engage with work. We can envision the same processes in prehistory, in which many aspects of production required routine but specialized inputs in the acquisition and preparation of raw materials, the cleaning and maintenance of work areas, and the transportation of raw materials, finished products, and waste (fig. 4.1). For example, metalworking encompasses many specialized tasks: gathering ore, smelting ore, making charcoal, building a fire, making bellows, working the bellows, and transporting both raw materials and finished products. There also is the aftermath of production seen in the specialized tasks of cleaning the furnace and preparing it for the next use. In the process of leather working, different individuals may slaughter the animal, skin it, tan the skin, cut the leather, sew the shoe or cloak, and deliver the finished product.

FIGURE 4.1. Small-scale manufacturing entails a variety of specialties includ-ing the making of objects but also packing, transportation, workshop clean-ing, and provision of raw materials

Types of Work

By expanding the notion of "work" to include both brain work and physical labor, we can evaluate how each individual constantly engages in decision making about the allocation of time and energy. One very basic form of work consists of watching and listening. The act of watching is not merely having one's eyes open but also consists of actively choosing to register what is in the field of vision. We all have the experience of seeing without seeing (for example, we might be facing the direction that would bring us a view of a friend picking his nose, but we accord a visual privacy by failing to "see" the action; the same is true of rural village life where people do not "see" others defecating nearby or, more soberingly, do not "hear" domestic violence). Perceptions of social behavior through seeing and hearing also can be transformed into pursuits that are more active. In small-scale societies, healers of physical or psychological ailments typically have some foreknowledge of the patient that predates the time of illness, and this foreknowledge conditions the prescribed forms of treatment. Similarly, the processes of memory and accumulated knowledge also enable adjudicators to mitigate disputes not merely as the resolution of past events but as the platform for further interactions within a community.

Information gathering also can be considered a form of work. Each individual's knowledge about the landscape in prehistory would have included the direct collection and communication of information about resources. The individual who received the information still had to use her or his cognitive skills to apply judgments about the potential accuracy of the notification passed on by others and the most suitable actions to take as a result of the information. Information of many kinds was critical to our ancestors' use of the environment and included not only the location and seasonality of resources but also knowledge of how to mitigate competition. While our earliest hominid ancestors would only have had to compete with each other for the location of durable items such as stone sources, they would have competed with a variety of other species for different types of food. Each type of food and its attendant competition involved variable risks: people would have competed with birds and primates for fruit and with pigs for tubers, but foraging for meat placed hominids in far more dangerous competition with swift, toothy predators.

The advent of sedentism, even without agriculture, would have increased information gathering to address new concerns about the growth cycles of available plants and animals and ways to keep stored food safe from rodents, bacteria, and other destructive elements. The development of communal architecture, which is often seen in sedentary societies, would have required the collection and pooling of knowledge about building materials, labor organization, structural engineering, and the optimal timing of construction activities. The development of agriculture would have vastly increased the amount of information that could be accumulated and shared, such as how to cultivate and process new foods and how to improve yields. The adoption of agriculture also would have necessitated a dramatic increase in the memory capacity needed to adjudicate matters of possession, access rights, and inheritance resulting from increased quantities of material goods.

One of the most energy-efficient ways of gathering information is through participation in social groups, in which the information-gathering components are an incidental outcome of the group's main purpose. Mark Granovetter's (1973) groundbreaking article "The Strength of Weak Ties" helps us to understand social networks that are made up of limited investments in socially distant contacts. While strong ties, such as bonds of kinship, certainly set the stage for many emotional interactions, they may not be the basis upon which to acquire the most diverse or accurate information. Granovetter illustrates how individuals in circumstances of passing acquaintance, such as membership in a club or working for the same company, succeed in spreading their social networks very thinly and widely. When people are not quite strangers but not quite friends, they constitute a network for garnering information on an as-needed basis. As a result, the efficient use of weak ties renders a high rate of return in an interconnected, multipurpose social network.

Even very passive activities can be considered "work" in the sense of time and energy expenditure. Although the understanding of ancient labor investment related to monuments often focuses on the construction of the venue, the elaborate preparations for feasting events, and the performance of rituals, we should recall that "being there" involves energy expenditure as well. Serving as a witness to a performance may result in the acquisition of some social and economic benefits by the individuals who gather at the ritual site. But it also involves costs: to be present, individuals forgo their other domestic tasks and incur the opportunity cost of the time that they might otherwise have spent in other activities, such as hunting, gathering, farming, or fishing. Being a spectator also involves specific risks associated with an absence from home. These include the generalized risk of having insufficient food en route, the specific hardships to young and old who might not have the strength to travel to and from the event, and the risks of an unattended dwelling being the target for theft or squatting.

The phenomenon of mass witnessing is familiar to us today in the form of sporting events and graduation ceremonies, in which hundreds or thousands of people assemble at a specific place, often at considerable expense, to watch a rite of passage or a performance. The gathering of large numbers of people for events that simultaneously encompassed ritual, economic, and social activities can be suggested for deep prehistory as well, because the small group sizes of foragers would have necessitated some mechanism to provide for greater genetic diversity. The focus of the earliest monuments was based not only on the act of construction but also on the notion of spectators as a component of ritual (Bradley 2005:12). Subsequent investments in these events are seen in the archaeological record of plazas and encircling spaces designed to organize viewers. In the opening pages of *Cultural Landscapes in the Ancient Andes*, Jerry Moore (2005) gives us a striking description of an Inka ritual, in which thousands of people undertake a pilgrimage to witness a sacrifice. Viewers take on hardships of hunger and thirst, fatigue and discomfort, and expense and uncertainty simply to be present throughout the long performance, which culminates in the dramatic slaughter of a llama.

Physical work, with its direct results that can be read in the archaeological record, constitutes one of the most readily recognizable forms of energy expenditure. More than a million years ago, the human capacity to act on the surrounding environment is evident through the recovery of stone tools that demonstrate that our ancestors engaged in the work of procuring raw materials and the modification of natural objects. Through the study of use-wear, archaeologists also infer the uses to which the tools were put after their manufacture, including hunting, carving, scraping, and drilling. Indirectly, these stone tools show other types of energy expenditure, such as the work of apprenticeship in both the teaching and the

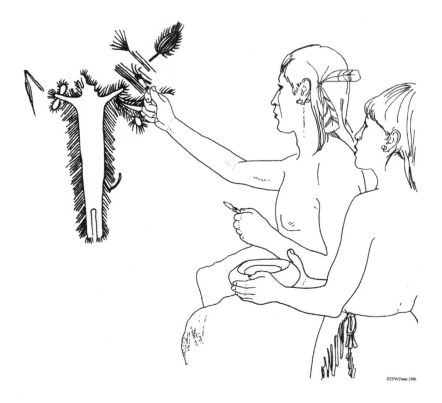

FIGURE 4.2. Energy investment in symbolic knowledge is made not only by those who create petroglyphs or ritual objects but also by those who witness and participate in their use.

learning of craft traditions. As Brooke Milne (2005) and L. Frink (2009) have shown, the "work" of making objects by hand is not limited to the physical outcome of a finished product but encodes social components of intergenerational teaching that encapsulate aspects of gender, landscape learning, and the capacity to interweave memory, planning, and idiosyncratic levels of expertise (fig. 4.2).

In addition to creating portable objects, humans make landscape alterations that often are preserved in the archaeological record. Although other species create durable signatures on the landscape (such as birds' nests and the mark of elephants' tusks on the interior of salt-bearing caves), human marks on the landscape are numerous and diverse. Deliberate actions range from well-planned efforts that require significant coordination, such as the creation of caches or monuments, to casual discard that serves as an incidental material signal of a person's existence. These utilitarian components encode a social intent as well, making use of the physical world to affirm identity, belonging, and possession. Individuals' use of the landscape encompasses both conscious creativity and the acceptance of habituation, often focused on particular components of the landscape such as rock formations and bodies of water. Simon Hall and Ben Smith (2000) provide the example of prehistoric South African rock shelter use, showing how rock shelters as a fixed feature were reinterpreted by herder, forager, and farmer communities. Rock shelters were areas of power for hunter-gatherers who modified and decorated them, but as farmers became dominant they "expropriated rock shelters by overwriting, adding to and subtracting from, and recycling hunter-gatherer deposits and images by imposing their own set of marks" (Hall and Smith 2000:30). Individual acts of physical modification became—like the example of language, in which repeated use leads to habituation—the beginnings of new traditions that were affirmed through the performance of each activity on a daily, annual, or lifetime basis.

Finally, energy expenditure is invested towards ritual and performance in ways that incorporate both brain work and physical labor. The construction of monumental architecture requires expertise not only in the design and engineering of the finished structure but also in the shaping of rocks, hauling of dirt, mixing of earth and water to make pisé, and manufacture of bricks. Ritual activities' tangible results also would be expressed in portable material goods, such as figurines or other ritually charged objects. Like work related to subsistence or other economic pursuits, ritual work involves more than just the specialist who memorizes incantations or is empowered to be the speaker or singer at ritual events. The work of ritual also can be found in the support systems needed: for example, bringing in the right kind of wood for a sacred fire (a task that could be relegated to the same individuals who carry wood for secular purposes), the preparation of beverages for a ritual occasion that are the same drinks for a secular work party, or the cleaning up needed after a ritual slaughter and feast. Work encompassed in ritual—just like any other type of work—involves time and energy expenditure, with the same calculations made about the trade-offs of time spent on ritual compared to the investments that could be made in other domains.

The Temporality of Work

Even relatively straightforward tasks such as hunting, gathering, and resource collection involve numerous steps in their execution, requiring the individual to cognize the steps involved, to calculate the time and energy required for the desired outcome, and to strategize how, when, and where the materials will be further transported, processed, and consumed. Time-motion studies of modern tasks such as food preparation show that what the practitioner might afterwards describe as a seamless process in fact comprises many actions, some of which must be done in a linear sequence and others of which may be interspersed at the maker's discretion through multitasking (one particularly affectionate anthropological case study is provided by Marvin Harris [1964], who diligently recorded all of the minute subtasks performed by his wife as she cooked a meal of potatoes and hamburgers). For our most distant ancestors as well, the phenomenon of food gathering and resource collection brought into play individual capacities of memory, landscape knowledge, timing, and coordination in the process of multitasking.

The creation of objects requires the input of raw materials and the artisan's understanding of both the linear and arbitrary components of the production sequence. The earliest stone tools are linked to our hominid ancestors about 2.5 million years ago, with cutting edges that are made by a relatively rapid process—one or two strategic blows produces enough of a sharp edge to make a stone more useful after modification than before. By around 1.6 million years ago, there were signs of greater energy expenditure on the stone tool form known as the Acheulean hand ax. A hand ax is made by the repeated hammering of a stone to make a bilaterally symmetrical form, which required a variety of calculations in manufacture. The individual making the hand ax had first to make some assessment of the initial piece of stone (was it long enough and thick enough to sustain repeated blows?) and had to follow this initial assessment with repeated hammering to flake off pieces and result in the desired shape while constantly turning the stone to ensure that it retained a symmetrical shape. Once started, each subsequent action required only a yes/no determination, in a relatively straightforward linear process that consisted of a string of simple binary decisions (fig. 4.3).

The next developments in stone tool making did not take place for many hundreds of thousands of years, but 250,000 years ago people

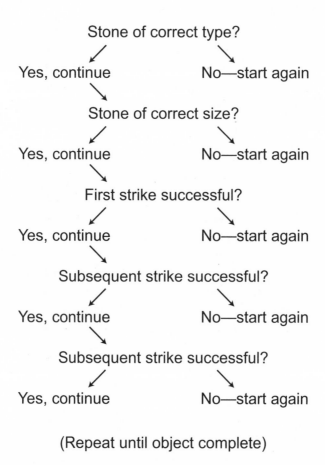

Stone of correct type?

Yes, continue   No—start again

Stone of correct size?

Yes, continue   No—start again

First strike successful?

Yes, continue   No—start again

Subsequent strike successful?

Yes, continue   No—start again

Subsequent strike successful?

Yes, continue   No—start again

(Repeat until object complete)

FIGURE 4.3. Lithic technology is the first archaeological record of repeated, deliberate human actions to create forms that were not seen in nature. Stone tool making is a subtractive technology, requiring a considerable imagination to correctly render a sequence of reduction steps.

started actualizing stone tool production in a two-step process in which there was first the preparation of a sturdy core and then the subsequent striking off of long, thin blades. As Sally McBrearty and Alison Brooks (2000:495) observe, "Blades are a more efficient use of lithic raw material than either core or flake tools, as they represent a greater length of cutting edge per unit volume of stone. . . . Blade production, whether by direct or indirect percussion, requires the cognitive skills to perceive artefact forms not preordained by the raw material and to visualize the manufacturing process in three dimensions, in addition to the dexterity to carry out a complex series of operations and corrections as the process advances." Utilizing blades made from cores meant that a core could be carried around and curated until new blades were needed, adding another element of short-term and long-term planning to the process of energy expenditure.

Only much later in the human repertoire of work were there production processes that were reversible, such as basketry and weaving in which the intertwined elements could be undone and redone. This capacity to undo and rework a material object at any point in the process may require the tolerance of extreme amounts of cognitive dissonance, which our earliest ancestors may not have been capable of sustaining. In this sense, we may be able to identify the moment of fully modern cognitive capacity at the juncture where reversible technologies of production became commonplace in the material culture repertoire, perhaps as early as 250,000 years ago in Africa (McBrearty and Brooks 2000:495). Through the material evidence for nonlinear production processes, we can see how human "creativity" through the constant envisioning of alternative outcomes was actualized on the autonomous cognitive level. Each person had to consciously assess the continued construction of the object, as well as the potential for reversal through dismantling and reordering of its component parts.

Few processes of manufacture are as simultaneously incremental, additive, and reversible as the manufacture of pottery. Until it is fired to a temperature of at least 600°C, clay can be shaped, reshaped, re-formed, built up, and collapsed numerous times without any negative consequences for the eventual finished product. Although fired clay objects were made much earlier than pottery, with the earliest clay figurines dated from 16,000–26,000 years ago (see Vandiver and Vasil'ev 2002), the use of clay to make vessels was a much later development often linked with the development of agriculture. The rationale for a lack of pottery vessels prior to the Neolithic period may not be due simply to the idea that pre-sedentary peoples had no use for breakable objects (as there are traditions of pottery manufacture among mobile groups in the historic period; see Eerkens 2003). In the combination of raw materials, shaping, and firing techniques, the development of pottery may have coincided with the development of agriculture in the sense that both require the activation of sophisticated cognitive processes (and not coeval merely because pottery was "useful" to sedentary people). Alternatively, the practical effects of multitasking have a finite limit; new technologies must be adopted not only because they are useful but also because their production can be integrated with other tasks. For example, Patricia Crown and her colleague W. H. Wills have proposed that "women maintained a heavy work load in the late Archaic and that scheduling conflicts might have *deterred* them from adding pottery manufacture to that work load until increased sedentism and greater dependence [on] cultigens required more frequent use of existing containers (baskets, bags, pits, and gourds) for storage and food processing" (1995; reported in Crown 2001:252; emphasis in original).

The timing of tasks within complementary technologies is not, however, infinitely flexible. Environmental, economic, and social parameters may guide individuals' assessment of what kinds of tasks may take place where, but in addition most sequences of production have some time-based elements that can be interrupted and restarted while others cannot. For example, in pottery production, inputs such as fuel can be incrementally brought in and stockpiled over a long period in preparation for use, but once the firing has started, the process requires a fixed and uninterruptible allocation of time and supervision. Even within distinct stages of production, potters make a range of time-investment decisions that change work inputs and the finished product. Some forms of decoration, such as painting, can be done on a dry pot whenever time permits, but other forms of decoration, such as incising the freshly made surface, have to be done at a specific time before the vessel becomes too dry. And, of course, potters can choose to decorate wares at different levels of care and intensity depending on tangible factors such as perceived market value or intangibles such as preference (e.g., Choksi 1998). In summary, for the production of durable goods, just as in the production of food, work outlays involve a series of contingent, ever-shifting circumstances of time and energy input that are consciously weighed by the participants in the course of interspersing their craft-making with other tasks.

One basic element of time management includes the temporality of the human body. Tasks related to objects are interspersed with corporeal needs for sleep and maintenance, the extent of which varies from season to season as well as at different points of the life cycle. Personal grooming encompasses constant energy inputs, ranging from the tending of hair, nails, and teeth to the fastening of clothing and footgear. Even the individual who spends no conscious time on appearance still takes some time for personal hygiene, as everyone eliminates bodily waste. Bodily functions introduce a physical necessity of time sequencing and "multitasking" in the daily sequence of events. The concept of "bathroom breaks" as a factor in contemporary labor law is only the most recent incarnation of the recognition that the human body has periodicities that can be controlled by the individual only within certain temporal limits. Nicole Boenke's (2007) study of coprolites found deep in the Iron Age salt mine of Dürrnberg shows that the interspersal of work with strategizing about the timing and location of bodily functions is a very old consideration indeed.

Individuals would have perceived decay and degradation in the natural environment through slow processes of weathering and decomposition, such as the slow rainy erasure of pictographs from rocks. Other natural processes are incremental and seasonal, such as the snowfall that in one afternoon can erase tracks and transform a landscape. Natural processes also included sudden, catastrophic events such as earthquakes, floods, and lightning-induced fires. The inherently perishable qualities of organic materials and architecture would have brought the perceptions of decay to the inside realm of human activity as well. In their dwellings, individuals would have been capable of noting the slow degradation of their surroundings and the need for maintenance and repair: wooden posts can become riddled with termites, baskets are subject to rot, textiles can be eaten away by insects, and floor coverings become worn and stained. Food stocks would have been a particularly acute source of the decomposition process, producing odors of mildew and other forms of spoilage that permeated the interiors of storage and living spaces.

Faced with both predictable and unpredictable forms of decay, multitasking humans would have calculated the relative value of maintaining and curating objects compared with the costs of replacement and would have interspersed the work of maintenance with other forms of energy expenditure. Some tools have low maintenance costs that involve only minor amounts of work to make them continually usable: for example, a metal knife can be sharpened, a stone grinding surface can be reroughened, and a piece of clothing that is torn can be mended. For objects such as these, repair requires considerably less energy expenditure than the crafting of a completely new object from raw materials. However, other types of maintenance entail significant expenditures of time and energy beyond what would be needed to make a new piece. For example, reflaking a stone tool to sharpen its edges may require more care and skill than making a new tool from pristine raw materials. While reflaking often is taken to indicate a shortage of raw materials, we also should consider how stone tools may have had "heirloom" qualities that influenced their users' decisions to make continued energy investments. This heirloom quality may help us to make sense of otherwise peculiar investments of labor seen in archaeological contexts, such as holes pierced in a broken pottery vessel to enable it to be tied back together.

Other natural factors that affect the periodicity of work include relatively stable environmental aspects such as topography and climate. Some fluctuations are predictable, including the changes that occur on a seasonal basis and daily fluctuations such as weather and the amount of light. Human factors affecting work include the development of social activities in tandem with the rhythms of nature, such as long harvest-season work hours followed by festivals, or lean-season periods of relatively low energy expenditure in which people concentrate on small-scale household tasks. Some forms of work have no biosocial constraints such as the ability of humans to mate and bear young year-round, meaning that a new infant can arrive in an otherwise busy or slack time of the year. Similarly, sudden accident or illness can result in a dramatic rearrangement of tasks not just by the afflicted individual but by the entire household or community.

Individuals can perceive their energy expenditure on a daily, seasonal, annual, and lifetime basis. The responses that can be generated through multitasking are thus themselves dependent on the temporality of the tasks and other external factors related to time. Work in the daily realm involves routine actions such as preparing food, acquiring resources, and tending to the needs of children and the elderly. These quotidian actions cannot be put off or postponed, because they represent basic biological needs. Seemingly simple choices about what to do at a given moment to address daily needs nonetheless interweave detailed calculations that capitalize on past behaviors and project future capacities. Seasonal opportunities also affect decision making about labor investment. For hunter-gatherers, extracting resources from the landscape is governed by the seasonal availability of favored plant and animal resources. Individuals may absent themselves from the group to target those resources, or the entire group may move. For farmers, seasons are equally important, because plants and animals reproduce at specific intervals. When the lambs are born or when the harvest is ready, there is a large amount of work in a short amount of time that cannot be put off if the abundance of the season is to be realized.

Melissa Hagstrum's (2001) examination of early agricultural activities in the American Southwest illustrates the many ways in which individuals take account of time on multiple scales simultaneously. She notes that in agricultural societies, there is considerable flexibility in the way that a surplus can be produced, because tasks have "complementary technologies" that enable people to take up different tasks not only throughout the seasons but also at different times of the day (Hagstrum 2001:49). Dick Whittaker and Jack Goody (2001) similarly have noted that our assessment of "traditional agriculture" as one of static subsistence farming is misplaced; in rural economies, there were often many ways in which people had seasonal labor or nonagricultural labor because of a lack of farmland (on the part of individuals) or because some family members were sent to do nonagricultural work (in the case of farming families).

Individuals' calculations of time investment involve trade-offs between the energy required to make an object and the energy required for its use. Patricia Crown (2001:254) discusses how adding steps in the manufacturing process of pottery, such as smoothing and polishing to reduce water transpiration and improve heat efficiency, can reduce energy expenditures in the subsequent cooking process: "Adding time in ceramic manufacturing tasks thus pays off significantly in reducing cooking time, as well as in preventing too much loss of vessel contents in the cooking process." Using case studies, she discusses other ways in which cooks in the prehistoric American Southwest engaged in trade-offs of energy investment: "Cooks saved time by using larger ground-stone tools, but they expended greater physical energy in doing so. They created new recipes that increase nutritional yields from a given quantity of food, but they expended greater time and energy in preparing those recipes. Cooking tools were made more durable and permanent but in some cases took more time to create

(Fratt and Biancaniello 1993)" (Crown 2001:260). The advent of storage also increased energy inputs, because, as Crown (2001:263) notes, "More intensive processing and long-term storage placed additional burdens on women's time, in part because dried foods require longer processing times than fresh foods."

A final component of the temporality of work involves the changes evident in the individual life span. Work in the lifetime involves the capacity for energy expenditure, which can vary considerably as a person ages. The development of strength and skill do not necessarily coincide, meaning that individuals must constantly reassess their capacities for particular tasks. Based on studies of modern Ache foragers, Hillard Kaplan and colleagues (2000:168) observed that while individuals may have maximum physical strength by young adult age, their acquisition of difficult-to-process foods such as palm starch does not peak until they are in their late twenties, and hunting success is not maximized until they are about thirty-five years old. The development of the individual thus involves factors beyond physical strength. Individuals do, however, make decisions in part on the basis of their self-assessment of physical capacities. Kaplan and colleagues (2000:168) further note that children's foraging is often focused on fruit, which is a relatively easily obtained food item, but that boys "switch from easier tasks, such as fruit collection, shallow tuber extraction, and baobab processing to honey extraction and hunting in their mid- to late teens." While we are accustomed to thinking of changes in action linked to major life events (such as a puberty ceremony or marriage), there are also many very small and incremental processes of self-directed decisions that define the life course of a person.

How does a small boy decide whether he will go honey hunting with his older cousins on the day that will mark his first foray? This is a significant decision and one that includes him in a different group, with a different task, and trying a new skill for the first time. But the decision-making process on subsequent occasions makes less of a mark. Each day he consciously makes the decision, until one day the thought of an alternative to honey hunting is no longer even considered. In this way, the decision of action is like the decision about the transitional object, in that the acquisition and first interaction mark a moment of conscious decision making with recognition of its significance, followed by a period of habituation, until there is a time when conscious decision making is no longer an essential component of the daily set of activities. The dynamic process of alternation between creativity and habituation in energy allocation is therefore similar to other processes of cognition and action, such as the distinction between short-term and long-term memory and the gradual drop-off of distinction noticed in new forms of language use.

The Spatiality of Work

Work takes place in space as well as in time. Resources are usually located in different portions of a landscape, and like many other mobile species our earliest hominid ancestors made use of differential natural distributions of food, water, and salt through judicious energy expenditure on a daily, seasonal, annual, and lifetime basis. Later, with the development of stone tool making, the location of outcrops and suitable raw materials were factored into the conscious perception and use of the landscape. Individuals engaged in multitasking through calculations that involved not only the distance to resources and potential for competition in their acquisition, but also the relative quality of the resource as a raw material for making artifacts. Over time, the increasingly diverse repertoire of objects meant that humans' perception of the landscape grew to include other economic elements, such as fuel, building materials, and ores. The adoption of agriculture and sedentism ten thousand to twelve thousand years ago meant an increased amount of extractive activity and investments in the landscape in the form of tending domesticated crops and herding domesticated animals.

The developmental trajectory of individually generated perceptions and use of the landscape encompassed social as well as economic aspects. Nearly all animals engage in territorial activity, and the human capacity to cognize the landscape in a territorial framework is inherited from a long mammalian tradition of competition among members of the same species. However, the notion of territory is more accurately described not as a single contiguous area but as a series of resource nodes and corridors of access (Smith 2007b). For humans, this ranged from passive senses of "belonging" to the active construction and demarcation of access rights and possession. Examining the role of possession in social activities, Timothy Earle (2000:40) has proposed that "[p]roperty is integral to all concepts of social institutions—how people are related to resources and to each other." The archaeological record shows that humans did not simply use the landscape but also created markers that incorporated notions of possession with the intertwined aspects of access rights and inheritance.

The reality of the hunter-gatherer economy means that individuals who make their living from the land are highly mobile. But ancient foragers used many types of modifications to mark their investments in productive areas, including rock carvings and paintings, and even simple caches of meat and tools to delineate territorial claims (Anderson and Zedeño 2009; Potter 2004). Burial monuments were another way in which mobile peoples made permanent markers. The use of the dead was a highly effective means of claiming a landscape, with collective labor that was concentrated at a single moment in time but yielded long-term visibility in the form of megaliths or mounds that stood as silent reminders to others of who belonged in that landscape. Even incidental remains—such as a scatter of debris from making a stone tool, the smoldering ashes from an abandoned fire, or a heap of discarded refuse—were signs that could be "read" by individuals as marking the presence of others.

The purposeful and incidental components of landscape marking continued after the development of settled village societies. Work had a strong spatial component in these eras as well, as not all members of a sedentary group actually reside in settlements and not all agricultural activities occur within a fixed radius of a village. Bruce Winterhalder and Carol Goland (1997:124) have examined the transition to agriculture and noted that one important mode of risk reduction for farmers would be the spacing out of fields. In smaller-scale agricultural societies, the use of field houses as temporary, seasonal accommodations in the vicinity of ripening fields enabled a greater spread of family members over the landscape (Snead 2008). The seasonal movement of some household members out from the main dwelling area might occur when individuals set up exterior camps for hunting, pottery, and brick production (Peacock 1982), the gathering of nuts or other wild resources, fishing, and other extractive activities. Individuals moving through the landscape for specific reasons, such as pastoralism, would engage in multitasking through the opportunistic acquisition of stone and other tradable items.

The advent of agriculture placed additional cultural delimitations on the landscape. Although we tend to think of territorial divisions, land rights, and property as consisting of a process of mutually exclusive boundary delimitations, people also could define their surroundings in ways that provided opportunities for sequential use by different parties: for example, the use of valley bottoms as summer farmland by agriculturalists, seasonal spring-fall pasture by mobile animal herders, and hunting land during the winter. Spatiality, risk, and time are intertwined factors in the process of energy expenditure in a landscape, because the availability and relative cost of resources can change considerably at different time scales. For example, although humans may compete with relatively few other predators during the day, nighttime resource collection can be considerably more dangerous. On a seasonal basis, high-altitude stone outcrops can become inaccessible, while on a lifetime basis, climate change or anthropogenic effects can alter the location of naturally growing plants, trees, and animals.

Increasing technological capacities accented the spatiality of work. New technologies that emerged in the human repertoire—lithic manufacture, pottery production, and the smelting of metal—were inserted into the spatiality of a landscape that was increasingly cultural rather than natural in its configurations. Inventions and their production processes might be associated with negative elements such as noise and noxious odors, and the archaeological evidence of technologies such as pottery and iron production shows that these production areas often were separated from habitation zones. The spatial segregation of these work areas might have led to social segregation of the craftsworkers as well, on the basis of either seeing literal dirtiness as a kind of spiritual pollution or viewing those who controlled mysterious technology as connected with potentially malevolent spirits (e.g., van der Merwe and Avery 1987).

The notion of inside versus outside constitutes another powerful spatial determinant of work patterns. The realities of climate mean that some work has to be done indoors or in a sheltered place, while other tasks can be undertaken in the open air. The determination of inside/outside components of energy investment is a basic aspect of task management—for example, cooking on a fire in the rain outdoors would be unworkable. However, the inside/outside distinction also is made for passive energy investments, such as storage. Storage space is by definition unifunctional, as a space full of stored items cannot be used for anything else. This is distinct from other types of interior spaces, which can be multifunctional and serve by turns as a sleeping space, a meeting place, a place of temporary storage, and a venue filled with different kinds of sounds, sights, and smells at different times of the day or year.

Spatiality also is intertwined with mobility at different scales of activity, ranging from daily foraging trips from a settled camp to the movement of entire populations across a landscape. From an individual perspective, mobility can be characterized as a temporary or permanent component of economic activity, as seen, for example, in the case of Ötzi the Ice Man, whose possessions suggested a wandering lifestyle. Migration also can mean the long-term absence of individuals from the household for the purposes of accumulating wherewithal, which is then sent back to the household in a faraway place. Migration is a very important topic today; although there is a global information economy that does not require the movement of people, labor flows clearly are still an important component of work. Today we experience migration at two ends of the economic scale. One end consists of highly skilled professionals who move to escape limiting conditions in their home countries in a process described as "brain drain." At the other end of the economic scale, migration brings people into low-wage jobs in farms, factories, and restaurants worldwide.

What was the role of migration in the past? For foragers, movement around the landscape was an essential component of their lifeways, a pattern of circulation that characterized most of our species' first two million years. Nor did the advent of agriculture and sedentism eliminate the idea of migration; instead, migration became part of the energy expenditure strategy of a subset of the population. Animal husbandry often includes the movement of people and animals, whether through the specialization of a subset of households or through the mutual interdependence of mobile pastoral and settled agricultural groups. Seasonal agricultural economies also experience "labor bottlenecks," which provide an incentive for some individuals to move around the landscape to fill the demands of field preparation or harvest (e.g., Barker 2006:46; Netting 1993). Migration is a factor in manufacturing whenever populations are too low or too dispersed to support permanent facilities; in recent European historical times, mobile work teams included brick makers (Peacock 1982:35), and even today metalworkers migrate from one community to another in central India. Skill levels also are an important component of the migration experience; D. P. S. Peacock (1982:35, citing Gault 1952) notes that at the tile-making workshop of Civry-la-Forêt in the early twentieth century, "[m]ost of the seasonal labour seems to have been recruited locally but the more skilled workers such as the tile moulders came from Normandy."

Although we tend to think of migration today as something that moves people from rural areas into cities, it is important to realize that in complex societies, reverse migration also occurs from populated areas out to rural zones for the purposes of agricultural work. Margaret Grieco's (1995) insightful article on nineteenth- and early-twentieth-century London describes how people migrated out from the city as seasonal laborers to the hop fields of southern England. The work was mostly done by women and children and was organized by women who would move out and re-create entire neighborhoods in the hop fields for several weeks a year. Medical facilities, recreational opportunities, religious services, and shops all migrated to the fields as well, resulting in what she calls the "movement of community over distance" (Grieco 1995:204). Other types of agricultural labor relying on London's urban dwellers included apple picking, which was done after the hops had been harvested, and pea picking, which was not communally organized but done as a matter of individuals engaging in day labor. Grieco (1995:201) emphasizes the social nature of all of these types of work, noting that interpersonal ties were essential to individual success and that "the social organisation of employment is frequently and typically complex, even at the 'bottom end' of the labour market."

Women and Men at Work

The study of gender is not merely the study of women but the study of the roles held by both women and men (Gutmann 1997; Meskell 1998). As seen in Grieco's work on London, the community organization of work and the expenditure of energy are affected by the gender and age of the individual participants as well as by environmental variables such as seasonality and climate. The different physical requirements of manual labor, as well as the fluctuating balance of skill and apprenticeship, are part of the conscious configuration of work inputs by individuals living in societies ranging from simple hunter-gatherers to globalized empires.

Through archaeological, ethnographic, and historic studies, we can evaluate the way in which male and female inputs of work were consciously crafted over time, mitigating natural parameters while creating and affirming social ones. Because work is the exchange of energy for wherewithal, observations about men and women at work indicate how these quotidian modes of energy expenditure were cognized and habituated to produce archaeologically visible patterns over time.

Information derived from observations on contemporary foraging peoples provides insights on the ways in which prehistoric men and women worked differently, just as in previous chapters we have seen that they sometimes ate differently and utilized objects differently. In the hunter-gatherer societies that exist today, men and women engage in different types of food gathering and other types of work. At the adult stage of life, men usually are engaged in long-distance hunting of larger animals in a process that can take them away from camp and family for days at a time; by contrast, women concentrate on plant foods and small game that are close at hand (Bird 1999; Kuhn and Stiner 2006). Skeletal evidence enables us to substantiate that those differences in physical exertion are visible in the premodern past as well. Christopher Ruff (1987) noted in his comparative study of male and female skeletons from forager, agriculturalist, and modern populations that foragers definitely had a distinct difference between males and females, with males having a more robust lower limb morphology indicative of activities such as running over long distances and over uneven terrain, a characteristic that he attributed to hunting. He noted that the same foraging patterns of male-female distinction are visible in the Upper Paleolithic and even earlier.

With the adoption of agriculture in many regions of the world starting ten thousand to twelve thousand years ago, there was a shift towards an annual cycle of planting and harvest that changed the configurations of work from one of daily foraging to long-term storage. There were many more types of work throughout the year, ranging from tending plants (watering, planting, and keeping away pests) to the disposition of stored foods. These many distinct tasks provided a greater scope for the division of work into roles held by men and women, young and old, skilled and unskilled. Although many agricultural tasks could be performed by either men or women, patterns of work were adapted from earlier ones, such that women specialized in close-in tasks and men specialized in longer-distance commuting. In the agricultural period, this "commuting" still included occasional big-game hunting but mostly concentrated on herding, tending distant fields, and procuring resources that might be found at a distance, such as grinding stones. But there was still the need for active considerations of the landscape by both women and men. As Gillian Bentley, Richard Paine, and Jasper Boldsen (2001) note, "sedentism" does not necessarily mean that everyone is staying in one location as if it were a hunter-gatherer camp simply frozen in place. Instead, "[o]ne of the constraints on residential mobility for horticulturalists is the location and relative permanence of their gardens and associated settlements. Paradoxically, this permanence often results in longer daily trips for women in search of supplementary wild foods, essential firewood, and to reach their garden plots" (Bentley, Paine, and Boldsen 2001:211).

Nonagricultural tasks developed after the adoption of sedentism often had a gendered division of labor as well. Pottery, weaving, and construction all include numerous production steps, and ethnoarchaeological research enables us to envision how these tasks can be specialized into male and female domains in a variety of combinations. Pottery production is a particularly well-studied process that provides models for understanding the division of female-male energy expenditure in the past. In some places, women are the gatherers of clay, while in other regions collecting and handling raw clay is the domain of males. Women and men also often divide the production process into distinct gendered subtasks; in South Asia, for example, women traditionally make hand-formed vessels but do not use, or even touch, the potter's wheel used by men. In some regions, the forming of all pottery is done by men while the decoration is done by women; in other regions, all of the fixed-place components of pottery production, from forming to decorating, are done by women while the firing, transporting, and selling are done by men (Peacock 1982:chap. 3).

The archaeological traces of similarly gendered activities can be recognized in burial populations, as male and female skeletons often are accompanied by different tool kits associated with different types of work. Sometimes, fingerprints that are left on durable surfaces such as clay can be divided into male and female sizes, enabling us to discern who handled the different steps of the production process. Archaeological evidence also shows that while some tasks seem to have been specifically relegated to women or men, other specialized jobs, such as being a medical practitioner, could be taken up by both men and women (as in ancient Egypt [Magner 1992]). The presence of tools, which allows us to abstract from them the social understandings of ancient gendered work patterns, also enables us to understand personalized aspects of the intimate connection between goods and work. Both the tools and the traditions of a deceased artisan could be inherited by others, with social relations that were materially transferred from one generation to the next. We should also envision how "intangible" professions related to music, drama, and adjudication resulted in wherewithal that had to be transferred, as suggested by the historically documented cases of women dancers who would adopt a girl "to follow in their profession and inherit their property" (Goody 1969:64, citing Mayne 1892:214).

Ancient people actively managed the effects of task specialization and the potential for disequilibrium among men and women. We should not assume that individuals simply accepted the gender parameters that they inherited; instead, they actively validated or changed those parameters through the act of working. Moreover, ethnographic research illustrates how individuals' active engagement with gender dynamics results in differential access to power and authority within a group. Among the very disparate groups examined by Ian Hodder (1982), women in both Western-based groups such as the Gypsies and the non-Western groups such as the Nuba in the Sudan had political and economic power that was couched and disguised in everyday actions. Hodder (1982:64) notes the way in which energy expenditure in Gypsy households is overlain with symbolic meaning that can be manipulated to accentuate or defuse interpersonal stresses: "Gypsy women act as intermediaries between the pure Gypsy male and the impure, polluting Gorgio society. They bring in food from that society and prepare it for the men, and its purification is in their trust." In the Gypsy case, the woman who acts, or even threatens to act, out of accordance with the prevailing social norm conveys a sense of power not only over her own identity but also over the identity of others. Thus, even routine, domestic work is subjected to oscillations of creativity and habituation by the individuals involved.

Archaeological evidence shows that women and men often had different patterns and types of work in prehistory. Human cognitive capacities would have been creatively engaged to interweave the inescapable realities of female and male physiology with social expectations that were the result of many acts of being and doing over the course of a lifetime. Patricia Crown (2001:227) discusses the way in which women's cooking transformed the outside, natural world into the inside, cultural one through the transformative effect of energy investment. Domestic actions as a form of energy transfer serve to establish and reinforce social parameters with each action undertaken by an individual. In the matter of meat allocation, Crown has suggested that particular cooking methods such as stews may have been a way for women to more equitably divide up hunted resources within a family unit (including getting more meat themselves [Crown 2001:255]). The expectations about male and female roles also could be utilized to secure entitlements by individuals, as Lotte Van de Pol and Erika Kuijpers (2005:45) note in their study of early modern European centers where women "had more difficulties in earning their bread but easier access to poor relief than [did] men."

If we view ordinary domestic actions, from cuisine to the use of goods, as having elements that are "ritualized" (see Bradley 2005:33–34) then we can evaluate the thought process that is enacted by individuals in the course of each specific occurrence. The creative input exercised by individuals through their interactions with daily-use goods enriches our potential to examine dynamic systems in the past, in a way that is distinct from simply examining the singular end-product of behavior such as a skeleton. Instead, both the body and the artifacts are the cumulative, physical record of long-term differential energy expenditure by women and men.

The Old and the Young at Work

Individuals' tasks and specializations vary by age as well as by sex, as is evident in the work undertaken by children, adults, and older people. Researchers have only recently begun to study children in the archaeological record, but these studies have shown how children's energy expenditures and contributions are a distinct, integral part of ancient economies (e.g., Baxter 2005; Crown 2007b). Childhood is a period of learning and apprenticeship, but it is also a time of energy expenditure that benefits the group and the household. Among foragers, children engage in important supporting tasks such as gathering fuel and collecting easy-to-capture plant foods. These routine support tasks are seen in sedentary contexts as well; for example, Nicole Boenke (2007) points to the recovery of small shoes within Iron Age salt mine galleries as evidence for the presence of child workers, who would have taken food and water to the miners as well as being involved in other tasks such as carrying tools in and salt out.

The adoption of a sedentary way of life meant that the rigors of moving the entire habitation were eliminated; one result was that children were not as much of a liability as they are for a highly mobile population. Moreover, each new mouth came with two tiny hands, which could be put to work almost as soon as the child could walk. Easy tasks such as chasing birds away from fields could be gradually upgraded as the child grew older to include herding animals, winnowing grain, collecting fuel, and, of course, tending the younger children. The advent of new technological processes meant that there were many additional jobs for children (and other physically underdeveloped or unskilled individuals) who could hold bellows, carry tools, fetch water, tend fires, and sort manufacturing debris for reuse.

Archaeological and ethnographic studies similarly show that elderly individuals take on particular kinds of tasks, with household impacts that differ by gender. Studies of twentieth-century foragers show that although adult life spans are quite short, there is a differential longevity for women and men. Kristen Hawkes and her colleagues have examined this unequal survival rate and proposed that female longevity had a long evolutionary trajectory (e.g., Hawkes, O'Connell, and Blurton Jones 1998; Hawkes et al. 1997; O'Connell, Hawkes, and Blurton Jones 1999). The resultant "grandmother hypothesis" interweaves the facts of juvenile dependency and humans' long postmenopausal survival rates to account for the differential longevity of females deep in prehistory. Subsequent work on the age distribution of ancestral populations by Rachel Caspari and Sang-Hee Lee (2004:10898) shows an increasing trend for longevity throughout the course of human evolution; however, this trend is one that builds up slowly, and not until the Upper Paleolithic do we see "for the first time . . . a larger amount of older adults than younger adults in the death distribution."

Whereas the role of elderly women is a phenomenon that appears to have a long trajectory in the human record, both the presence of and the role for elderly men may not have emerged until relatively recent times.

Studies of the transition from foraging to farming as measured by skeletal populations show that people lived longer in the agricultural period both in the Old World (Eshed et al. 2004) and in the Americas (Buikstra and Konigsberg 1985). What were these older individuals doing? For women, the shift from foraging to farming probably had relatively little qualitative change. Women's energy expenditure would have continued a pattern of close-to-home work involving child care and food preparation, and elderly women would have been particularly valued as individuals who had survived past the risky reproductive age to contribute to the upbringing of their grandchildren. For men, however, the advent of agriculture brought into existence an entirely new demographic category: the older male. In forager economies, older males are relatively rare because of deaths through violence and hunting accidents; with sedentism, males were subjected to fewer such risks. Moreover, elderly males and females alike could make use of stored resources and soft foods such as porridge that are more suitable for fragile elderly teeth. As a result, elderly males probably took up social roles that were either new to or accentuated by the sedentary lifestyle, such as the adjudication of property, storytelling, and serving as the holders of household and communal memory.

The interaction of generations also enabled the sequential buildup and transfer of specialized skills through the process of apprenticeship. The give-and-take between master craftsmaker and apprentice constitutes "a complex cognitive process in which memory, attention, and motivation interact" (Wallaert 2008:179). In many production systems, such as smithing, weaving, potting, and other crafts, young people may be apprenticed to older, skilled individuals. As beginners, workers trade energy and time for the opportunity to learn skills that will enhance their future productivity. Apprentices usually start their training by serving as uncompensated workers who carry fuel, tools, water, and raw materials, as well as sweeping, cleaning, and preparing work surfaces. Apprenticeship also may involve learning intangibles such as incantations, epic poems, songs, or movements such as dance. Medicinal apprenticeship may encompass the learning not only of skills but also of capacities for observation and persuasion. Apprenticeship involves conscious decision making on the part of both the learner and the teacher, in which new skills are acquired through the processes of observation and imitation, as well as through processes of idiosyncratic trial and error (Wallaert 2008:180).

The Substance and Symbolism of Work

Human time and energy expenditure can be divided into two categories: work as a mechanism for the direct acquisition of desired items, and work as a social mechanism of cohesion and cooperation. The example of the apprentice and the master craftsmaker shows how economic and social aspects of work are intertwined at many levels, from the process of learning a craft to the relationships between artisans and others who supply them with materials or accept their products in return. The metaphor of teaching and learning is one that is applicable to nearly every realm of human energy expenditure, because people learn even the most basic skills from others. Among foragers, this would include the location and behavior of prey, the preparation of food, and the treatment of illness or injury; for sedentary peoples, the process of learning and teaching would encompass a further diversity of tasks, including the making of containers, the creation and maintenance of storage facilities, and the pursuit of increasing knowledge about the productive characteristics of plants and animals. Both forager and sedentary groups also would have had ritual knowledge, which would have been passed along from one person to another as a process of teaching and learning. All of these components of work have as their foundation the individual who uses the body and the brain to transfer energy in the physical realm.

Can we say that prehistoric people also experienced symbolism in the creation of goods and food, even prior to the development of institutionalized political hierarchies? The ability of our earliest hominid ancestors to consistently replicate certain shapes in stone tools suggests that there was a sense of learning, a concept of exacting craftsmanship, and a recognition of virtuosity in the everyday tasks of energy expenditure. For more recent time periods, the sense of identity created through the exercise of craft traditions is seen in the inclusion of pottery production tools in the burials of women in early Southeast Asia (e.g., Higham 1989:77) and the inclusion of both life-size and votive tools in early Egyptian tombs (Bard 2000:86).

Research on the social components of work shows how symbolism is attached not only to the finished product but also to the act of manufacture. Some of these approaches utilize ethnographic studies, such as research in West Africa that has shown the extent to which ritual is an essential component of metallurgy (Schmidt and Mapunda 1997). Although most transformative processes involving fire require skill, metallurgy is particularly unusual because the transformation of a rock through extreme temperature to become a piece of shiny metal is one that required specific skills on the part of the producer. The very striking and lengthy ritual preparations that accompany the transformation of ore in the ethnographic record have inspired archaeologists to think more carefully about the magical elements of these transformations in the past (e.g., Bradley 2005; Rowlands and Warnier 1993). With a skill set that was the result of many years of apprenticeship, the metalsmith utilized a precise "recipe" of charcoal, heat, time, and ore that was outside the realm of most individuals' experience, rending the metalworker as a person to be viewed with both respect and trepidation.

Sometimes it was the shape of a finished item that required special expertise in manufacture, even if the material was something that could be worked in a basic way by anyone. Tristan Carter (2007) has discussed the way in which stone blades of dramatically different length are found in the context of settlement and burial sites of the Cycladic Bronze Age (fourth millennium BC). This differentiation was not just a matter of choice in the disposition of finished goods, but the result of two different types of techniques used on the same material. The thin and elegant blades from burial sites would have required special expertise that might have involved traveling artisans for the performance of what he calls "necrolithic theatrics" at the funeral site (Carter 2007:96). And in many cases, the application of human energy on wild products enabled individuals to create socially valued goods from easily available or even "free" components, as seen in the transformation of flowers into garlands or gourds into containers (fig. 4.4).

Everyday acts of energy transfer on food and goods gave ordinary people the opportunity to create symbolically charged effects on daily-use items. Foragers would greet the seasonality of plant foods or the opportunistic capture of a favored prey with the emotionally laden enthusiasm reflective of individual or group food preferences. Seasonality would particularly affect agriculturalists, who would see their weeks and months of work rewarded in the space of a few days of harvest; they would continue to utilize the surrounding natural world for medicine, flavoring, dyes, and fuel that similarly would have involved not only the economic

FIGURE 4.4. Energy expenditure can transform low-cost or wild materials into objects that can be exchanged for wherewithal; this Aztec flower seller, for example, has sewn blooms together into garlands.

knowledge of their existence but also the symbolic recognition of unseen powers that brought wild resources into fruition. The existence of harvest festivals in both ancient texts and contemporary agricultural societies shows a universal recognition of the precarious relationship between consistent energy expenditure and the potentially fickle natural world.

Symbolic actions also are invested in the use of "extra" work to create a particular effect, a factor that is particularly evident in the preparation of food. Humans can eat most foods prepared in a very basic manner of roasting or boiling, but the human propensity to create variations is a way to demonstrate care for family and guests through energy expenditure. Haute cuisine is a particularly useful way to understand the transformation of basic ingredients into edible substances with social status. Many of the most distinct and widely known examples of French cooking, for example, actually involve very simple ingredients. An omelette is a skillful presentation of eggs, and a sauce is a carefully tended boiling down of leavings from a pan of roasted meat. Combining the simple ingredients of eggs, milk, flour, and butter can yield a soufflé, a crêpe, or a crème brûlée. In all cases, the application of time, energy, and skill—rather than the ingredients themselves—is what makes these dishes distinct. The evidence for ancient cuisine indicates the range of energy expenditure that could be utilized to produce a "finer" product. Mesopotamian beer was unfiltered and drunk through a straw (Sherratt 1987:94), but one can imagine that for some occasions a time-consuming process of filtering through cloth might have enabled the individual to show an extra level of care and respect for the guest. After the advent of sedentism, corn in the American Southwest was sometimes ground to a very fine flour, perhaps to make it cook more quickly as a fuel-saving measure (Crown 2001:247); alternatively, one can envision that extra care in food preparation enabled the cook to project a level of virtuosity on this symbolically charged staple.

Work as a Mechanism for the Acquisition of Desired Things

Humans are characterized by a desire for a high level of diversity in the items that we eat, wear, display, and discard. How do individuals actually acquire those items? In some cases, they can manufacture items themselves, utilizing raw materials that they collect and modifying those materials to result in the desired item. In most cases, however, the distinctive attributes desired by humans and evident at least fifty thousand years ago include at least some aspects that would have required the input of other people. The skills required for making objects, as well as the knowledge required for their use, were the result of information transfer from one person to another. Unusual raw materials or specialized tools used to fashion the finished product would have passed through the hands of other individuals who would have been compensated, or at least recognized, for their contribution to the finished product.

To avoid the restrictive and historically loaded terms *capital* and *purchasing power*, I instead propose using the term *wherewithal* to explain the ways in which both physical vigor and socially valued skills (such as art and memory) are transformed into the direct or delayed acquisition of desired objects such as food and goods. Wherewithal can take the form of physical accumulations, either as goods or as raw materials that can be stockpiled and traded away. However, wherewithal also can be represented by an investment in intellectual achievements for which there is a potential for lifelong recompense by others (such as medicine, music, storytelling, and ritual knowledge). People can work to establish a skill set as a long-term investment, the expression of which is directed by the individual on an autonomous basis.

Sometimes people acquire things that are provided by others through bonds of kinship without expectation of immediate return. Children in their earliest days are incapable even of moving themselves to sources of food, so they must be cared for by others. But as individuals grow older and more physically independent, they spend their days selecting from a range of potential objects and comestibles. Possibly the most basic form of energy transfer for the purpose of achieving wherewithal is encompassed in the exchange of sex for compensation. Colloquially known as "the world's oldest profession," this scenario of exchange is relatively common in our primate relatives, which suggests a similarly long history among our human ancestors. The determination of what to exchange in return for sexual access is a highly compelling example of the human capacity to calculate short-term benefits compared to long-term costs and risks. For a female, engaging in sex may provide short-term access to wherewithal but with a potential long-term energy cost in the form of pregnancy and child rearing.

Most nonsexual transactions are financed by the production of food or objects that can be either traded away for other goods or, through feasts and donations, converted into social standing. Exchange networks would have included trades of common materials among immediate neighbors in times of variable household surplus and need. Exchange also included items transferred across long distances. As Zofia Sulgostowska's (2002) study of European "chocolate flint" shows, people transported materials two hundred kilometers or more on a routine basis even ten thousand to fourteen thousand years ago, a pattern that is not uncommon in other parts of the world for the same era. Transportation would have involved individual energy expenditure under two principal mechanisms: direct long-distance transportation and the incremental transfer over shorter distances.

From our modern-day perspective, the thought of walking across difficult terrain carrying bulky goods is unappealing, except if we are hiking and camping for recreational purposes. However, most objects in ancient times were transported by human labor, and ethnographic studies show the surprisingly large quantities of materials that can be moved this way. Research on human porters in the Himalayan nation of Nepal shows that people regularly carry over 100 percent of their own body weight when transporting goods long distances over mountain paths (Malville 2001).

It is important also to keep in mind that there were no beasts of burden domesticated until ten thousand to twelve thousand years ago (and that some parts of the world such as North America, Mexico, and Australia never had domestic pack animals until European contact). Work as porters would have been a specialized task requiring particular skills—not only physical strength but also the ability to memorize routes and landscapes, predict weather and strategize the timing and pace of movement, and possess the social skills required to move from place to place while acquiring food and shelter en route.

In addition to the direct long-distance movement of objects, there is also the phenomenon known as "down-the-line" trade, a process first defined by Colin Renfrew (1975:41–43). He describes this as a series of short-distance exchanges that succeed in eventually moving an object for a long distance. Down-the-line trade makes use of the social interactions that already exist among near neighbors in a landscape, as the short-distance exchanges are encompassed in regular interactions among kin and familiar individuals whose memories of exchange patterns would grow and accumulate over the course of a lifetime. In these transactions, individuals would calculate worth and value not only on objectively measurable and commonly known aspects such as distance to the source material, or the time required to manufacture an item, but also on the past and predictive social investments that were symbolized in the process.

Who Works for Whom?

The effects of energy expenditure can be measured in both the physical and the social realm. Within both simple and complex societies, there are many configurations in which one individual works for another, including apprenticeship, indentured servitude, sharecropping, and outright slavery. Apprenticeship is a formal agreement in which one person provides strength in return for the knowledge of a skill or craft. The corollary of labor investment in apprenticeship is the increased cost of supervision from the point of view of the skilled craftsmaker. Supervisors organize the work of others who are focused on the gross motor components of production that set the stage for the master to proceed directly to sophisticated detail work. While more work can be done when people perform specialized tasks within a team, it also means that the nature of the supervisor's work shifts from direct participation to a role of oversight that includes a variety of new tasks: teaching, quality assessment, mentoring, scolding or exhorting, and correcting or mitigating errors. Apprenticeship thus captures the intersections of young and old, skilled and unskilled, and physical labor and intellectual input that characterize the multicomponent nature of the work process.

Indentured servitude is another type of social relationship that is focused on the exchange of individuals' energy expenditure for support and sustenance. Indenture can be the result of short-term affiliations for a specific purpose (such as earning bride-price) or longer-term dependencies that result from unequal resource control (such as debt-bondage that occurs when crop failures or poverty enable resource holders to gain access to others' labor). Debt-bondage usually reflects one-way energy input in the form of brawn rather than brain, hence the frequency of debt-bondage as a characteristic of agricultural societies to address issues of labor bottlenecks at seasons of planting or harvest.

Slavery is a form of economic interaction for which contemporary anthropological theorizing is hopelessly inadequate. Our modern perceptions of slavery are conditioned by some of the worst excesses of the modern era, including sex slavery rings that continue to take advantage of young women worldwide and, of course, the legacy of colonial slavery, in which millions of Africans, South Asians, and Native Americans were displaced and forced to work against their will. If, however, we can manage to conceptualize slavery—and other types of work-based interdependence—as the temporary or permanent ownership of one person's work capacity by another person, we can evaluate systems of long-term bonded labor that were fairly common in the ancient world.

Much information on ancient slavery comes from the Classical Greco-Roman Mediterranean, where poems, plays, and philosophical works along with texts on law enable us to assess social and economic conditions. Slavery could result from the large-scale misfortunes of war as well as the small-scale misfortunes of a household, and in the ancient world slavery was not necessarily focused on particular ethnic groups. Documents show that while most slaves probably spent their lives under the control of an owner, there was also a significant category of freed slaves who could gain normal social status upon manumission. Slaves worked at different types of tasks, ranging from agricultural labor to household work, and these occupations appear to have affected their status later in life; F. Hugh Thompson (2003:60) notes that the slaves who continued to work for their masters after being freed "were mostly engaged in household work, as personal attendants, or as handicraft workers." In sum, slavery could be a permanent, or semipermanent, relationship among individuals and could be crafted on a highly individualized basis ranging from outright labor capture to dynamic gradations of patronage and clientage.

Long-term agreements of mutual dependence also are evident in the development of caste systems in various parts of the world. Although the term *caste* is today associated most closely with the Indian subcontinent, the idea of caste can be more widely referred to as the phenomenon of social groups that are endogamous and economically specialized and whose designation includes moral overtones (Smith 2005b). The economic specialization of caste groups usually includes necessary, basic services such as making pottery, barbering, metalworking, and undertaking that are required by all members of society (e.g., for India, see Dumont 1966; for Africa, see Tamari 1991). Nonetheless, these groups are encumbered with strict moral injunctions against social interactions with the dominant group, ranging from taboos against intermarriage to prohibitions against sharing food. The apparent economic perversity of denigrating those upon whom dominant groups depend provides an opportunity to evaluate the historical roots of these relationships. Using the idea of "entitlements" (*sensu* Sen 1981:1), we can view the development of caste systems as a historically contingent one that occurs at moments of precipitous social decline, in which groups of occupational specialists accept low social rank in exchange for a permanent entitlement in which they must be supported by groups of higher social rank (Smith 2005b).

Beyond patronage, caste relationships, debt-bondage, and indentured servitude, there were other forms of socially sanctioned energy capture at the level of the individual and the household. These include adoption, fostering, and the extension of fictive kinship to disadvantaged individuals seeking to exchange energy inputs for food and shelter. Adoption, for example, is a relationship of long-term labor dependence overlain with the expectations and obligations of kinship. Adoption might be carried out largely to ensure offspring for the sake of inheriting property and carrying out essential rituals for the dead, but it also had economic implications; in Greece, for example, an adopted son could not make his own will regarding the disposition of property that he had inherited as a result of the adoptive relationship (Goody 1969:61). The economic inputs of adopted or fostered offspring also could include the rights to earnings as well as expectations about the long-term financial outlay for rituals to the deceased.

Work and the Development of Social Complexity

The preceding sections indicate how the process of work is cognized and activated at the individual level. Through the oscillations of creativity and habituation, individuals engage in work through a multitasking strategy that makes use of time, space, resource availability, and perceptions of value. Gender, age, and expertise constitute the community parameters of individual responses. These parameters were modified as populations increased and hierarchical social levels were added to the person-to-person interactions sustained at the small group sizes of deep prehistory. The earliest division of labor was between males and females, a biological concept that acquired cultural importance through the assumption of gendered roles in both social and economic activities. The first articulation of this behavioral pattern may have been at the time of the australopithecine-*Homo* transition starting around two million years ago, a time when socialized divisions of labor might have compensated for (or propelled) the reduction of sexual dimorphism between males and females.

By a million years ago, our ancestors had begun to engage in the transformation of energy into wherewithal when they first began to loan, share, trade, exploit, and benefit from the energy inputs of others in cycles of interdependence. Humans have the capacity of memory, a long infantile development, and a long life span coupled with a transition from greater physical skill in youth to a greater store of experience in old age that means that the conditions of interdependence are constantly shifting. These conditions can even shift catastrophically, as, for example, when a woman dies in childbirth, leaving an infant to be raised by others, or when a man is injured in the course of hunting and afterwards depends on others for food and shelter. As a result, the capacity and productivity of the individual are subject to continual recalculation both by the individual and by the surrounding household and community members.

Although humans are not the only species observed to have life-long recognition of kin relationships, the increased amounts of goods and increased density of social networks combine to make energy transfers between human individuals a matter of continual adjustment. Our primate relatives generally do not share food and appear to have little sense of obligation between generations or among individuals. By contrast, humans thrive as they increase the ways that one person can work for another when the number of household and community members increases. Children and the elderly contribute differently to household tasks, with their contributions ranging from brute force to wisdom and expertise. Even among simple forager societies, the daily work of carrying foraged foods, fuel, and water back to camp means that there is work for everyone. This is accented in times of extraordinary demands on human energy, such as moving camp or adjusting to seasonal bonuses and deprivations. In sedentary societies, the number of routine and repetitive tasks increases exponentially. Food preparation and the manufacture of the simplest objects have steps that can be managed even by those who lack the skill or stamina to complete the process or envision its outcome.

Work beyond the family also exists in even the simplest societies. Differential levels of skill or experience mean that some individuals may be more adept at hunting certain types of animals or at locating certain types of plants. Some individuals are inevitably more skilled than others at storytelling, ritual interventions, and healing and are disproportionately called upon, depending on the need of the surrounding community. Some individuals also are more skilled at leadership and in exhorting others to collectively accomplish tasks that involve energy expenditure beyond the capacity of the individual. Most tasks beyond individual artifact crafting involve this type of coordination: hunting activities, construction of dwellings and ritual spaces, warfare and raiding, adjudication of disputes, and even the mass witnessing of events such as marriages, ritual events, and funerals.

Jeanne Arnold (1996:60) has proposed that one of the markers of social complexity is the regular appropriation of labor and that a "critical evolutionary change that must have been experienced by the most complex hunter-gatherer groups and early agricultural chiefdoms . . . was the restructuring of labor involved in manufacturing, subsistence, facilities construction, or other activities." However, this evolutionary change was undertaken within the context of energy expenditure in which individuals were already consciously engaged with the multitasking process. The advent of communal labor activities involves the coordination of energy expenditure by numerous individuals who each cognize the effects of adding more work into their already-existing repertoires. Communal work itself may fall under a range of temporal and spatial types, ranging from singular acts (such as the creation of a monument, a ditch, or a stockade) to repeated activities (such as the seasonal cleaning of canals). Communal work may be planned and the tasks known well in advance (such as the annual cycle of festivals) or may be rapidly imposed through natural disasters such as earthquakes or cultural upheavals such as warfare. Within communal activities, preexisting social bonds and networks are integrated into the task at hand, with factors of expertise, apprenticeship, gender, age, and health resulting in effects that can vary widely among individuals. These factors also affected the perception of new opportunities for both elites and non-elites at the transition to increased social complexity, as the growth of population centers provided the scope for otherwise "unskilled" individuals to make a living through engaging in transportation, serving, packing, and cleaning.

An examination of the role of managers also sheds light on the process of multitasking, energy expenditure, and coordination. Managers are an essential component of the elicitation of work by elites in the development of social complexity, but the process of management involves numerous stages of planning as well as preparation for contingencies (fig. 4.5). The manager must ensure that the call for workers is effectively broadcast and must ensure that the workers assemble in the appropriate place at the appropriate time. Workers must either bring their own tools or be provided with tools (even simple ones such as hoes or baskets), another factor of preparation that must be competently undertaken by the manager. Only then can the work begin, and for this stage the manager has to be present to coordinate the work of many individuals at different levels of age, skill, and motivation. If work is undertaken under the rubric of taxation or labor tribute, there must be an investment in mechanisms of control; if work is undertaken in exchange for compensation, then the manager incurs additional responsibilities. Standardized currency is a surprisingly recent development in human economic systems; prior to about 600 BC, there was no coinage, and most compensations were

FIGURE 4.5. The development of segmented production processes introduces the role of managers who engage in multitasking as they supervise workers, monitor the quality and quantity of output, and provide compensation in the form of rations or payment.

delivered in kind. If the reward for work consisted of rations, the manager had to arrange for the appropriate foods to be elicited from farmers or from the state stockpiles and then transported to the area where workers would be compensated. If the reward for work was a feast, then the manager would also have had to arrange for someone to cook the food (which involves the transport and cleaning of vessels as well as the collection of fuel and water for cooking).

In complex societies, individual calculations of acquisition and distribution become interwoven with increasingly large-scale processes including markets and institutional redistribution. However, the actual transactions within those institutions still are carried out by individuals who seek out, acquire, use, and discard the objects that are the focus of the exchange. In a study of production and consumption at the third-millennium site of Kurban Hoyuk in Mesopotamia, Patricia Wattenmaker (1994) noted that domestic contexts of non-elite dwellings had household-produced goods such as pottery and lithics, as well as specialist-produced pottery. Textual evidence indicates that while the contents of containers may have been controlled, the production of pottery was not; in any case, the widespread availability of pottery suggests that vessels were markers of ethnic or social display rather than of hierarchy. She concluded that rural access to specialist goods was therefore not simply the result of donation or permission from urban elites but was a consumer-driven phenomenon with increased social differentiation in which "rural nonelite households were active participants in the material component of the social system" (Wattenmaker 1994:115).

As households became integrated into larger and larger realms of contact, the phenomenon of work still required individuals' conscious calculations. Insights on this process are provided by the tiny hamlet of Ceren in El Salvador, often called the "Pompeii of the New World" because it was buried by ash from a volcano circa AD 600. Based on his observations that each household produced some surplus beyond its needs, Payson Sheets (2000:217) has concluded that there was considerable autonomy in economic decision making and that "commoner individual and household choice was far greater than would have been anticipated by economic models emphasizing the elite." In his view, the small-scale but ubiquitous production of surplus goods was traded not only between households within Ceren but also in local centers, resulting in a highly flexible trading network "quite different from the view of the top of the pyramid which generally depicts commoners as the exploited class at the bottom of a powerful political and economic hierarchy" (Sheets 2000:217).

The perspective raised by the Ceren example shows that the autonomous cognitive capacity evident in prehistory is retained in transactions that take place after the advent of social complexity. Individuals apply an assessment of value and utilize both the objects and the transaction to express identity. One way in which we can see the active participation of individuals in the crafting of identity is in the Roman world, where new research shows the reciprocal dynamic between colonial powers and subject populations. In an insightful treatment of the relationship between an expanding Roman empire and the local societies of northern Europe, Peter Wells (1999) sees the provisioning of Roman military camps as a way that local, small-scale artisans beyond the boundaries of the empire produced objects such as pottery and metalwork in exchange for desired Roman trade goods. These goods were incorporated into local customs such as burials, and emulation of "Roman" tastes was popular; yet, a few generations later, new local pottery styles were developed that incorporated older pre-Roman elements, a retro style that provided an expression of resurgent indigenous identity.

The emergence of hierarchies in which there is taxation or tribute in labor should be seen not as a completely new development in the history of human energy transfer but as an elaboration of the cognitive assessments of energy transfer that were already a million-plus years in the making. In a community, who works for whom means daily or lifetime allotments of energy transfer from individuals to others.

Summary

Work is both cognized and actualized at the individual level. Defined as energy transfer, work involves the engagement of both the brain and the body. The purpose of work is to achieve an effect on the physical environment that results in desired outcomes for the individual undertaking the energy transfer. At its most basic level, work enables the individual to engage with the physical landscape to acquire food through the strategic use of memory, skill, knowledge, and planning. Through communication with other people, the individual can engage in a wide variety of strategies to improve energy capture from the landscape through cooperation in hunting, gathering, plant cultivation, and animal husbandry. These skills also factor into the development of exchange relationships in which individuals accumulate the wherewithal to acquire food and goods at a temporal or spatial distance.

Work also serves to enable individuals to create, foster, and demonstrate long-term commitments within a group. Group sizes may vary from the household to the nation-state, but regardless of the size of the group, individuals make use of their multitasking abilities to factor in new and changing parameters of ritual, social, and communal behavior. At the same time, individuals create and substantiate those patterns of behavior, with the potential for stasis and change inherent in each act of energy expenditure. Although our expectations about "work" and "labor" are heavily conditioned by the moral and political expectations of our own time, the many forms of decision making about energy expenditure indicate that work is a basic component of what it means to be human.

CHAPTER 5

Multitasking and Social Complexity

A PREHISTORY OF ORDINARY PEOPLE concerns the vast majority of those who have lived in the past. Viewing the ordinary person as an autonomous cognitive entity richly enables us to understand how our species has developed from being small-group-living primates to having the capacity for large-scale group interactions with elaborate symbolic systems, language, and communication abilities. Through this autonomous cognitive capacity, individuals have the ability to comprehend a variety of time scales, with effects at the personal, household, and community level through both creativity and habituation. At any level of sociopolitical complexity, humans have the capacity to be habituated to patterns of behavior and at the same time possess the potential for reflexive self-awareness and change.

The development of cities and states in the past six thousand years is a remarkably recent event in human history. These densely populated and spatially extensive formations could not have been initiated without the active participation of individuals who utilized their skills of perception and time allocation to add new tasks to their repertoire. Long before the emergence of cities and states, humans exhibited a wide array of characteristics that were manifested at the individual level: perceptions of health, illness, and value; the capacity for language, communication, and memory; and the experience of time, space, and landscapes. These capacities eventually made possible an increasing diversity of technologies, an increasing density of social networks, and an increasing number of multiple, overlapping hierarchical configurations of ritual and political authority.

Often anonymous in the historical sense, each individual leaves some material record of her or his actions in the physical world. From very young childhood, each person engages with the basic means of survival by eating food, using objects, and seeking shelter. All of these actions leave their mark in the form of abandoned goods, discarded food waste, and the tools used to make and repair objects. Even the most minimal life experience leaves an archaeological trace, if only through the preservation of a skeleton. However, we know that most of the archaeological record reflects much more than mere survival and death. The material remains of the past show the capacity of individuals to make goods with more decoration than is functionally necessary, to change objects on the basis of fashion and style, to creatively modify foodways in response to changes in resource availability, and to consciously engage with others to modify the surrounding environment.

Multitasking is the mechanism by which members of our species expend energy in the course of daily activities. Multitasking involves the capacity to discern among multiple potential outcomes, with flows of planning and energy expenditure that integrate more than one activity simultaneously. Multitasking also involves the capacity to restart tasks after interruptions and to incorporate new information and inputs as they occur. The earliest multitasking was inherent in the bodily specialization of two limbs for walking and two for carrying, a simple division of energy that along with growing capacities for memory and communication enabled an enormous amount of creativity on the part of each individual even when engaged in the most routine activity. Starting more than a million years ago, our ancestors made daily determinations balancing energy expenditure against projected outcomes based on their own experience as well as the shared communication of others. These first steps of multitasking are seen in the archaeological record through the evidence of stone tool making in which there was a purposeful integration of raw-material procurement, transportation, and modification. The process of tool making was eventually augmented by the creation of environmental knowledge and ritual, the development of landscape modifications such as agriculture and animal husbandry, and the development of intricate social and political hierarchies.

The study of food, goods, and energy expenditure demonstrates how individuals exhibited the habituation of behavioral patterns as well as the capacity for creative innovation, alteration, and rejection of cultural parameters. By evaluating the sequence of specific actions in time and space, we can see how individuals acted to achieve particular outcomes that can inform us about the dynamics of stasis and change over the long term. Each person has a body whose physiological characteristics include strength, longevity, fertility, intelligence, and biological determinants of sex. To this can be added social expectations that govern the range of choices perceived by the individual related to food, possessions, dress, ornamentation, hairstyle, communication, and opportunities for energy expenditure.

The physical landscape, with its many sudden and subtle changes, provided another set of parameters for individual action. "Inside" activities were related to kinship, hearth, home, and shelter, and "outside" activities were related to the larger surroundings. Symbolic investments were selectively made in both inside and outside activities, in which ritual was manifested in the everyday, and everyday needs were often satisfied within the course of elaborate, infrequent rituals. These ritual capacities provide some of the most promising forms of future archaeological research; we cannot reconstruct belief systems in the abstract, but we can utilize understandings of individual cognitive capacities, as well as landscape studies, symbolic artifacts, and the ritual of the quotidian to understand the human trajectory towards increasingly elaborate belief systems.

The appearance of extensive symbol systems starting forty thousand to fifty thousand years ago was not instantly accompanied by the development of cities, chiefdoms, and states. Instead, the first appearance of purposeful burials, nonutilitarian artifacts, personal ornaments, and increasingly sophisticated uses of the landscape for sustenance were followed by about thirty thousand years' worth of small-group living in which individuals each engaged with the physical and social environment. Political hierarchies did not develop because elites were more cognitively capable than others were; instead, those individuals made use of the cognitive skills already exercised at the autonomous level in matters related to food, goods, and work. For the individuals supplying objects and energy expenditure to newly emergent political hierarchies, the exhortations of elites were merely one additional factor in the exercise of an already wellestablished cognitive mechanism of task scheduling.

Even after the development of the permanent hierarchies that began to separate elites from non-elites, high-ranking people had only a limited control over daily life. Individual activities continued to generate the vast majority of the artifacts and structures found in the archaeological record. For ordinary people, the emergence of sociopolitical hierarchies starting around six thousand years ago may not even have been particularly dramatic. Instead, the transition to sedentism (and its frequent correlate, agriculture) starting ten thousand to twelve thousand years ago is likely to have had more-profound effects on the individual's relationship to the surrounding environment and community. Sedentism requires significant changes at the individual cognitive level: attention to long-term planning, the acceptance of sunk costs as a daily event of work without immediate return, and the capacity to accumulate resources on a seasonal basis but distribute them on an incremental basis.

Through the examination of food, goods, and work, we can identify the specific actions that were retained at the individual cognitive level and augmented in the course of the development of cities, states, and empires. In the realm of food, the practice of ordinary foodways continued to be enacted on the household level with individuals engaged in multitasking to address basic social and biological needs. With increasing social and political complexity, new foods were added, feasting became a prominent mode of political activity, and elites devoted resources to the creation of production systems. The human propensity to seek out and consume preferred foods was a strong aspect in the creation of the new foodways: the concept of luxury foods was an enhancement of the concept of preferences, and sumptuary rules were the enhancement of the concept of food taboos that already existed to guide consumption based on gender, age, and other temporary or permanent characteristics.

Political leaders might control some of the food some of the time, but they could not control all foods all of the time. Multitasking at the individual and household level continued to govern the acquisition, use, presentation, and disposal of food even after the advent of social complexity in ways that suggest a high level of awareness and creativity on the part of individuals. Patrick Kirch and Sharyn Jones O'Day (2003:493) have noted in their archaeological analysis of early Hawaii that commoner households have a much higher proportion of rats consumed as food and that the middens of commoner households also had nineteen more varieties of shellfish than did middens associated with elite contexts. Their work shows that the development of food preferences and taboos associated with social complexity did not always result in the disenfranchisement of non-elites; instead, the diversity of foods consumed shows a strategy of multitasking in which the type, variety, and timing of food preparation and processing were established, enacted, and reaffirmed in each act of consumption by ordinary households.

Similarly, the increasing diversity of goods seen in the past million years of the archaeological record provided the substrate of basic consumption that was augmented in the development of social complexity. In cities and states, some aspects of the production process were controlled by elites to produce goods of distinction, as, for example, through the oversight of workshops or the control of raw material resource zones. There might also be selective investments in mechanisms of transportation (such as the creation of an official fleet or the construction of roads and bridges) or distribution (such as the control of markets by the Aztec political leaders, who created "the court that sat without interruption at one end of the market, where three judges continually took turns and gave their verdict on the spot" [Soustelle 1996:43]). The specific types of materials consumed at the household level were, however, established through the oscillation of creativity and habituation exercised by individuals in their acquisition and use of goods. Ideas about style and the distinction among goods through decoration, form, shape, and place of origin continued to be acted upon by individuals who considered elite emulation as an additional factor in the selection of objects for acquisition, use, and discard (see Cool 2006:158; Miller 1985).

The archaeological record of complex societies shows the sustained nature of individual decision-making processes in goods acquisition. In the pre-Columbian Valley of Mexico, Leah Minc, Mary Hodge, and M. James Blackman (1994:160) conducted a statistical analysis on archaeologically recovered pottery and showed that the proportion of "foreign" pottery was roughly the same in hamlets, villages, and local centers and that these wares "were clearly not restricted in their distribution to larger sites or political centers." Chen Shen notes the recovery of a rare phoenix-design stone pendant, usually associated with elites, from a lower-class tomb at the first-millennium BC site of Yan-Xiadu in China. The recovery of this item in the unusual context of the low-status grave "suggests that the grave owner must have obtained these items from markets and guarded them with his or her life" (Shen 2003:304). A similar case of curating rare objects usually associated with elites is cited by Julia Hendon (2000) at the site of Ceren in El Salvador. As Hendon (2000:46–47) notes, even a modest amount of durables in storage holds an important place of collective memory for that family or domestic group: "While seven jade beads may seem a rather picayune set of inalienable possessions . . . their presence in one farming family's storehouse argues that the desire to retain valued objects around which memory accrues is not restricted to one particular social class or centered on only one kind of object."

The development of cities and states provided more opportunities and more realms of meaning that could be applied by individuals to material objects, but these activities built upon the materialization of human cognitive realms such as health, memory, and ritual that long predated social complexity (see Joyce 2003:122; Lillios 1999). Meaning and memory encoded in objects provided the shared basis upon which elites made further distinctions, providing a bottom-up creation of meanings of space and place through material goods. Cynthia Robin (2002) provides an example of ritual continuities from elites to non-elites from the modest site of Chan Nòohol in the hinterlands of the ancient Maya ceremonial center of Xunantunich. She found a small cache of ordinary cobbles and a broken greenstone ax in one of the structures, interpreting it as "an ordinary farming family's version of a dedicatory cache, which consecrated their farmstead as the center of the world axes" that were commonly expressed in elite iconography as well (Robin 2002:255). Shared perceptions of meaning provided a platform for elite action that capitalized on already-existing cultural practices, rendered acceptable precisely because they grew from shared traditions. Just as in the case of elite-sponsored medical treatises that inscribed common medical knowledge or the elite subsidizing of agricultural infrastructure to provide increased quantities of preferred foods, the elite support of ritual in the Maya world and elsewhere was the materialization of a shared ideology that was already sustained within the group but magnified, consolidated, and aggrandized through leader-directed actions.

One of the hallmarks of complex societies is evidence for the allocation of time and energy to communal projects. Hierarchical leadership is associated with the development of elaborate tombs, temples, and other monuments that are manifestations of the organization of work and expressions of social power. These physical markers also are very distinctive in the landscape, constituting some of the best-known archaeological remains from ancient chiefdoms and states. But while monuments are very noticeable in the landscape, the steps involved in their construction may not have been strikingly different to those who contributed the labor. For them, the concept of mundane, repetitive work such as carrying stones or lifting baskets of earth as a tradeoff for the rights to food and shelter may have been merely an elaboration of the many preexisting configurations of working for others, as seen in relationships of apprenticeship, gendered household task management, and the intergenerational dependence of older and younger individuals.

Prior to the development of complex societies six thousand years ago, individuals' allocations of energy expenditure revolved around the day-to-day acquisition, use, and discard of ordinary goods and around the manipulation of the landscape that was already cognized in multiple time frames of daily, seasonal, and annual tasks interspersed with predictable and unpredictable fluctuations. In complex societies, actions of leaders encompassing tribute and labor demands, as well as warfare, were added to what was already a very elaborate repertoire of multitasked considerations. The resultant organization of settlement systems was the product of "individual and community choices regarding where and how to live . . . informed by many factors, from economic realities to environmental conditions to the political landscape" (Casana 2007:197). These observations are leading to new and compelling archaeological research projects to examine this human-nature dynamic. One such project has been carried out by Anabel Ford, Keith Clarke, and Gary Raines (2009:509), who have successfully utilized predictive modeling and Geographic Information Systems (GIS) to show that ordinary Maya farmers in the ancient period calculated a variety of landscape characteristics in their choice of settlement areas, a factor that "underscore[s] the importance of farmer choice in the selection of residential site locations. These locations would be the natural focus for the development of civic centers that would have responded to established settlement areas."

New archaeological research projects such as these provide the opportunity to examine the details of archaeological sites not only as the manifestation of large-scale cultural patterns but also as the result of discrete, intentional daily actions by real people. Although leadership had been evident even in simple societies through the organization of occasional events such as communal rituals, the institution of permanent leadership in complex societies may have been a form of "meta-multitasking" applied to the social realm. The acceptance of permanent leaders as decision makers for some domains of activity may have enabled individuals to mitigate the cognitive overload inherent in the amounts of information related to increasing types of work, greater numbers of people, more choices involved in each aspect of energy investment, and more goods and styles resulting from the dynamic relationship of production and consumption. The development of institutionalized leadership, and even the development of elites as models for emulation, was a means by which individuals engaged in cognitive shortcuts to preserve working memory, much as language and the development of a sophisticated material repertoire had freed up working memory in simple societies. The integrative function of leadership in the earliest complex societies also is indicated by the fact that leaders' actions tended to reinforce already-existing cultural behaviors and expectations related to foodways, ritual, and the symbolic use of goods, a cost-effective elite strategy that was based in cultural consensus.

A prehistory written from the ordinary person's point of view has the capacity to challenge both our theoretical and our methodological approaches to the past. Equally important is that such a perspective reduces the singular emphasis on elites, political hierarchy, and leadership as the principal explanatory factors in the development of social complexity. Considerations of the mutually constructed relationships among hierarchical levels within social groups have led scholars to propose that a strict division between elites and non-elites, or between "top-down" and "bottom-up" approaches, is unrealistic given what is known about the dynamics of human interactions (e.g., Bell 2002:258; Janusek and Kolata 2004; Robin 2003:318). Instead, a view of social complexity as a collective process with strongly shared cultural elements enables us to see not only why entities such as cities and states were developed but also how they have become and continue to be the dominant form of social integration today.

References

Abu-Lughod, Janet

1969   Migrant Adjustment to City Life: The Egyptian Case. In *The City in Newly Developing Countries*, edited by Gerald Breese, 376–88. Prentice Hall, Englewood Cliffs, NJ.

Agency for International Development

1985   *Background Paper and Guide to Addressing Bellmon Amendment Concerns on Potential Food Aid Disincentives and Storage.* Agency for International Development, Washington, DC.

Ahearn, Laura M.

2001a   Language and Agency. *Annual Review of Anthropology* 30:109–37.

2001b   *Invitations to Love: Literacy, Love Letters, and Social Change in Nepal.* University of Michigan Press, Ann Arbor.

Alt, Kurt W., Joachim Burger, Angela Simons, Werner Schön, Gisela Grupe, Susanne Hummel, Birgit Grosskopf, et al.

2003   Climbing into the Past—First Himalayan Mummies Discovered in Nepal. *Journal of Archaeological Science* 11:1529–35.

Ames, Kenneth M.

2003   The Northwest Coast. *Evolutionary Anthropology* 12 (1): 19–33.

Anderson, Arthur J. O., and Charles E. Dibble

1963   *General History of the Things of New Spain: Florentine Codex.* Vol. 11. School of American Research, Santa Fe, NM; and University of Utah, Salt Lake City.

Anderson, Derek, and Maria Nieves Zedeño

2009   Returning to the Country: Hunter-Gatherer Territory Formation. Paper presented at the 74th Annual Society for American Archaeology Meeting, Atlanta.

Anderson, Robin L.

2007   *Sources in the History of Medicine.* Pearson, Upper Saddle River, NJ.

Appadurai, Arjun

1981   Gastro-Politics in Hindu South Asia. *American Ethnologist* 8 (3): 494–511.

Armstrong, Douglas V., and Kenneth G. Kelly

2000   Settlement Patterns and the Origins of African Jamaican Society: Seville Plantation, St. Ann's Bay, Jamaica. *Ethnohistory* 47 (2): 369–97.

Arnold, Jeanne E.

1996   Organizational Transformations: Power and Labor among Complex Hunter-Gatherers and Other Intermediate Societies. In *Emergent Complexity: The Evolution of Intermediate Societies*, edited by Jeanne E. Arnold, 59–73. International Monographs in Prehistory Archaeological Series 9. Ann Arbor, MI.

Arnott, Robert

2002   Disease and Medicine in Hittite Asia Minor. In *The Archaeology of Medicine*, edited by Robert Arnott, 41–52. British Archaeological Reports 1046. Archaeopress, Oxford.

Arrowsmith, William

1959   *Petronius: The Satyricon*. New American Library, New York.

Arthur, John

2003   Brewing Beer: Status, Wealth and Ceramic Use Alteration among the Gamo of South-Western Ethiopia. *World Archaeology* 34 (3): 516–28.

Ascenzi, Antonio, Aidan Cockburn, and Ekkehard Kleiss

1980   Miscellaneous Mummies. In *Mummies, Disease, and Ancient Cultures*, edited by Aidan Cockburn and Eve Cockburn, 224–38. Cambridge University Press, Cambridge.

Ashmore, Wendy, Jason Yaeger, and Cynthia Robin

2004   Commoner Sense: Late and Terminal Classic Social Strategies in the Xunantunich Area. In *The Terminal Classic in the Maya Lowlands: Collapse, Transition, and Transformation*, edited by Arthur Demarest, Prudence M. Rice, and Don S. Rice, 302–23. University Press of Colorado, Boulder.

Atalay, Sonya, and Christine A. Hastorf

2006   Food, Meals, and Daily Activities: Food *Habitus* at Neolithic Çatalhöyük. *American Antiquity* 71 (2): 283–319.

Bard, Kathryn A.

2000   The Emergence of the Egyptian State (c. 3200–2686 BC). In *The Oxford History of Ancient Egypt*, edited by Ian Shaw, 61–88. Oxford University Press, Oxford.

Barker, Graeme

2006   *The Agricultural Revolution in Prehistory: Why Did Foragers Become Farmers?* Oxford University Press, Oxford.

Bar-Yosef, Ofer

2002   The Upper Paleolithic Revolution. *Annual Review of Anthropology* 31:363–93.

Baxter, Jane Eva

2005   *The Archaeology of Childhood: Children, Gender, and Material Culture*. Alta Mira, Walnut Creek, CA.

Beck, Margaret E., and Matthew E. Hill Jr.

2004   Rubbish, Relatives, and Residence: The Family Use of Middens. *Journal of Archaeological Method and Theory* 11 (3): 297–333.

Bell, Alison

2002   Emulation and Empowerment: Material, Social, and Economic Dynamics in Eighteenth- and Nineteenth-Century Virginia. *International Journal of Historical Archaeology* 6 (4): 253–98.

1999   Contextualizing Post-Colonial "Conspicuous Consumption." Paper presented at the Annual Meeting of the American Anthropological Association, Chicago, IL.

Belloc, Hilaire

1902   *The Path to Rome*. Longman, Greens and Co., New York.

Benson, John, and Nicky Britten

2002   Patients' Decisions about Whether or Not to Take Antihypertensive Drugs: Qualitative Study. *British Medical Journal* 325:873–77.

Bentley, Amy

2004   From Culinary Other to Mainstream America: Meanings and Uses of Southwestern Cuisine. In *Culinary Tourism*, edited by Lucy M. Long, 209–25. University Press of Kentucky, Lexington.

Bentley, Gillian R., Richard R. Paine, and Jesper L. Boldsen

2001   Fertility Changes with the Prehistoric Transition to Agriculture: Perspectives from Reproductive Ecology and Paleodemography. In *Reproductive Ecology and Human Evolution*, edited by Peter T. Ellison, 203–31. Aldine de Gruyter, New York.

Benveniste, Emile

1971   Subjectivity in Language [1958]. Reprinted in Benveniste, *Problems in General Linguistics*. Translated by Mary Elizabeth Meek. University of Miami Press, Miami.

Bersaglieri, Todd, Pardis C. Sabeti, Nick Patterson, Trisha Vanderploeg, Steve F. Schaffner, Jared A. Drake, Matthew Rhodes, David E. Reich, and Joel N. Hirschhorn

2004   Genetic Signatures of Strong Recent Positive Selection at the Lactase Gene. *American Journal of Human Genetics* 74:1111–20.

Bettie, Julie

2000   Women Without Class: Chicas, Cholas, Trash, and the Presence/Absence of Class Identity. *Signs* 26 (1): 1–35.

Bijker, Wiebe

1997   *Of Bicycles, Bakelites, and Bulbs: Toward a Theory of Sociotechnical Change*. MIT Press, Cambridge, MA.

Billman, Brian R.

2002   Irrigation and the Origins of the Southern Moche State on the North Coast of Peru. *Latin American Antiquity* 13 (4): 371–400.

Billson, Janet Mancini, and Kyra Mancini

2007   *Inuit Women: Their Powerful Spirit in a Century of Change*. Rowman and Littlefield, Lanham, MD.

Bird, Rebecca

1999   Cooperation and Conflict: The Behavioral Ecology of the Sexual Division of Labor. *Evolutionary Anthropology* 8 (2): 65–75.

Blanton, Richard E., Gary M. Feinman, Stephen A. Kowalewski, and Peter N. Peregrine

1996   A Dual-Processual Theory for the Evolution of Mesoamerican Civilization. *Current Anthropology* 37 (1): 1–14.

Bletter, Nathaniel, and Douglas C. Daly

2006   Cacao and Its Relatives in South America: An Overview of Taxonomy, Ecology, Biogeography, Chemistry, and Ethnobotany. In *Chocolate in Mesoamerica: A Cultural*

History of Cacao, edited by Cameron L. McNeil, 31–68. University Press of Florida, Gainesville.

Blurton Jones, Nicholas G.

1987   Tolerated Theft, Suggestions about the Ecology and Evolution of Sharing, Hoarding and Scrounging. *Social Science Information* 26 (1): 31–54.

Bobe, René, and Anna K. Behrensmeyer

2004   The Expansion of Grassland Ecosystems in Africa in Relation to Mammalian Evolution and the Origin of the Genus *Homo*. *Palaeogeography, Palaeoclimatology, Palaeoecology* 207:399–420.

Boenke, Nicole

2007   Human Excrement from a Prehistoric Salt Mine: A Window onto Daily Life. In *The Archaeology of Food and Identity*, edited by Katheryn C. Twiss, 69–84. Center for Archaeological Investigations, Southern Illinois University Carbondale Occasional Paper 34. Carbondale.

Boserup, Esther

1970   *Woman's Role in Economic Development*. Allen and Unwin, London.

Bourdieu, Pierre

1984   *Distinction*. Trans. Richard Nice. Harvard University Press, Cambridge, MA.

Bowman, D. M. J. S.

1998   Tansley Review No. 101: The Impact of Aboriginal Landscape Burning on the Australia Biota. *New Phytologist* 140:385–410.

Bradley, Richard

2005   *Ritual and Domestic Life in Prehistoric Europe*. Routledge, London.

2002   Access, Style and Imagery: The Audience for Prehistoric Rock Art in Atlantic Spain and Portugal, 4000–2000 BC. *Oxford Journal of Archaeology* 21 (3): 231–47.

Brady, James E.

1997   Settlement Configuration and Cosmology: The Role of Caves at Dos Pilas. *American Anthropologist* 99:602–18.

Brady, James E., and Wendy Ashmore

1999   Mountains, Caves, Water: Ideational Landscapes of the Ancient Maya. In *Archaeologies of Landscape: Contemporary Perspectives*, edited by Wendy Ashmore and A. Bernard Knapp, 124–45. Blackwell, Malden, MA.

Brady, James E., and Keith M. Prufer

1999   Caves and Crystalmancy: Evidence for the Use of Crystals in Ancient Maya Religion. *Journal of Anthropological Research* 55 (1): 129–44.

Bratlund, Bodil

1996   Hunting Strategies in the Late Glacial of Northern Europe: A Survey of the Faunal Evidence. *Journal of World Prehistory* 10 (1): 1–48.

Brested, James Henry

1930   *The Edwin Smith Surgical Papyrus*, vol. 1. University of Chicago Press, Chicago.

Brody, J. J.

1977   *Mimbres Painted Pottery*. School of American Research Press, Santa Fe, NM.

Brody, Jane E.

2007   The "Poisonous Cocktail" of Multiple Drugs. *New York Times*, September 18, 2007.

Browman, David L., Gayle J. Fritz, and Patty Jo Watson

2005   Origins of Food-Producing Economies in the Americas. In *The Human Past*, edited by Chris Scarre, 306–49. Thames and Hudson, London.

Brugge, David M.

1983   Navajo Activity Areas. In *Forgotten Places and Things: Archaeological Perspectives on American History*, edited by Albert E. Ward, 185–91. Center for Anthropological Studies, Albuquerque, NM.

Brumfiel, Elizabeth M.

1995   Origins of Social Inequality. In *Research Frontiers in Anthropology*, edited by Carol R. Ember, Melvin Ember, and Peter N. Peregrine, 103–20. Prentice-Hall, Englewood Cliffs, NJ.

1991   Weaving and Cooking: Women's Production in Aztec Mexico. In *Engendering Archaeology: Women and Prehistory*, edited by Joan M. Gero and Margaret W. Conkey, 224–51. Basil Blackwell, Oxford, UK.

1987   Elite and Utilitarian Crafts in the Aztec State. In *Specialization, Exchange and Complex Societies*, edited by Elizabeth Brumfiel and Timothy Earle, 102–18. Cambridge University Press, Cambridge.

Buikstra, Jane E., and Lyle W. Konigsberg

1985   Paleodemography: Critiques and Controversies. *American Anthropologist* 87 (2): 316–33.

Burgess, Paul W., Emma Veitch, Angela de Lacy Costello, and Tim Shallice

2000   The Cognitive and Neuroanatomical Correlates of Multitasking. *Neuropsychologia* 38 (6): 848–63.

Capasso, Luigi

1998   5300 Years Ago, the Ice Man Used Natural Laxatives and Antibiotics. *Lancet* 352:1864.

Carter, Tristan

2007   The Theatrics of Technology: Consuming Obsidian in the Early Cycladic Burial Arena. In *Rethinking Craft Specialization in Complex Societies: Archaeological Analyses of the Social Meaning of Production*, edited by Zachary X. Hruby and Rowan K. Flad, 88–107. Archeological Papers of the American Anthropological Association 17. Washington, DC.

Casana, Jesse

2007   Structural Transformations in Settlement Systems of the Northern Levant. *American Journal of Archaeology* 112:195–221.

Caspari, Rachel, and Sang-Hee Lee

2004   Old Age Becomes Common Late in Human Evolution. *Proceedings of the National Academy of Sciences* 101 (30): 10895–900.

Casson, Lionel

1989   *The Periplus Maris Erythraei*. Princeton University Press, Princeton.

Charles, Douglas K., and Jane E. Buikstra

2002   Siting, Sighting, and Citing the Dead. In *The Space and Place of Death*, edited by David B. Small and Helaine Silverman, 13–35. Archeological Papers of the American Anthropological Association 11. Wiley InterScience, Malden, MA.

Chase, B. A.

2005   Butchers, Bones, and Plastic Bags: An Ethnoarchaeological Study of a Specialized Meat Distribution System in the Indian Punjab. In *South Asian Archaeology 2003*, edited by U. Franke-Vogt and H. Weisshaar, 123–36. Lindensoft, Aachen.

Chelliah, J. V. (trans.)

1985   *Pattupattu: Ten Tamil Idylls*. Tamil University, Thanjavur.

Childe, V. Gordon

1951   *Social Evolution*. Watts and Co., London.

Choksi, Archana

1998   Pottery Manufacturing Techniques: The Role of Technical Constraints and Personal Choices. *Man and Environment* 23 (2): 107–18.

Cilliers, L., and F. P. Retief

2000   Poisons, Poisoning and the Drug Trade in Ancient Rome. *Akroterion* 45:88–100.

Claassen, Cheryl

1986   Shellfishing Seasons in the Prehistoric Southeastern United States. *American Antiquity* 51 (1): 21–37.

Cline, Eric H.

1999   Coals to Newcastle, Wallbrackets to Tiryns: Irrationality, Gift Exchange, and Distance Value. In *Meletemata: Studies in Aegean Archaeology Presented to Malcolm H. Wiener*, edited by Philip B. Betancourt, Vassos Karageorghis, Robert Laffineur, and Wolf-Dietrich Niemeier, 119–23. Université de Liège, Belgium.

Coleman, Simon, and John Elsner

1995   *Pilgrimage: Past and Present in the World's Religions*. Harvard University Press, Cambridge.

Colombijn, Freek

1994   *Patches of Padang: The History of an Indonesian Town in the Twentieth Century and the Use of Urban Space*. Centre of Non-Western Studies, Leiden University, Leiden.

Conkey, Margaret W., and Christine Hastorf (eds.)

1990   *The Uses of Style in Archaeology*. Cambridge University Press, Cambridge.

Cook, Lauren, J., Rebecca Yamin, and John P. McCarthy

1996   Shopping as Meaningful Action: Toward a Redefinition of Consumption in Historical Archaeology. *Historical Archaeology* 30 (4): 50–65.

Cool, H. E. M.

2006   *Eating and Drinking in Roman Britain*. Cambridge University Press, Cambridge.

Cooper, R. A., P. C. Molan, and K. G. Harding

2002   The Sensitivity to Honey of Gram-Positive Cocci of Clinical Significance Isolated from Wounds. *Journal of Applied Microbiology* 93:857–63.

Costin, Cathy Lynne

1991   Craft Specialization: Issues in Defining, Documenting, and Explaining the Organization of Production. In *Archaeological Method and Theory*, vol. 3, edited by Michael B. Schiffer, 1–56. University of Arizona Press, Tucson.

Crown, Patricia L.

2007a   Life Histories of Pots and Potters: Situating the Individual in Archaeology. *American Antiquity* 72 (4): 677–90.

2007b   Learning about Learning. In *Archaeological Anthropology*, edited by James M. Skibo, Michael W. Graves, and Miriam T. Stark, 198–217. University of Arizona Press, Tucson.

2001   Women's Role in Changing Cuisine. In *Women and Men in the Prehispanic Southwest: Labor, Power, and Prestige*, edited by Patricia L. Crown, 221–66. School of American Research Press, Santa Fe, NM.

1991   Evaluating the Construction Sequence and Population of Pot Creek Pueblo, Northern New Mexico. *American Antiquity* 56 (2): 291–314.

Crown, Patricia L., and W. H. Wills

1995   The Origins of Southwestern Ceramic Containers: Women's Time Allocation and Economic Intensification. *Journal of Anthropological Research* 51:173–86.

Cruz, Juan Cruz

1997   *Dietética medieval: Apéndice con la versión castellana del régimen de salud de Arnaldo de Vilanova*. La Val de Onsera, Zaragoza.

D'Altroy, Terence N., and Timothy K. Earle

1985   Staple Finance, Wealth Finance, and Storage in the Inka Political Economy. *Current Anthropology* 26 (2): 187–206.

David, Nicholas, and Carol Kramer

2001   *Ethnoarchaeology in Action*. Cambridge University Press, Cambridge.

Deal, Michael, and Melissa B. Hagstrum

1995   Ceramic Reuse Behavior among the Maya and Wanka. In *Expanding Archaeology*, edited by James M. Skibo, William H. Walker, and Axel E. Nielsen, 111–25. University of Utah, Salt Lake City.

Deaux, Kay

2000   Identity. In *Encyclopedia of Psychology*, edited by Alan E. Kazdin, 222–25. American Psychological Association, Washington, DC.

DeCorse, Christopher R.

2001   *An Archaeology of Elmina: Africans and Europeans on the Gold Coast, 1400–1900*. Smithsonian Institution Press, Washington, DC.

DeMarrais, Elizabeth, Luis Jaime Castillo, and Timothy Earle

1996   Ideology, Materialization, and Power Strategies. *Current Anthropology* 37 (1): 15–31.

Díaz-Andreu, Margarita, and Sam Lucy

2005   Introduction. In *The Archaeology of Identity: Approaches to Gender, Age, Status, Ethnicity and Religion*, edited by Margarita Díaz-Andreu, Sam Lucy, Staša Babić, and David Edwards, 1–12. Routledge, London.

Dickson, James H., Michael P. Richards, Richard, J. Hebda, Petra J. Mudie, Owen Beattie, Susan Ramsay, Nancy J. Turner, et al.

2004   Kwäday Dän Ts'ìnchí, The First Ancient Body of a Man from a North American Glacier: Reconstructing His Last Days by Intestinal and Biomolecular Analyses. *Holocene* 14 (4): 481–86.

Dietler, Michael

2007   Culinary Encounters: Food, Identity, and Colonialism. In *The Archaeology of Food and Identity*, edited by Katheryn C. Twiss, 218–42. Center for Archaeological Investigations, Southern Illinois University Carbondale Occasional Paper 34. Carbondale.

1996   Feasts and Commensal Politics in the Political Economy: Food, Power and Status in Prehistoric Europe. In *Food and the Status Quest: An Interdisciplinary Perspective*, edited by Polly Wiessner and Wulf Schiefenhövel, 87–125. Berghahn, Providence, RI.

1995   Greeks, Etruscans, and Thirsty Barbarians: Early Iron Age Interaction in the Rhône Basin of France. In *Centre and Periphery: Comparative Studies in Archaeology*, edited by T. C. Champion, 127–41. Routledge, New York.

Diner, Hasia R.

2001   *Hungering for America: Italian, Irish, and Jewish Foodways in the Age of Migration*. Harvard University Press, Cambridge, MA.

Dobres, Marcia-Anne, and John E. Robb

2000   Agency in Archaeology: Paradigm or Platitude? In *Agency in Archaeology*, edited by Marcia-Anne Dobres and John E. Robb, 3–17. Routledge, London.

Douglas, Mary, and Baron Isherwood

1996   *The World of Goods: Towards an Anthropology of Consumption*. Routledge, London. (Orig. pub. 1979.)

Dowson, Thomas A.

1994   Reading Art, Writing History: Rock Art and Social Change in Southern Africa. *World Archaeology* 25 (3): 332–45.

D'Souza, Frances

1988   Famine: Social Security and an Analysis of Vulnerability. In *Famine*, edited by G. A. Harrison, 1–56. Oxford University Press, Oxford.

Duistermaat, Kim

2008   *The Pots and Potters of Assyria*. Brepols, Turnhout.

Dumont, Louis

1966   *Homo hierarchicus, essai sur le système des castes*. Éditions Gallimard, Paris.

Earle, Timothy K.

2000   Archaeology, Property, and Prehistory. *Annual Review of Anthropology* 29:39–60.

1997   *How Chiefs Come to Power*. Stanford University Press, Stanford.

1990   Style and Iconography as Legitimation in Complex Chiefdoms. In *The Uses of Style in Archaeology*, edited by Margaret Conkey and Christine Hastorf, 73–81. Cambridge University Press, Cambridge.

Eerkens, Jelmer W.

2003   Residential Mobility and Pottery Use in the Western Great Basin. *Current Anthropology* 44 (5): 728–37.

Eide, Wenche Barth

2000   The Promotion of Human Rights Perspective on Food Security: Highlights of an Evolving Process. In *Food Aid and Human Security*, edited by Edward Clay and Olav Stokke, 326–50. Frank Cass, London.

El-Najjar, Mahmoud Y., and Thomas M. J. Mulinski

1980   Mummies and Mummification Practices in the Southwestern and Southern United States. In *Mummies, Disease, and Ancient Cultures*, edited by Aidan Cockburn and Eve Cockburn, 103–17. Cambridge University Press, Cambridge.

Erlandson, Jon M.

1988   The Role of Shellfish in Prehistoric Economies: A Protein Perspective. *American Antiquity* 53 (1): 102–9.

Erman, Adolf

1894   *Life in Ancient Egypt.* Translated by H. M. Tirard. Macmillan, London.

Eshed, Vered, Avi Gopher, Timothy B. Gage, and Israel Hershkovitz

2004   Has the Transition to Agriculture Reshaped the Demographic Structure of Prehistoric Populations? New Evidence from the Levant. *American Journal of Physical Anthropology* 124:315–29.

Etkin, Nina L.

2006   *Edible Medicines: An Ethnopharmacology of Food.* University of Arizona Press, Tucson.

Etkin, Nina L., and Paul J. Ross

1982   Food as Medicine and Medicine as Food: An Adaptive Framework for the Interpretation of Plant Utilization among the Hausa of Northern Nigeria. *Social Science and Medicine* 16:1559–73.

Evans, Susan T.

1990   The Productivity of Maguey Terrace Agriculture in Central Mexico during the Aztec Period. *Latin American Antiquity* 1 (2): 117–32.

Fagan, Brian M.

1998   *People of the Earth: An Introduction to World Prehistory.* 9th edition. Longman, New York.

Feder, Kenneth L.

2004   *The Past in Perspective: An Introduction to Human Prehistory*, 3rd edition. Mayfield Publishing, Mountain View, CA.

Feinman, Gary M.

1998   Scale and Social Organization: Perspectives on the Archaic State. In *Archaic States*, edited by Gary M. Feinman and Joyce Marcus, 95–133. School of American Research, Santa Fe, NM.

Feinman, Gary, and Jill Neitzel

1984   Too Many Types: An Overview of Prestate Societies in the Americas. In *Advances in Archaeological Method and Theory*, edited by Michael Schiffer, 39–102. Academic Press, Orlando, FL.

Flood, Ann Barry, W. Richard Scott, and Wayne Ewy

1984   Does Practice Make Perfect? Part I: The Relation between Hospital Volume and Outcomes for Selected Diagnostic Categories. *Medical Care* 22 (2): 98–114.

Fogelin, Lars

2004   Sacred Architecture, Sacred Landscape: Early Buddhism in North Coastal Andhra Pradesh. In *Archaeology as History in Early South Asia*, edited by Himanshu Prabha Ray and Carla M. Sinopoli, 376–91. Aryan Books, New Delhi.

Forbes, H.

1989   Of Grandfathers and Grand Theories: The Hierarchised Ordering of Responses to Hazard in a Greek Rural Community. In *Bad Year Economics*, edited by Paul Halstead and John O'Shea, 87–97. Cambridge University Press, Cambridge.

Ford, Anabel, Keith C. Clarke, and Gary Raines

2009   Modeling Settlement Patterns of the Late Classic Maya Civilization with Bayesian Methods and Geographic Information Systems. *Annals of the Association of American Geographers* 99 (3): 496–520.

Foucault, Michel

1966   *Les mots et les choses: Une archéologie des sciences humaines.* Gallimard, Paris.

Fowler, Chris

2004   *The Archaeology of Personhood: An Anthropological Approach.* Routledge, London.

Frei, Karin Margarita, Irene Skals, Margarita Gleba, and Henriette Lyngstram

2009   The Huldremose Iron Age Textiles, Denmark: An Attempt to Define Their Provenance Applying the Strontium Isotope System. *Journal of Archaeological Science* 36:1965–71.

Frink, L. M.

2009   The Social Role of Technology in Coastal Alaska. *International Journal of Historical Archaeology* 13:282–302.

Gamble, Clive, and Martin Porr

2005   From Empty Spaces to Lived Lives: Exploring the Individual in the Palaeolithic. In *The Hominid Individual in Context: Archaeological Investigations of Lower and Middle Paleolithic Landscapes, Locales and Artefacts*, edited by Clive Gamble and Martin Porr, 1–12. Routledge, London.

Garnsey, Peter

1983   Grain for Rome. In *Trade in Ancient Rome*, edited by Peter Garnsey, Keith Hopkins, and C. R. Whittaker, 118–30. University of California Press, Berkeley.

Garvey, Pauline

2001   Organized Disorder: Moving Furniture in Norwegian Homes. In *Home Possessions*, edited by Daniel Miller, 47–68. Berg, Oxford.

Gault, A.

1952   L'ancienne tuilerie de Civry-la-Forêt. *Bulletin Folklorique d'Ile de France*, n.s., 14:426–29.

Geier, Andrew, Paul Rozin, and Gheorghe Doros

2006   Unit Bias: A New Heuristic that Helps Explain the Effect of Portion Size on Food Intake. *Psychological Science* 17 (6): 521–25.

Giddens, Anthony

1984   *The Constitution of Society: Outline of the Theory of Structuration.* University of California Press, Berkeley.

Glassie, Henry

2000   *Vernacular Architecture.* Indiana University Press, Bloomington.

Glob, P. V.

1951   *Ard og Plov i Nordens Oldtid* (Ard and Plough in Prehistoric Scandinavia). Aarhus University Press, Aarhus, Denmark.

Goody, Jack

1976   *Production and Reproduction: A Comparative Study of the Domestic Domain.* Cambridge University Press, Cambridge.

1969   Adoption in Cross-Cultural Perspective. *Comparative Studies in Society and History* 11 (1): 55–78.

Gooldin, Sigal

2003   Fasting Women, Living Skeletons and Hunger Artists: Spectacles of Body and Miracles at the Turn of a Century. *Body and Society* 9 (2): 27–53.

Gradwohl, David M., and Nancy M. Osborn

1984   *Exploring Buried Buxton: Archaeology of an Abandoned Iowa Coal Mining Town with a Large Black Population.* Iowa State University Press, Ames.

Granovetter, Mark S.

1973   The Strength of Weak Ties. *American Journal of Sociology* 78 (6): 1360–80.

Gregory, C. A.

1982   *Gifts and Commodities.* Academic Press, London.

Greif, Marissa L., Deborah G. Kemler Nelson, Frank C. Keil, and Franky Gutierrez

2006   What Do Children Want to Know about Animals and Artifacts? Domain-Specific Requests for Information. *Psychological Science* 17 (6): 455–59.

Grieco, Margaret

1995   Transported Lives: Urban Social Networks and Labour Circulation. In *The Urban Context: Ethnicity, Social Networks and Situational Analysis,* edited by Alisdair Rogers and Steven Vertovec, 189–212. Berg, Oxford, UK.

Gutmann, Matthew C.

1997   Trafficking in Men: The Anthropology of Masculinity. *Annual Review of Anthropology* 26:385–409.

Haaland, Randi

2007   Porridge and Pot, Bread and Oven: Food Ways and Symbolism in Africa and the Near East from the Neolithic to the Present. *Cambridge Archaeological Journal* 17 (2): 165–82.

Hagstrum, Melissa

2001   Household Production in Chaco Canyon Society. *American Antiquity* 66 (1): 47–55.

Hall, Jenny

2005   The Shopkeepers and Craft-Workers of Roman London. In *Roman Working Lives and Urban Living,* edited by Ardle MacMahon and Jennifer Price, 125–44. Oxbow Books, Oxford, UK.

Hall, Simon, and Ben Smith

2000   Empowering Places: Rock Shelters and Ritual Control in Farmer-Forager Inter-
        actions in the Northern Province. In *African Naissance: The Limpopo Valley
        1000 Years Ago*, edited by Mary Leslie and Tim Maggs, 30–46. Goodwin Series 8.
        South African Archaeological Society, Cape Town.

Halperin, Edward C.

2004   Paleo-Oncology: The Role of Ancient Remains in the Study of Cancer. *Perspec-
        tives in Biology and Medicine* 47 (1): 1–14.

Halstead, Paul, Ian Hodder, and Glynis Jones

1978   Behavioural Archaeology and Refuse Patterns: A Case Study. *Norwegian Archae-
        ological Review* 11 (2): 118–31.

Harris, Marvin

1964   *The Nature of Cultural Things*. Random House, New York.

Hasselmo, Michael E., and Chantal E. Stern

2006   Mechanisms Underlying Working Memory for Novel Information. *Trends in
        Cognitive Sciences* 10 (11): 487–93.

Hawass, Zahi, and Mark Lehner

1997   Builders of the Pyramids. *Archaeology* 50 (1): 30–38.

Hawkes, K., J. F. O'Connell, and N. G. Blurton Jones

1997   Hadza Women's Time Allocation, Offspring Provisioning, and the Evolution of
        Long Postmenopausal Life Spans. *Current Anthropology* 38 (4): 551–77.

Hawkes, K., J. F. O'Connell, N. G. Blurton Jones, H. Alvarez, and E. L. Charnov

1998   Grandmothering, Menopause, and the Evolution of Human Life Histories. *Pro-
        ceedings of the National Academy of Sciences* 95:1336–39.

Hayden, Brian

2009   Funerals as Feasts: Why Are They So Important? *Cambridge Archaeological Jour-
        nal* 19 (1): 29–52.

2001   Fabulous Feasts: A Prolegomenon to the Importance of Feasting. In *Feasts:
        Archaeological and Ethnographic Perspectives on Food, Politics and Power*, edited
        by Michael Dietler and Brian Hayden, 23–64. Smithsonian Institution Press,
        Washington, DC.

1996   Feasting in Prehistoric and Traditional Societies. In *Food and the Status Quest*,
        edited by Polly Wiessner and Wulf Shiefenhovel, 127–47. Berghahn, Provi-
        dence, RI.

1990   Nimrods, Piscators, Pluckers, and Planters: The Emergence of Food Production.
        Journal of Anthropological Archaeology 9:31–69.

Hayes, Bryan D., Wendy Klein-Schwartz, and Fermin Barrueto Jr.

2007   Polypharmacy and the Geriatric Patient. *Clinics in Geriatric Medicine* 23 (2):
        371–90.

Helms, Mary W.

1993   *Craft and the Kingly Ideal: Art, Trade and Power*. University of Texas Press,
        Austin.

1979   *Ancient Panama: Chiefs in Search of Power*. University of Texas Press, Austin.

Hendon, Julia A.

2000   Having and Holding: Storage, Memory, Knowledge, and Social Relations. *American Anthropologist* 102 (1): 42–53.

Herlihy, David V.

2004   *Bicycle: A History*. Yale University Press, New Haven, CT.

Higham, Charles

1989   *The Archaeology of Mainland Southeast Asia: From 10,000 B.C. to the Fall of Angkor*. Cambridge University Press, Cambridge.

Hill, J. D.

1995   *Ritual and Rubbish in the Iron Age of Wessex*. British Archaeological Reports British Series 242. Tempus Reparatum, Oxford, UK.

Hill, James N.

1985   Style: A Conceptual Evolutionary Framework. In *Decoding Prehistoric Ceramics*, edited by Ben A. Nelson, 362–85. Southern Illinois University Press, Carbondale.

Hill, James N., and Joel Gunn (eds.)

1977   *The Individual in Prehistory: Studies of Variability in Style in Prehistoric Technologies*. Academic Press, New York.

Hindmarsh, Bruce

2002   Transported Food: Convict Food Habits in Australia. In *Food in the Migrant Experience*, edited by Anne J. Kershen, 134–48. Ashgate, Aldershot, Hampshire, UK.

Hodder, Ian

2000   Agency and Individuals in Long-Term Processes. In *Agency in Archaeology*, edited by Marcia-Anne Dobres and John Robb, 21–33. Routledge, London.

1982   *The Present Past: An Introduction to Anthropology for Archaeologists*. B. T. Batsford, London.

Holden, Constance

2001   Ötzi Death Riddle Solved. *Science* 293:795.

Hollan, Douglas

1997   The Relevance of Person-Centered Ethnography to Cross-Cultural Psychiatry. *Transcultural Psychiatry* 34 (2): 219–34.

Hutson, Scott R.

2010   *Dwelling, Identity, and the Maya: Relational Archaeology at Chunchucmil*. Altamira, Lanham, MD.

Hutson, Scott R., and Travis W. Stanton

2007   Cultural Logic and Practical Reason: The Structure of Discard in Maya Households. *Cambridge Archaeological Journal* 17 (2): 123–44.

Ihde, D.

2006   The Designers Fallacy and Technological Imagination. In *Defining Technological Literacy: Towards an Epistemological Framework*, edited by J. R. Dakers, 121–31. Palgrave Macmillan, New York.

Ingold, Tim

1987   *The Appropriation of Nature: Essays on Human Ecology and Social Relations*. University of Iowa Press, Iowa City.

Inomata, Takeshi, and Lawrence S. Coben

2006   Overture: An Invitation to the Archaeological Theater. In *Archaeology of Performance: Theaters of Power, Community, and Politics*, edited by Takeshi Inomata and Lawrence S. Coben, 11–44. Altamira, Lanham, MD.

Isaac, Glynn Ll.

1978   Food Sharing and Human Evolution: Archaeological Evidence from the Plio-Pleistocene of East Africa. *Journal of Anthropological Research* 34 (3): 311–25.

James, Susan E.

2000   Some Aspects of the Aztec Religion in the Hopi Kachina Cult. *Journal of the Southwest* 42 (4): 897–926.

Janusek, John Wayne, and Alan L. Kolata

2004   Top-Down or Bottom-Up: Rural Settlement and Raised Field Agriculture in the Lake Titicaca Basin, Bolivia. *Journal of Anthropological Archaeology* 23:404–30.

Jarrige, Jean-François

1995   Introduction. In *Mehrgarh Field Reports, 1974–1985: From Neolithic Times to the Indus Civilization*, edited by Catherine Jarrige, Jean-François Jarrige, Richard H. Meadow, and Gonzague Quivron, 51–103. Department of Culture and Tourism, Government of Sindh, Pakistan.

Jones, Andrew

2007   *Memory and Material Culture*. Cambridge University Press, Cambridge.

Jones, Martin

2007   *Feast: Why Humans Share Food*. Oxford University Press, Oxford.

2002   Eating for Calories or for Company? Concluding Remarks on Consuming Passions. In *Consuming Passions and Patterns of Consumption*, edited by Preston Miracle and Nicky Milner, 131–36. McDonald Institute Monographs, Cambridge.

Jones, Todd

2005   How Many New Yorkers Need to Like Bagels Before You Can Say "New Yorkers Like Bagels?" Understanding Collective Ascription. *Philosophical Forum* 36 (3): 279–306.

Joyce, Arthur, Laura Arnaud Bustamante, and Marc N. Levine

2001   Commoner Power: A Case Study From the Classic Period Collapse on the Oaxaca Coast. *Journal of Archaeological Method and Theory* 8 (4): 343–85.

Joyce, Rosemary A.

2003   Concrete Memories: Fragments of the Past in the Classic Maya Present (500–1000 AD). In *Archaeologies of Memory*, edited by Ruth M. Van Dyke and Susan E. Alcock, 104–25. Blackwell, Malden, MA.

Kaplan, Hillard, Kim Hill, Jane Lancaster, and A. Magdalena Hurtado

2000   A Theory of Human Life History Evolution: Diet, Intelligence, and Longevity. *Evolutionary Anthropology* 9 (4): 156–85.

Kardulias, P. Nick

2003   Stone in an Age of Bronze: Lithics from Bronze Age Contexts in Greece and Iran. In *Written in Stone: The Multiple Dimensions of Lithic Analysis*, edited by P. Nick Kardulias and Richard W. Yerkes, 113–24. Lexington, Lanham, MD.

1992   The Ecology of Bronze Age Flaked Stone Tool Production in Southern Greece: Evidence from Agios Stephanos and the Southern Argolid. *American Journal of Archaeology* 96 (3): 421–42.

Karlin, C., and M. Julien

1994   Prehistoric Technology: A Cognitive Science? In *The Ancient Mind: Elements of Cognitive Archaeology*, edited by Colin Renfrew and Ezra B. W. Zubrow, 152–64. Cambridge University Press, Cambridge.

Kaye, Barbara K., and Barry S. Sapolsky

2001   Offensive Language in Prime Time Television: Before and After Content Ratings. *Journal of Broadcasting and Electronic Media* 45 (2): 303–19.

Keith, Kathryn

2003   The Spatial Patterns of Everyday Life on Old Babylonian Neighborhoods. In *The Social Construction of Ancient Cities*, edited by Monica L. Smith, 56–80. Smithsonian Institution Press, Washington, DC.

Kemp, Barry

1989   *Ancient Egypt: Anatomy of a Civilization*. Routledge, London.

Kenoyer, Jonathan Mark

1998   *Ancient Cities of the Indus Valley Civilization*. Oxford University Press, Karachi.

Kiernan, Kevin, Rhys Jones, and Don Ranson

1983   New Evidence from Fraser Cave for Glacial Age Man in South-West Tasmania. *Nature* 301:28–32.

Kirch, Patrick V., and Sharyn Jones O'Day

2003   New Archaeological Insights into Food and Status: A Case Study from Precontact Hawaii. *World Archaeology* 34 (3): 484–97.

Klein, Richard

2009   Hominin Dispersals in the Old World. In *The Human Past*, 2nd ed., edited by Chris Scarre, 84–123. Thames and Hudson, London.

Kleine, Robert E., III, Susan Schultz Kleine, and Jerome B. Kernan

1993   Mundane Consumption and the Self: A Social-Identity Perspective. *Journal of Consumer Psychology* 2 (3): 209–35.

Kliks, Michael

1975   *Paleoepidemiological Studies of Great Basin Coprolites: Estimation of Dietary Fiber Intake and Evaluation of the Ingestion of Anthelmintic Plant Substances*. Archaeological Research Facility, University of California, Berkeley.

Kopytoff, Igor

1986   The Cultural Biography of Things: Commoditization as Process. In *The Social Life of Things: Commodities in Cultural Perspective*, edited by Arjun Appadurai, 64–91. Cambridge University Press, Cambridge.

Kracke, E. A., Jr.

1947   Family vs. Merit in Chinese Civil Service Examinations under the Empire. *Harvard Journal of Asiatic Studies* 10:103–23.

Krief, Sabrina, Claude Marcel Hladik, and Claudie Haxaire
2005   Ethnomedicinal and Bioactive Properties of Plants Ingested by Wild Chimpan-
        zees in Uganda. *Journal of Ethnopharmacology* 101:1–15.
Kuhn, Steven L., and Mary C. Stiner
2006   What's a Mother to Do? The Division of Labor among Neandertals and Modern
        Humans in Eurasia. *Current Anthropology* 47 (6): 953–80.
Kuhn, Steven L., Mary C. Stiner, David S. Reese, and Erksin Güleç
2001   Ornaments of the Earliest Upper Paleolithic: New Insights from the Levant. *Pro-
        ceedings of the National Academy of Sciences* 98 (13): 7641–46.
Laden, Greg, and Richard Wrangham
2005   The Rise of the Hominids as an Adaptive Shift in Fallback Foods: Plant Under-
        ground Storage Organs (USOs) and Australopith Origins. *Journal of Human Evo-
        lution* 49:482–98.
Larco Hoyle, Rafael
1939   *Los Mochicas*, vol. 2. Empresa Editorial, Rimac, Lima.
LeCount, Lisa J.
2001   Like Water for Chocolate: Feasting and Political Ritual among the Late Classic
        Maya at Xunantunich, Belize. *American Anthropologist* 103 (4): 935–53.
Lévi-Strauss, Claude
1964   *Le cru et le cuit (The Raw and the Cooked)*. Librarie Plon, Paris.
Lewis, Krista
2007   Fields and Tables of Sheba: Food, Identity, and Politics in Early Historic South-
        ern Arabia. In *The Archaeology of Food and Identity*, edited by Katheryn C. Twiss,
        192–217. Center for Archaeological Investigations, Southern Illinois University
        Carbondale Occasional Paper 34. Carbondale.
Lewis-Williams, J. D., and T. A. Dowson
1988   The Signs of All Times: Entoptic Phenomena in Upper Paleolithic Art. *Current
        Anthropology* 29 (2): 201–45.
Lightfoot, Kent G., Antoinette Martinez, and Ann M. Schiff
1998   Daily Practice and Material Culture in Pluralistic Social Settings: An Archae-
        ological Study of Culture Change and Persistence from Fort Ross, California.
        American Antiquity 63 (2): 199–222.
Lillios, Katina
1999   Objects of Memory: The Ethnography and Archaeology of Heirlooms. *Journal of
        Archaeological Method and Theory* 6 (3): 235–62.
Loasby, Brian J.
2001   Cognition, Imagination and Institutions in Demand Creation. In *Escaping
        Satiation: The Demand Side of Economic Growth*, edited by Ulrich Witt, 13–27.
        Springer, Berlin.
2000   Patterned Variations: Evolution, Psychology and Economic Institutions (Com-
        ment on Ekkehart Schlict). In *Cognition, Rationality, and Institutions*, edited
        by Manfred E. Streit, Uwe Mummert, and Daniel Kiwit, 55–60. Springer,
        Berlin.

Lohse, Jon C., and Fred Valdez Jr. (eds.)

2004   *Ancient Maya Commoners*. University of Texas, Austin.

Longacre, William A.

1991a   Ceramic Ethnoarchaeology: An Introduction. In *Ceramic Ethnoarchaeology*, edited by William A. Longacre, 1–10. University of Arizona Press, Tucson.

1991b   Sources of Ceramic Variability among the Kalinga of Northern Luzon. In *Ceramic Ethnoarchaeology*, edited by William A. Longacre, 95–111. University of Arizona Press, Tucson.

Loren, Diana DiPaolo

2001   Manipulating Bodies and Emerging Traditions at the Los Adaes Presidio. In *The Archaeology of Traditions*, edited by Timothy R. Pauketat, 58–76. University Press of Florida, Gainesville.

Lowe, E. J.

1998   Personal Experience and Belief: The Significance of External Symbolic Storage for the Emergence of Modern Human Cognition. In *Cognition and Material Culture: The Archaeology of Symbolic Storage*, edited by Colin Renfrew and Chris Scarre, 89–96. McDonald Institute for Archaeological Research, University of Cambridge, England.

Lukacs, John

1996   Sex Differences in Dental Caries Rates with the Origin of Agriculture in South Asia. *Current Anthropology* 37 (1): 147–53.

Mack, Alexandra

2004   One Landscape, Many Experiences: Differing Perspectives of the Temple Districts of Vijayanagara. *Journal of Archaeological Method and Theory* 11 (1): 59–81.

Magner, Lois N.

1992   *A History of Medicine*. Marcel Dekker, New York.

Malville, Nancy J.

2001   Long-Distance Transport of Bulk Goods in the Pre-Hispanic American Southwest. *Journal of Anthropological Archaeology* 20:230–43.

Manning, Peter K., and Betsy Cullum-Swan

1994   Narrative, Content and Semiotic Analysis. In *Handbook of Qualitative Research*, edited by Norman K. Denzin and Yvonna S. Lincoln, 463–77. Sage Publications, Thousand Oaks, CA.

Marcus, Joyce

2004   Maya Commoners: The Stereotype and the Reality. In *Ancient Maya Commoners*, edited by Jon C. Lohse and Fred Valdez Jr., 255–83. University of Texas, Austin.

1998   The Peaks and Valleys of Ancient States: An Extension of the Dynamic Model. In *Archaic States*, edited by Gary M. Feinman and Joyce Marcus, 59–94. School of American Research, Santa Fe, NM.

Marshall, Douglas A.

2002   Behavior, Belonging, and Belief: A Theory of Ritual Practice. *Sociological Theory* 20 (3): 360–80.

Marshall, Yvonne, and Alexandra Maas

1997   Dashing Dishes. *World Archaeology* 28 (3): 275–90.

Martin, Alex

1998   Organization of Semantic Knowledge and the Origin of Words in the Brain. In *The Origin and Diversification of Language*, edited by Nine G. Jablonski and Leslie C. Aiello, 69–88. Memoirs of the California Academy of Sciences 24. San Francisco, CA.

Martin, Angela K., and Sandra Kryst

1998   Encountering Mary: Ritualization and Place Contagion in Postmodernity. In *Places Through the Body*, edited by Heidi J. Nast and Steve Pile, 207–29. Routledge, London.

Mauss, Marcel

1990   *The Gift*. Translated by W. D. Halls. W. W. Norton, New York. (Orig. pub. 1954.)

Maxham, Mintcy D.

2000   Rural Communities in the Black Warrior Valley, Alabama: The Role of Commoners in the Creation of the Moundville I Landscape. *American Antiquity* 65 (2): 337–54.

McBrearty, Sally, and Alison S. Brooks

2000   The Revolution That Wasn't: A New Interpretation of the Origin of Modern Human Behavior. *Journal of Human Evolution* 39:453–563.

McIntosh, Roderick J.

2005   *Ancient Middle Niger: Urbanism and the Self-Organizing Landscape*. Cambridge University Press, Cambridge.

McIntosh, Roderick J., and Susan Keech McIntosh

2003   Early Urban Configurations on the Middle Niger. In *The Social Construction of Ancient Cities*, edited by Monica L. Smith, 103–20. Smithsonian Institution Press, Washington, DC.

McKee, Larry

1995   The Earth Is Their Witness. *Sciences* 35 (2): 36–41.

McKendrick, Neil

1982   The Consumer Revolution of Eighteenth-Century England. In *The Birth of a Consumer Society: The Commercialization of Eighteenth-Century England*, edited by Neil McKendrick, John Brewer, and J. H. Plumb, 9–33. Indiana University Press, Bloomington.

Meskell, Lynn

1998   An Archaeology of Social Relations in an Egyptian Village. *Journal of Archaeological Method and Theory* 5 (3): 209–43.

Miles, Steven, and Ronan Paddison

1998   Urban Consumption: An Historiographical Note. *Urban Studies* 35 (5/6): 815–23.

Miller, Daniel

1995   Consumption and Commodities. *Annual Review of Anthropology* 24:141–61.

1987   *Material Culture and Mass Consumption*. Basil Blackwell, London.

1985   *Artefacts as Categories*. Cambridge University Press, Cambridge.

Miller, Nancy Houston

1997   Compliance with Treatment Regimens in Chronic Asymptomatic Diseases. *American Journal of Medicine* 102 (2A): 43–49.

Miller, R. L.

1991   Paleoepidemiology, Literacy, and Medical Tradition among Necropolis Workmen in New Kingdom Egypt. *Medical History* 35:1–24.

Mills, Barbara J. (ed.)

2004   *Identity, Feasting, and the Archaeology of the Greater Southwest*. University Press of Colorado, Boulder.

Milne, S. Brooke

2005   Palaeo-Eskimo Novice Flintknapping in the Eastern Canadian Arctic. *Journal of Field Archaeology* 30 (3): 329–45.

Minc, Leah D., Mary G. Hodge, and M. James Blackman

1994   Stylistic and Spatial Variability in Early Aztec Ceramics: Insights into Pre-imperial Exchange Systems. In *Economies and Polities in the Aztec Realm*, edited by Mary G. Hodge and Michael E. Smith, 133–73.

Miracle, Preston

2002   Mesolithic Meals from Mesolithic Middens. In *Consuming Passions and Patterns of Consumption*, edited by Preston Miracle and Nicky Milner, 65–88. McDonald Institute Monographs, Cambridge.

Mithen, S. J.

2003   Handaxes: The First Aesthetic Artefacts. In *Evolutionary Aesthetics*, edited by E. Voland, 261–75. Springer, Berlin.

Mohanty, R. K., and M. L. Smith

2008   *Excavations at Sisupalgarh, Orissa*. Indian Archaeological Society, New Delhi.

Moore, Jerry D.

2005   *Cultural Landscapes in the Ancient Andes: Archaeologies of Place*. University Press of Florida, Gainesville.

Morey, Darcy F., George M. Crothers, Julie K. Stein, James P. Fenton, and Nicholas P. Hermann

2002   The Fluvial and Geomorphic Context of Indian Knoll, an Archaic Shell Midden in West-Central Kentucky. *Geoarchaeology* 17 (6): 521–53.

Mullins, Paul R.

1999   *Race and Affluence: An Archaeology of African American and Consumer Culture*. Kluwer, New York.

Myers, Garth Andrew

1996   Naming and Placing the Other: Power and the Urban Landscape in Zanzibar. *Journal of Economic and Social Geography* 87 (3): 237–46.

Netting, Robert McC.

1993   *Smallholders, Householders: Farm Families and the Ecology of Intensive, Sustainable Agriculture*. Stanford University Press, Stanford.

Ntole, Kazadi

1996   Objects and People: Relationships and Transformations in the Culture of the Bambala. In *African Material Culture*, edited by Mary Jo Arnoldi, Christraud M. Geary, and Kris L. Hardin, 130–41. Indiana University Press, Bloomington.

O'Connell, J. F., K. Hawkes, and N. G. Blurton Jones

1999   Grandmothering and the Evolution of *Homo erectus*. *Journal of Human Evolution* 36:461–85.

Oeggl, Klaus, Werner Kofler, Alexandra Schmidl, James H. Dickson, Eduard Egarter-Vigl, and Othmar Gaber

2007   The Reconstruction of the Last Itinerary of "Ötzi," the Neolithic Iceman, by Pollen Analyses from Sequentially Sampled Gut Extracts. *Quaternary Science Reviews* 26:853–61.

Paducheva, A. L.

1956   Certain Peculiarities of Metabolism in Breeds of Sheep. *Bulletin of Experimental Biology and Medicine* 41 (1): 55–59.

Parker Pearson, Mike

2000   Eating Money: A Study in the Ethnoarchaeology of Food. *Archaeological Dialogues* 7 (2): 217–32.

Patterson, Thomas C.

2005   The Turn to Agency: Neoliberalism, Individuality, and Subjectivity in Late-Twentieth-Century Anglophone Archaeology. *Rethinking Marxism* 17 (3): 373–84.

Paynter, Robert

2000   Historical Archaeology and the Post-Columbian World of North America. *Journal of Archaeological Research* 8 (3): 169–217.

Peacock, D. P. S.

1982   *Pottery in the Roman World*. Longman, London.

Peck, William H.

1980   Mummies of Ancient Egypt. In *Mummies, Disease, and Ancient Cultures*, edited by Aidan Cockburn and Eve Cockburn, 11–28. Cambridge University Press, Cambridge.

Perry, George H., Nathaniel J. Dominy, Katrina G. Claw, Arthur S. Lee, Heike Fiegler, Richard Redon, John Werner, et al.

2007   Diet and the Evolution of Human Amylase Gene Copy Number Variation. *Nature Genetics* 39:1256–60.

Pieroni, A.

1999   Gathered Wild Food Plants in the Upper Valley of the Serchio River (Garfagnana), Central Italy. *Economic Botany* 53 (3): 327–41.

Pinker, Steven

1998   The Evolution of the Human Language Faculty [1997]. In *The Origin and Diversification of Language*, edited by Nine G. Jablonski and Leslie C. Aiello, 69–88. Memoirs of the California Academy of Sciences 24. University of California Press, Berkeley.

Pliny the Elder

1980   *Histoire naturelle* (Natural History), Book VI. Edited by J. André and J. Filliozat. Société d'Édition "Les Belles Lettres," Paris.

1949   *Histoire naturelle* (Natural History), Book XII. Edited by A. Ernout. Société d'Édition "Les Belles Lettres," Paris.

Possehl, Gregory L.

2002   *The Indus Civilization: A Contemporary Perspective.* Altamira, Walnut Creek, CA.

Potter, James M.

2004   The Creation of Person, the Creation of Place: Hunting Landscapes in the American Southwest. *American Antiquity* 69 (2): 322–38.

Potter, James M., and Scott G. Ortman

2004   Community and Cuisine in the Prehispanic American Southwest. In *Identity, Feasting, and the Archaeology of the Greater Southwest*, edited by Barbara J. Mills, 173–91. University Press of Colorado, Boulder.

Pottier, Johan

1999   *Anthropology of Food: The Social Dynamics of Food Security.* Polity Press, Cambridge, UK.

Prahalad, C. K.

2005   *The Fortune at the Bottom of the Pyramid: Eradicating Poverty through Profits.* Wharton School Publishing, Upper Saddle River, NJ.

Pretty, Graeme L., and Angela Calder

1980   Mummification in Australia and Melanesia. In *Mummies, Disease, and Ancient Cultures*, edited by Aidan Cockburn and Eve Cockburn, 194–209. Cambridge University Press, Cambridge.

Redman, Charles L.

1977   The "Analytic Individual" and Prehistoric Style Variability. In *The Individual in Prehistory: Studies of Variability in Style in Prehistoric Technologies*, edited by James N. Hill and Joel Gunn, 41–53. Academic Press, New York.

Reed, Kaye A.

1997   Early Hominid Evolution and Ecological Change through the African Plio-Pleistocene. *Journal of Human Evolution* 32: 289–322.

Rehman, S. U., P. J. Nietert, D. W. Cope, and A. O. Kilpatrick

2005   What to Wear Today? Effect of Doctor's Attire on the Trust and Confidence of Patients. *American Journal of Medicine* 118 (11): 1279–86.

Reid, J. Jefferson, Michael B. Schiffer, and William L. Rathje

1975   Behavioral Archaeology: Four Strategies. *American Anthropologist* 77 (4): 864–69.

Renfrew, Colin

2001   Symbol before Concept: Material Engagement and the Early Development of Society. In *Archaeological Theory Today*, edited by Ian Hodder, 122–40. Polity Press, Cambridge, UK.

1975   Trade as Action at a Distance: Questions of Integration and Communication. In *Ancient Civilization and Trade*, edited by Jeremy Sabloff and C. C. Lamberg-Karlovsky, 3–59. School of American Research, Santa Fe, NM.

Richerson, Peter J., Robert Boyd, and Robert L. Bettinger
2001   Was Agriculture Impossible during the Pleistocene but Mandatory during the Holocene? A Climate Change Hypothesis. *American Antiquity* 66 (3): 387–411.

Robin, Cynthia
2003   New Directions in Classic Maya Household Archaeology. *Journal of Archaeological Research* 11 (4): 307–56.
2002   Outside of Houses: The Practices of Everyday Life at Chan Nòohol, Belize. *Journal of Social Archaeology* 2 (2): 245–67.

Rockman, Marcy, and James Steele (eds.)
2003   *Colonization of Unfamiliar Landscapes: The Archaeology of Adaptation.* Routledge, London.

Rolle, R., and M. Satin
2002   Basic Requirements for the Transfer of Fermentation Technologies to Developing Countries. *International Journal of Food Microbiology* 75:181–87.

Rollo, Franco, Massimo Ubaldi, Luca Ermini, and Isolina Marota
2002   Ötzi's Last Meals: DNA Analysis of the Intestinal Content of the Neolithic Glacier Mummy from the Alps. *Proceedings of the National Academy of Sciences* 99:12594–599.

Rosenberg, Karen, and Wenda Trevathan
2002   Birth, Obstetrics and Human Evolution. *BJOG: An International Journal of Obstetrics and Gynaecology* 109 (11): 1199–1206.

Rowlands, Michael, and Jean-Pierre Warnier
1993   The Magical Production of Iron in the Cameroon Grassfield. In *The Archaeology of Africa: Food, Metals and Towns*, edited by Thurstan Shaw, Paul Sinclair, Bassey Andah, and Alex Okpoko, 512–50. Routledge, London.

Ruff, Christopher
1987   Sexual Dimorphism in Human Lower Limb Bone Structure: Relationship to Subsistence Strategy and Sexual Division of Labor. *Journal of Human Evolution* 16:391–416.

Sackett, James R.
1977   The Meaning of Style in Archaeology: A General Model. *American Antiquity* 42 (3): 369–80.

Sahlins, Marshall
1972   *Stone Age Economics.* Aldine, Chicago.

Saitta, Dean J.
2007   *The Archaeology of Collective Action.* University Press of Florida, Gainesville.

Sakurai, Kiyohiko, and Tamotsu Ogata
1980   Japanese Mummies. In *Mummies, Disease, and Ancient Cultures*, edited by Aidan Cockburn and Eve Cockburn, 211–23. Cambridge University Press, Cambridge.

Salas-Salvadó, Jordi, Maria D. Huetos-Solano, Pilar García-Lorda, and Mònica Bulló
2006   Diet and Dietetics in al-Andalus. *British Journal of Nutrition* 96, supp. 1: S100–103.

Salvucci, Dario D., and Niels A. Taatgen
2008   Threaded Cognition: An Integrated Theory of Concurrent Multitasking. *Psychological Review* 115 (1): 101–30.

Sato, Tomoi, and Go Miyata
2000   The Nutraceutical Benefit, Part III: Honey. *Nutrition* 16:468–69.

Schiffer, Michael Brian
2005   The Devil Is in the Details: The Cascade Model of Invention Processes. *American Antiquity* 70 (3): 485–502.
1991   *The Portable Radio in American Life.* University of Arizona Press, Tucson.

Schiffer, Michael Brian, with Andrea R. Miller
1999   *The Material Life of Human Beings: Artifacts, Behavior, and Communication.* Routledge, London.

Schiffer, Michael Brian, and James M. Skibo
1997   The Explanation of Artifact Variability. *American Antiquity* 62 (1): 27–50.

Schmidt, Peter R., and Bertram B. Mapunda
1997   Ideology and the Archaeological Record in Africa: Interpreting Symbolism in Iron Smelting Technology. *Journal of Anthropological Archaeology* 16:73–102.

Scott, Elizabeth M.
2007   Pigeon Soup and Plover in Pyramids: French Foodways in New France and the Illinois Country. In *The Archaeology of Food and Identity*, edited by Katheryn C. Twiss, 243–59. Center for Archaeological Investigations, Southern Illinois University Carbondale Occasional Paper 34. Carbondale.

Scott, James C.
1985   *Weapons of the Weak: Everyday Forms of Peasant Resistance.* Yale University Press, New Haven, CT.

Scott, Joan Wallach
1986   Gender: A Useful Category of Historical Analysis. *American Historical Review* 91 (5): 1053–75.

Sen, Amartya
1981   *Poverty and Famines: An Essay in Entitlement and Deprivation.* Clarendon Press, Oxford, UK.

Shanks, Michael
1997   Photography and Archaeology. In *The Cultural Life of Images: Visual Representation in Archaeology*, edited by Brian Leigh Molyneaux, 73–107. Routledge, London.

Shaw, Julia, John Sutcliffe, Lindsay Lloyd-Smith, Jean-Luc Schwenninger, and M. S. Chauhan
2007   Ancient Irrigation and Buddhist History in Central India: Optically Stimulated Luminescence Dates and Pollen Sequences from the Sanchi Dams. *Asian Perspectives* 46 (1): 166–201.

Shea, John J.
2006   Interdisciplinary Approaches to Hominid Diets. *Evolutionary Anthropology* 15:204–6.

Sheets, Payson

2000   Provisioning the Ceren Household: The Vertical Economy, Village Economy, and Household Economy in the Southeastern Maya Periphery. *Ancient Mesoamerica* 11:217–30.

Shen, Chen

2003   Compromises and Conflicts: Production and Commerce in the Royal Cities of Eastern Zhou, China. In *The Social Construction of Ancient Cities*, edited by Monica L. Smith, 290–310. Smithsonian Institution Press, Washington, DC.

Sherratt, Andrew

1987   Cups That Cheered. In *Bell Beakers of the Western Mediterranean: Definition, Interpretation, Theory and New Site Data*, part 1, edited by William H. Waldren and Rex Claire Kennard, 81–102. BAR International Series 331. British Archaeological Reports, Oxford.

Shipman, Pat

1986   Scavenging or Hunting in Early Hominids: Theoretical Framework and Tests. *American Anthropologist* 88 (1): 27–43.

Silliman, Stephen

2001   Agency, Practical Politics and the Archaeology of Culture Contact. *Journal of Social Archaeology* 1 (2): 190–209.

Simpson, St. John

1997   Prehistoric Ceramics in Mesopotamia. In *Pottery in the Making: Ceramic Traditions*, edited by Ian Freestone and David Gaimster, 38–43. Smithsonian Institution Press, Washington, DC.

Singer, Hans, John Wood, and Tony Jennings

1987   *Food Aid: The Challenge and the Opportunity*. Clarendon Press, Oxford, UK.

Smith, Adam

1776   *An Inquiry into the Nature and Causes of the Wealth of Nations*. W. Strahan and T. Cadell, London.

Smith, Bruce D.

2001   Low-Level Food Production. *Journal of Archaeological Research* 9 (1): 1–43.

Smith, Michael E., and Frances F. Berdan

2000   The Postclassic Mesoamerican World System. *Current Anthropology* 41 (2): 283–86.

Smith, Monica L.

2007a   Inconspicuous Consumption: Non-display Goods and Identity Formation. *Journal of Archaeological Method and Theory* 14:412–38.

2007b   Territories, Corridors and Networks: A Biological Model for the Premodern State. *Complexity* 12 (4): 28–35.

2006a   How Ancient Agriculturalists Managed Yield Fluctuations through Crop Selection and Reliance on Wild Plants: An Example from Central India. *Economic Botany* 60 (1): 39–48.

2006b   The Archaeology of Food Preference. *American Anthropologist* 108 (3): 480–93.

2005a   Networks, Territories and the Cartography of Ancient States. *Annals of the Association of American Geographers* 95 (4): 832–49.

2005b   Discussant for "Casting Roles: Are Caste Groups Visible in the Archaeological Record?" Society for American Archaeology Annual Meeting, Salt Lake City.

1999   The Role of Ordinary Goods in Premodern Exchange. *Journal of Archaeological Method and Theory* 6 (2): 109–35.

Smyth, Michael P.

1998   Surface Archaeology and Site Organization: New Methods for Studying Urban Maya Communities. In *Surface Archaeology*, edited by Alan P. Sullivan III, 43–60. University of New Mexico Press, Albuquerque.

Snead, James E.

2008   *Ancestral Landscapes of the Pueblo World*. University of Arizona Press, Tucson.

Sosis, Richard

2003   Why Aren't We All Hutterites? Costly Signaling Theory and Religious Behavior. *Human Nature* 14 (2): 91–127.

Soustelle, Jacques

1996   Daily Life of the Aztecs on the Eve of the Spanish Conquest [1964]. In *I Saw a City Invincible: Urban Portraits of Latin America*, edited by Gilbert M. Joseph and Mark D. Szuchman, 35–47. Scholarly Resources, Wilmington, DE.

Southall, Aidan

1998   *The City in Time and Space*. Cambridge University Press, Cambridge.

Spencer, Charles S.

1997   Evolutionary Approaches in Archaeology. *Journal of Archaeological Research* 5 (3): 209–64.

1987   Rethinking the Chiefdom. In *Chiefdoms in the Americas*, edited by Robert D. Drennan and Carlos A. Uribe, 369–90. University Press of America, Lanham, MD.

Standage, Tom

2005   *A History of the World in 6 Glasses*. Walker, New York.

Steedman, Ian

2001   *Consumption Takes Time*. Routledge, London.

Stiner, Mary C.

1994   *Honor among Thieves: A Zooarchaeological Study of Neandertal Ecology*. Princeton University Press, Princeton.

Strauss, Claudia

2007   Blaming for Columbine: Conceptions of Agency in the Contemporary United States. *Current Anthropology* 48 (6): 807–32.

Streicker, Joel

1997   Spatial Reconfigurations, Imagined Geographies, and Social Conflicts in Cartagena, Colombia. *Cultural Anthropology* 12 (1): 109–28.

Sulgostowska, Zofia

2002   Flint Raw Material Economy during the Late Glacial and Early Postglacial in the Oder-Daugava-Prypet Basin. In *Lithic Raw Material Economies in Late Glacial and Early Postglacial Europe*, edited by Lynn E. Fisher and Berit Valentin Eriksen, 7–17. BAR International Series 1093. British Archaeological Reports, Oxford.

Summers, Kyle

2005   The Evolutionary Ecology of Despotism. *Evolution and Human Behavior* 26:106–35.

Swami Madhavananda (trans.)

1965   *The Brihadaranyaka Upanisad*. Advaita Ashrama, Calcutta.

Tamari, Tal

1991   The Development of Caste Systems in West Africa. *Journal of African History* 32:221–50.

Tambiah, Stanley J.

1985   *Culture, Thought, and Social Action: An Anthropological Perspective*. Harvard University Press, Cambridge, MA.

Tardío, J., H. Pascual, and R. Morales

2005   Wild Food Plants Traditionally Used in the Province of Madrid, Central Spain. *Economic Botany* 59 (2): 122–36.

Teaford, Mark F., and Peter S. Ungar

2000   Diet and the Evolution of the Earliest Human Ancestors. *Proceedings of the National Academy of Sciences* 97 (25): 13506–511.

Terry, Richard E., Fabian G. Fernández, J. Jacob Parnell, and Takeshi Inomata

2004   The Story in the Floors: Chemical Signatures of Ancient and Modern Maya Activities at Aguateca, Guatemala. *Journal of Archaeological Science* 31:1237–50.

Thapar, Romila

1997   *Aśoka and the Decline of the Mauryas*. Rev. ed. Oxford University Press, Delhi.

Thompson, F. Hugh

2003   *The Archaeology of Greek and Roman Slavery*. Duckworth, London.

Toll, H. Wolcott

2001   Making and Breaking Pots in the Chaco World. *American Antiquity* 66 (1): 56–78.

Tomasello, Michael

1999   The Human Adaptation for Culture. *Annual Review of Anthropology* 28:509–29.

Toth, Nicholas, and Kathy Schick

2005   Hominin Dispersals in the Old World. In *The Human Past*, edited by Chris Scarre, 46–83. Thames and Hudson, London.

Treherne, Paul

1995   The Warrior's Beauty: The Masculine Body and Self-Identity in Bronze Age Europe. *Journal of the European Association of Archaeologists* 3 (1): 105–44.

Trigg, Heather B.

2005   *From Household to Empire: Society and Economy in Early Colonial New Mexico*. University of Arizona Press, Tucson.

Turner, Terence S.

1980   The Social Skin. In *Not Work Alone*, edited by Jeremy Cherfas and Roger Lewin, 112–40. Temple Smith, London.

Twiss, Katheryn C. (ed.)

2007   *The Archaeology of Food and Identity*. Center for Archaeological Investigations, Southern Illinois University Carbondale Occasional Paper 34. Carbondale.

Van de Pol, Lotte, and Erika Kuijpers

2005   Poor Women's Migration to the City: The Attraction of Amsterdam Health Care and Social Assistance in Early Modern Times. *Journal of Urban History* 32 (1): 44–60.

van der Merwe, Nikolaas, and Donald H. Avery

1987   Science and Magic in African Technology: Traditional Iron Smelting in Malawi. *Africa* 57 (2): 143–72.

van der Veen, Marijke

2007   Food as an Instrument of Social Change: Feasting in Iron Age and Early Roman Southern Britain. In *The Archaeology of Food and Identity*, edited by Katheryn C. Twiss, 112–29. Center for Archaeological Investigations, Southern Illinois University Carbondale Occasional Paper 34. Carbondale.

2003   When Is Food a Luxury? *World Archaeology* 34 (3): 405–27.

VanDerwarker, Amber M., C. Margaret Scarry, and Jane M. Eastman

2007   Menus for Families and Feasts: Household and Community Consumption of Plants at Upper Saratown, North Carolina. In *The Archaeology of Food and Identity*, edited by Katheryn C. Twiss, 16–49. Center for Archaeological Investigations, Southern Illinois University Carbondale Occasional Paper No. 34. Carbondale, Il.

Vandiver, Pamela B., and Sergey A. Vasil'ev

2002   A 16,000-Year-Old Ceramic Human-Figurine from Maina, Russia. *Materials Research Society Symposium Proceedings* 712, II6.9.1–11.

Van Dyke, Ruth M., and Susan E. Alcock

2003   Archaeologies of Memory: An Introduction. In *Archaeologies of Memory*, edited by Ruth M. Van Dyke and Susan E. Alcock, 1–13. Blackwell, Malden, MA.

VanPool, Christine S., and Todd L. VanPool

1999   The Scientific Nature of Postprocessualism. *American Antiquity* 64:33–53.

Vardi, A., Z. Barzilay, N. Linder, H. A. Cohen, G. Paret, and A. Barzilai

1998   Local Application of Honey for Treatment of Neonatal Postoperative Wound Infection. *Acta Paediatrica* 87 (4): 429–32.

Veblen, Thorstein

1899   *The Theory of the Leisure Class*. MacMillan, London.

Voss, Barbara L.

2005   The Archaeology of Overseas Chinese Communities. *World Archaeology* 37 (3): 424–39.

Vreeland, James M. Jr.

1998   Mummies of Peru. In *Mummies, Disease and Ancient Cultures*, 2nd edition, edited by Aidan Cockburn, Eve Cockburn, and Theodore A. Reyman, 154–89. Cambridge University Press, New York.

Wallaert, Hélène

2008   The Way of the Potter's Mother: Apprenticeship Strategies among Dii Potters from Cameroon, West Africa. In *Cultural Transmission and Material Culture: Breaking Down Boundaries*, edited by Miriam T. Stark, Brenda J. Bowser, and Lee Horne, 178–98. University of Arizona Press, Tucson.

Wansink, Brian

2006   *Mindless Eating: Why We Eat More than We Think.* Bantam-Dell, New York.

Wansink, Brian, James E. Painter, and Jill North

2005   Bottomless Bowls: Why Visual Cues of Portion Size May Influence Intake. *Obesity Research* 13 (1): 93–100.

Wansink, Brian, and Jeffery Sobal

2007   Mindless Eating: The 200 Daily Food Decisions We Overlook. *Environment and Behavior* 39 (1): 106–23.

Wattenmaker, Patricia

1994   State Formation and the Organization of Domestic Craft Production at Third-Millennium B.C. Kurban Hoyuk, Southeast Turkey. In *Archaeological Views from the Countryside*, edited by Glenn M. Schwartz and Steven E. Falconer, 109–20. Smithsonian Institution Press, Washington, DC.

Weiner, Steve, Qinqi Xu, Paul Goldberg, Jinyi Liu, and Ofer Bar-Yosef

1998   Evidence for the Use of Fire at Zhoukoudian, China. *Science* 281:251–53.

Weismantel, Mary

2004   Moche Sex Pots: Reproduction and Temporality in Ancient South America. *American Anthropologist* 106 (3): 495–505.

Weiss, Brad

1997   Forgetting Your Dead: Alienable and Inalienable Objects in Northwest Tanzania. *Anthropological Quarterly* 70 (4): 164–72.

Welch, Paul D.

1991   *Moundville's Economy.* University of Alabama Press, Tuscaloosa.

Wells, Peter S.

1999   Production Within and Beyond Imperial Boundaries: Goods, Exchange, and Power in Roman Europe. In *World-Systems Theory in Practice: Leadership, Production, and Exchange*, edited by P. Nick Kardulias, 85–101. Rowman and Littlefield, Lanham, MD.

Whittaker, Dick, and Jack Goody

2001   Rural Manufacturing in the Rouergue from Antiquity to the Present: The Examples of Pottery and Cheese. *Comparative Studies in Society and History* 43 (2): 225–45.

Wiessner, Polly

1983   Style and Social Information in Kalahari San Projectile Points. *American Antiquity* 48 (2): 253–76.

Wilkinson, T. J.

1982   The Definition of Ancient Manured Zones by Means of Extensive Sherd-Sampling Techniques. *Journal of Field Archaeology* 9 (3): 323–33.

Wills, W. H., and Patricia L. Crown

2004 Commensal Politics in the Prehispanic Southwest. In *Identity, Feasting, and the Archaeology of the Greater Southwest*, edited by Barbara J. Mills, 153–72. University Press of Colorado, Boulder.

Winnicott, D. W.

1971 *Playing and Reality*. Tavistock Publications, London.

Winterhalder, Bruce, and Carol Goland

1997 An Evolutionary Ecology Perspective on Diet Choice, Risk, and Plant Domestication. In *People, Plants, and Landscape: Studies in Paleoethnobotany*, edited by Kristen J. Gremillion, 123–60. University of Alabama Press, Tuscaloosa.

Witt, Ulrich

2001 Consumption, Demand and Economic Growth: An Introduction. In *Escaping Satiation: The Demand Side of Economic Growth*, edited by Ulrich Witt, 1–10. Springer, Berlin.

Wobst, H. Martin

1977 Stylistic Behavior and Information Exchange. In *For the Director: Research Essays in Honor of James B. Griffin*, edited by Charles E. Cleland, 317–42. Anthropological Papers of the Museum of Anthropology 61. University of Michigan, Ann Arbor.

Wrangham, Richard W., James Holland Jones, Greg Laden, David Pilbeam, and Nancy-Lou Conklin-Brittain

1999 The Raw and the Stolen: Cooking and the Ecology of Human Origins. *Current Anthropology* 40 (5): 567–94.

Wright, Henry T.

1984 Pre-State Political Formations. In *The Evolution of Complex Societies: The Harry Hoijer Lectures for 1982*, edited by Timothy Earle, 41–78. Undena Press, Malibu, CA.

Yoffee, Norman

1993 Too Many Chiefs? (Or, Safe Texts for the '90s). In *Archaeological Theory: Who Sets the Agenda?* edited by Norman Yoffee and Andrew Sherratt, 60–78. Cambridge University Press, Cambridge.

Zajonc, Robert B., and Hazel Markus

1982 Affective and Cognitive Factors in Preferences. *Journal of Consumer Research* 9 (2): 123–31.

Zappler, Georg

1996 *Learn about . . . Texas Indians*. Texas Parks and Wildlife Department, Austin.

Zeder, Melinda A., and Brian Hesse

2000 The Initial Domestication of Goats (*Capra hircus*) in the Zagros Mountains 10,000 Years Ago. *Science* 287:2254–57.

Zimmerman, Michael R.

1980 Aleutian and Alaskan Mummies. In *Mummies, Disease, and Ancient Cultures*, edited by Aidan Cockburn and Eve Cockburn, 118–34. Cambridge University Press, Cambridge.

zur Nedden, Dieter, Klaus Wicke, Rudolf Knapp, Horst Seidler, Harald Wilfing, Gerhard
Weber, Konrad Spindler, William A. Murphy, Gertrud Hauser, and Werner Platzer
1994   New Findings on the Tyrolean "Ice Man": Archaeological and CT-Body Anal-
        ysis Suggest Personal Disaster before Death. *Journal of Archaeological Science*
        21:809–18.

Figure Credits

1.1 Making stone tools. From *Learn About . . . Texas Indians*, by Georg Zappler, illustrations by Elena T. Ivy, consulting editor Juliann Pool, copyright © 1996, p. 8; reproduced by permission of the University of Texas Press.

1.2 Food, goods, and energy expenditure. Illustration © John Sibbick; reprinted with permission.

1.3 Manufacture of pottery. From Kim Duistermaat, *The Pots and Potters of Assyria* (2008), 381; reprinted with permission.

1.5 Creative actions and habituation. Illustration by Monica L. Smith, Redrawn by Robert Mion.

1.6 Marking identity on the body. From Thomas A. Dowson, "Reading Art, Writing History: Rock Art and Social Change in Southern Africa," *World Archaeology* 25, no. 3 (1994): 338; reprinted by permission of Taylor & Francis Ltd., http://www.informaworld.com

1.7 Relationship among food, goods, and work. Illustration by Monica L. Smith, redrawn by Robert Mion.

2.1 Early European images of plowing. From P. V. Glob, *Ard og Plov i Nordens Oldtid*, Jutland Archeological Society Publications (Aarhus: Aarhus University Press, 1951), 1:93, 94; reproduced by permission of the Jutland Archeological Society.

2.2 Food storage area at Çatalhöyük. Reproduced by permission of the Society for American Archaeology from Sonya Atalay and Christine Hastorf, "Food, Meals, and Daily Activities: Food *Habitus* at Neolithic Çatalhöyük," *American Antiquity* 71, no. 2 (2006): 292, illustration by Kathryn Killackey, copyright Çatalhöyük Research Project.

2.3 Types of waste. Adapted from J. D. Hill 1995:25.

2.5 Bowls, jars, and cups. From the Archaeology Collections Facility of the Fowler Museum at UCLA; photograph by the author.

2.6 Statuette of woman grinding grain. Egyptian, Old Kingdom, Dynasty 5, 2500–2350 B.C.; from Egypt, Giza, Tomb G 2185; limestone; 19.5 × 8.2 cm (7 11/16 × 3 1/4 in.); Harvard University—Boston Museum of Fine Arts Expedition, 12.1486; photograph © 2010 Museum of Fine Arts, Boston; reproduced by permission.

2.7 Moche food and political activity. From Rafel Larco Hoyle, *Los Mochicas* (Lima, 1939), 2:147, pl. 31; reproduced by permission of the Museo Larco, Lima, Peru.

3.1 Making an Acheulean hand ax. From Brian M. Fagan, *People of the Earth: An Introduction to World Prehistory*, 9th ed. © 1998, p. 90; reprinted by permission of Pearson Education, Inc., Upper Saddle River, NJ.

3.2   Buddhist rock art panel. © 1997 Heidelberger Akademie der Wissenschaften; reproduced with permission.

3.3   Tzeltal Maya uses of broken pottery. Adapted from Deal and Hagstrum 1995:125; reproduced by permission of the University of Utah Press.

4.1   Specialized and routine tasks in manufacturing. From Hall 2005:133; drawings by Derek Lucas, reproduced by permission of the Museum of London.

4.2   Experiencing and creating objects and symbols. From *Learn about . . . Texas Indians*, by Georg Zappler, illustrations by Elena T. Ivy, consulting editor Juliann Pool, copyright © 1996, p. 16; reproduced by permission of the University of Texas Press.

4.4   Aztec flower seller in the *Florentine Codex*. From *Florentine Codex*, Book 11 (Anderson and Dibble 1963:11:741); reproduced by permission of the University of Utah Press.

4.5   Multitasking by managers. From Adolf Erman, *Life in Ancient Egypt*, trans. H. M. Tirard (London: Macmillan, 1894), 448).

Index

adoption, 33, 157, 168–69

age, 127–28; human experience and, 17, 32, 36, 41, 46, 159, 170, 181; physical changes and, 29–30, 35, 86, 87–89, 117; work and, 15, 116, 154, 155, 158–60, 167, 169–70, 171

agriculture, 53, 56, 60, 84, 103, 124–25, 129; animal husbandry and, 12, 19, 34–37, 58, 59, 174, 176; crops and, 19–20, 37, 71, 80, 94, 167, 174; development of, 66, 77, 170; domestication and, 67, 68, 70, 71, 74, 79, 90, 150, 161; gender and, 19, 24, 39, 155, 160; harvest and, 2, 19, 153, 154, 162, 163; health and, 61, 75, 87, 160; landscape and, 37, 42, 180, 181; manure and, 19, 129, 131; seasonality of, 55, 68, 75, 151–52; status and, 92–94, 180; time and, 4, 34; work and, 153, 154, 155–56, 159, 167

animals, 18, 135, 150, 152, 166; domestic, 12, 19, 34, 35, 36, 37, 58, 59, 66, 67, 68, 70, 71, 129, 151–53, 156, 159; meat of, 43, 55, 62, 63, 65, 67, 73, 115, 151, 155, 158; predators, 2, 21, 25, 65, 152; as prey, 53, 63, 64, 66, 68, 70, 74, 77, 78, 79, 81, 84, 85, 86, 115, 161, 162

apprenticeship, 104, 154, 158, 160, 161, 162, 166–67, 171, 181

archaeology, 1, 8; "great leader" model and, 6–7; historical, 121; person-centered, 13, 15, 51, 133, 175–76; post-processual (postmodern), 9–10, 20–21; structuration theory and, 21

beverages, 50, 54, 58, 61, 62, 71, 72, 74, 82–86, 88, 93, 121, 163–64

burials, 2, 7, 11, 36, 61–62, 127–28, 156; energy expenditure and, 26, 161; individuals and, 13, 43, 131; landscape and, 151, 177; material culture and, 111, 121, 132, 173

children, 29, 35, 36, 42; cognition and, 107–9, 111; food and, 71, 78, 97, 108; household economy and, 38, 64, 169; material culture and, 115, 175; nurturing, 2, 32, 39, 159, 160, 165, 169; work and, 135, 158–60, 170

cities: population density and, 12, 131, 171; social complexity and, 2, 5, 175, 177, 179–82; subsistence and, 132, 178; tradition and, 121; work and, 26, 103, 153

clothing, 1, 7, 18–19, 26, 28, 42; individual actions and, 3, 5, 98, 164, 177; making of, 39, 135; styles of, 12, 20, 31, 104, 111, 120–21

cognition, 27, 28, 35, 37, 50–52, 173–82; change and, 17, 36, 39, 41–42; energy expenditure and, 4, 23, 38, 155, 157–58; food and, 56, 65, 91, 95, 96; individuality and, 7, 10, 14, 16, 34, 49; material culture and, 107–11, 122, 129, 133; multitasking and, 24–25, 30, 44, 67, 100, 105–6; ritual and, 45, 161; social complexity and, 2, 11, 48; work and, 134, 160–61, 169, 171

communication, 40–41, 63, 67, 108, 174; interaction and, 13, 22, 120, 175, 177; memory and, 43, 107, 109, 180; physical means of, 12, 98, 100, 111, 130, 133, 151; work and, 134, 164, 169

community, 2, 5, 13, 61, 73, 169; cooperation and, 23, 65, 108–9; food and, 79,
84, 85, 91; identity and, 6, 14–15, 76,
109, 125; individual actions and, 3, 98,
129, 131, 174–75; material culture and,
110, 122, 130; memory and, 160, 179–80;
ritual and, 45, 56, 181; rural, 15, 154,
172–73; work and, 154, 171
consumption, 106, 111, 179; direct, 4, 50,
51, 55, 76, 115; elites and, 7, 73, 93, 97,
101–5, 177–78; individuals and, 89,
100–106, 131, 133, 173; meaning of, 120,
122, 123
cooking, 36, 53–55, 64, 70–74, 80, 83–85,
121–22, 172; gender and, 39, 77, 157, 160;
as process, 46, 57, 89, 163; types of, 4, 65,
79, 82, 91, 105, 158
craftsmakers, 4, 7, 14, 81, 98, 101, 105, 131,
152, 157, 160–62, 166, 173
creativity, 37, 40–41, 66, 86; cognition and,
xv, 6, 20, 36, 108, 175; food and, 53, 56,
72, 73, 75, 81, 96, 178; habituation and,
20–21, 24, 34, 39, 49, 122, 179; material
culture and, 98, 100, 109, 111, 120, 158,
176; work and, 157–58, 163, 169

decision making, 22, 23, 52, 160; food and,
53, 80, 82, 96, 113; individuals and,
17–18, 49, 68, 72–73, 118–19, 137, 179;
material culture and, 4, 50, 115–16, 123,
131; social complexity and, 2, 52, 94,
181–82; technology and, 18–20, 48, 175;
work and, 134–35, 174
discard, 23, 123–29, 151, 179; as individual
action, 3, 20, 120, 133, 164, 172, 175, 181;
middens and, 61, 92, 124–29
display, 3, 20, 111, 120, 164; purposes of, 12,
36, 50, 51, 118, 119–23, 128

economic systems, 53, 80, 135, 153, 157–59;
consumption and, 102, 105, 133, 172–73;
decision making and, 24, 118, 128, 161;
exchange and, 47–49, 95, 96; labor and,
166–68, 171–72; political hierarchy and,
7, 94–95, 101–2, 132
elites, 87–88, 171; cognition and, 5, 7–8,
26–27, 39, 177; food and, 92–93, 95, 97,
178; material culture and, 101–2, 104,
172–73, 179–80, 182
empires, 2, 12, 26, 51, 52, 130, 154, 178.
See also states
exchange: as economic interaction, 47–49,
50, 103, 115–16, 119, 122–23, 165–166; food
and, 53, 86, 96, 168; individuals and, 18,
118–19, 130; networks for, 9, 14, 91, 112,
113; as social interaction, 118, 134, 136,
170, 174; surplus and, 69, 76, 95, 101,
148, 165, 173

feasting, 11, 79, 91–93, 95, 106, 119, 130, 165,
172, 178; "feast failure," 93
fire, 43, 127, 159; destructive, 36, 42, 59, 87;
as tool, 25, 37, 42–43, 49, 64, 73, 74, 90,
134, 151, 152, 162
food, 96–97; access to, 11, 12, 25, 26, 36,
48, 94, 164, 166, 168, 169, 177; archaeological record and, xiv, 56–64, 70, 72,
74, 75, 77, 81, 91–94; biological need
for, 1, 4, 33, 49, 50–51, 96, 175, 178;
consumption of, 106, 113, 178; creativity
and, 72, 76, 78, 81–82, 163, 164; culture
and, 81, 93–97, 104, 113, 130; distribution of, 12, 50, 78, 92, 94, 150; energy
expenditure and, 54, 56, 80–81, 83–85,
92, 106, 164, 174; exotic, 92, 93, 97, 113,
121, 122, 178; fasting and, 78–79; funerals
and, 62, 128; habituation and, 23, 46, 82;
illness and, 22, 91–92; individual choice
and, 3, 5, 50, 77, 82, 95, 97, 106, 158,
177, 178; liquid, 82–85; material culture
and, 113, 122, 129; meals and, 10, 69, 85;
medicine and, 27–28, 73, 88–89, 91, 94;
multitasking and, 53–54, 178; as payment, 12, 27, 172, 181; pilgrimage and, 47;
as poison, 86, 90–91; preferences for,
xiv, 49–50, 69–74, 77, 78, 81, 93–94,

113, 162, 178, 180; preparation of, 4, 13, 34, 42, 53, 54–55, 58, 61, 65, 69, 70, 73, 161; preserving, 43, 67; purification and, 157; salt as, 62, 75, 150, 159; seasonality and, 33, 34; serving, 13, 53, 83, 113, 159; sharing, 36, 64, 68, 115, 168, 170; shortage, 74–76, 91, 94; status and, 63, 73, 77, 79, 92–94, 95, 104–5; technology and, 26, 58, 79, 80, 84, 98; toxins in, 65, 73, 90–91; transporting, 12, 58, 93, 159, 170, 172; waste and, 61, 65, 71, 72, 81, 91, 125, 126, 175

foodways, 69, 81–82, 84, 91, 96, 121–22, 176, 178, 182

foraging, 9, 67, 103, 115, 151–53; food and, 4, 11, 20, 55, 58, 61, 70, 82, 174; social organization and, 51, 65, 170; and wild plants, 34, 66, 75, 76, 155, 158—62

gender, 19, 32, 37–39, 169, 181; food and, 50, 77, 80, 122, 126, 157, 160, 178; material culture and, 104, 111, 115, 122; sex and, 165, 167; work and, 15, 24, 154–58, 159, 169, 171

gifts, 30, 50, 111, 115–18, 123

goods, 31–32, 47, 120–23, 170–72, 174–79; acquiring, 30, 33, 45, 50, 51, 115–19, 123, 129–31; cognition and, 5, 23, 107–11, 158; cost of, 106, 129, 151, 157; distribution of, 7, 13, 26, 27, 115; diversity in, 116, 150, 164, 181–82; exotic/rare, 103, 105, 118; funerary, 128, 161, 162; manufacture of, 14, 98–102, 105–6, 112, 134–35; nonlocal, 100, 112, 165; reuse/recycling and, 123–24, 129, 133; use of, 102–6, 111–14, 129–31, 181. See also material culture

grain, 26, 54, 55, 66, 77, 89, 159; consumption of, 63, 69, 71, 78, 79–80; fermentation and, 85, 90; "grandmother hypothesis," 159; grinding, 61, 67, 84, 87, 164; significance of, 62, 94, 132; storage of, 34, 42, 59

habituation, xv, 23, 35–39, 45, 50, 108, 155, 175, 176; creativity and, 20–21, 24, 34, 49, 122, 179; food and, 53, 73, 79, 96, 121; material culture and, 100, 111, 121; memory and, 22, 44; work and, 51, 157, 169

hierarchy: "costly signaling" and, ix, 31, 122; food and, 92–94, 161; material culture and, 7, 26–27, 101, 104, 105, 116, 117, 119, 120, 122, 130, 172; social complexity and, 6–8, 11–12, 48, 95, 97, 132, 175–79, 181–82; work and, 169, 174, 180

household: archaeological record and, 15, 61, 63; economies of, 53, 56, 76, 80, 83, 123, 126, 151, 159, 167, 173; energy expenditure and, 19, 153, 157, 158, 168, 177; food and, 79, 84, 91–92, 96, 97, 178; gender and, 38, 159, 169, 181; individual actions and, 3, 13, 14, 54, 95, 98, 175; labor in, 168–70, 174; material culture and, 122, 129, 130–32, 179; production and, 15, 68, 172

hunting, 10, 39, 45–46, 53, 64, 86, 103, 115, 155, 169; food and, 48, 58, 61, 70, 76, 79, 174; migration and, 21, 57, 82; mobility and, 151, 156; organizing, 11, 63, 170; seasonality and, 2, 35, 55; social organization and, 51, 65, 116, 117; time and, 4, 33, 34

identity: discard and, 125, 128; food and, 67, 69, 76–78, 81–82; markers of, 31–32, 36, 96, 97, 98, 109–11, 120, 122, 130, 172; perception and, xiv, 107–8; social complexity and, 6, 132, 173; social roles and, 30–31, 33, 79, 119–20, 128, 131, 157

invention cascade model, 18, 48, 84, 113

labor, 93–94, 153–54, 165–66: socioeconomic organization and, 7, 11–12, 27, 39, 95, 116, 167, 169, 174, 180; wage, 103, 116, 146, 154. See also work

language, 25, 46, 50, 56, 96, 119; change
in, 1, 17, 77; cognition and, 41, 107,
175; memory and, 43, 110, 182; social
complexity and, 11, 39–40, 108; written,
28, 45, 48, 121

managers, 93, 134, 166–67, 171, 172
material culture: cognition and, 27, 48–49,
52, 98–99, 107–11, 182; "cheap signaling"
and, 122; "costly signaling" and, ix, 31,
122; environment and, 1, 4, 36, 47, 107–8;
food and, 53, 58, 74; hierarchy and,
101–2, 105, 121, 132; human engagement
with, 2, 16, 18, 25, 108, 129–30, 132–33,
175; identity and, 31–32, 98, 110, 119, 122,
125, 130, 172; industrialization and, 18, 78,
98, 103; meaning and, 50, 106, 111, 113,
127, 128, 131, 177; production and, 126,
165; reuse and, 36, 106, 123; sedentism
and, 26, 34, 129; social complexity and, 7,
10, 12, 129–32; social roles and, 30–31, 109,
111, 112–13, 119–20, 122; styles of, 100, 104,
119, 122–23, 130, 131, 179, 182; subsistence
goods and, 103, 132, 170; symbolism and,
114, 123, 125–28, 177, 182; talismans as, 31,
113; utility and, 118, 120–21, 130, 172–73,
176; variation in, 14, 16–17, 19–20
medicine, 27–30, 73, 76, 86, 88–91, 94,
160, 162, 164
memory, 46, 47, 118, 129, 166; cognition
and, 5–6, 22, 160, 169, 175, 182; community, 28, 36, 43, 160, 179–80; encoding,
37, 41, 44–45, 115; food and, 25, 26, 33,
48, 65, 67, 75, 91, 96, 174; material culture and, 100, 105, 107, 109, 110, 116–17;
social complexity and, 2, 11, 176; work
and, 34, 135, 137, 164
metallurgy/metalworking, 7, 14, 129, 132,
135, 150, 152, 153, 160, 161–62, 168, 173
migration, 57, 66; cognition and, 2, 21, 22,
75; as economic activity, 65, 76, 82, 152,
153–54; food preference and, xiv, 69,
77, 81, 82

monuments, 37, 114, 125, 138, 139, 141, 151,
171, 180
multitasking, 24–25, 86; cognition and,
5–6, 23, 27, 100, 106, 169; energy
expenditure and, 26, 51, 98, 134–35,
150, 151, 171, 172, 174, 176; food and,
53–54, 65, 67, 75, 84, 85, 93, 96, 97,
178; material culture and, 105, 106, 109,
131, 156; memory and, 44, 109; "meta-
multitasking," 181

pilgrimage, 47, 86, 139
planning, 5–6, 41, 127; food and, 53, 65, 67,
75, 91, 93, 96, 174; material culture and,
105, 107, 131; social complexity and, 2,
11, 48; work and, 34, 43, 134, 135, 171
political organization, 5, 36, 157; cultural
change and, 2, 6–7, 49, 101, 132; food
and, 92–94, 116; hierarchies and, 5, 6,
11–12, 26–27, 101–2, 161, 175–78, 182;
material culture and, 104, 105, 116,
121, 130, 131, 179; multitasking and, 24,
52, 181
pottery, 34, 53, 83, 90, 104, 121, 128, 152;
archaeological record and, 2, 58, 74, 113,
125; for food, 3, 54, 59, 61, 64, 70, 71, 80,
84, 92, 130; making of, 4, 14, 42, 48, 132,
151, 168; raw materials for, 7, 34, 156;
reuse of, 123–24, 131; ritual and, 114, 127;
skills and, 15, 116, 160, 161, 172; trade in,
113, 121, 173, 179
production, 152, 156, 165; of food, 55, 78,
83–84, 92, 94, 178; of goods, 98, 100–102,
104–6, 112, 131, 170; as process, 129–30,
134, 161–62, 164, 168, 170–72, 176, 179;
scale of, 132, 135–36, 153; skill sets and,
15, 136, 160, 161, 166–67, 170; waste
from, 126, 159

ritual: authority and, 12, 15, 26, 175, 181,
182; complex societies and, 12–13; consumption and, 104–5, 113; death and,
26, 33, 61, 113, 128, 168–69; discard and,

126–28; energy expenditure and, 26–27, 31, 47, 86, 126, 134, 138–41, 158, 170, 174; food and, 56, 68, 79, 94, 96; memory and, 46, 180; pilgrimage and, 86, 139; renewal and, 43, 126; social connections and, 43, 45–46, 138–39, 140, 161, 164; space and, 47, 170, 177; utility and, 114; work and, 134, 141, 161–62, 176

skills, 157, 170–71; age and, 35, 116, 159, 169, 170; energy expenditure and, 19, 26, 44, 105, 169; food and, 57, 64, 163, 174; individual actions and, 3, 14, 164, 175; specialization and, 95, 135, 136, 153–54, 155, 157, 160–62, 166–67, 168, 172
slavery, 7, 12, 69–70, 95, 97, 166–68
societies, complex, 8–9, 10, 151; core-periphery relationships and, 102, 132, 180; food and, 82, 91–95, 96–97, 177–78; human evolution and, 2, 5, 6–7, 11–12, 16, 25, 51, 101; landscape and, 150–51; material culture and, 103, 110–11, 130, 133, 179; organization of, 24, 26, 169; work and, 153, 154, 170–73, 181–82 ·
societies, simple/small-scale, 11, 51, 95, 96, 97, 111, 137, 170, 181, 182
space, 16, 35–37, 67, 96; discard and, 124–26, 128, 129; "inside" vs. "outside," 2, 35–36, 56, 60, 61, 98, 152–53, 158, 177; material culture and, 106, 107, 110, 124; meaning of, 46, 47, 79, 170, 180; modification of, 2, 4, 13; public, 127, 130; social complexity and, 6, 108, 150–51, 174, 175; work and, 135, 152, 153, 169
states, 6–8, 12, 52, 182; material culture and, 130, 133, 180; social complexity and, 2, 5, 6, 51, 132, 175, 177–80; work and, 24, 26, 101–2, 174. *See also* empires
status, 7–8, 15, 63, 73, 87–88, 92–93, 104–5, 111, 116, 119–23, 125, 131, 163, 167–68, 178
storage, food, 60, 71, 81, 84, 91, 113, 152–53, 155, 161; access to, 11, 12, 36, 67, 70, 160;

crops and, 19, 42, 75, 80; destruction of, 56, 59, 80; individual actions and, 4, 53, 115; meat and, 43, 64, 67, 151; multitasking and, 26, 55
structures, 19, 36, 43, 126–27; archaeological record and, 2, 13, 15, 67, 113–14, 125, 180; construction of, 18, 36, 121, 134, 156, 170, 180; fire and, 42, 127; food and, 59, 60, 80; materials for, 124, 131, 150, 151; use of space and, 35, 36, 37, 46, 98, 127, 131, 180
"sunk costs," 67, 178

taxation/tribute, 26, 52, 95, 103, 131, 171, 174, 181
time, 17, 23, 33, 46, 67, 110, 111, 126–27; food and, 54–55, 81, 91, 96, 97; invest-ment of, 12, 53, 68, 175; multitasking and, 54, 65, 106, 135, 169; scales of, 34, 44, 79, 175, 181; social complexity and, 6, 16, 26, 134, 174, 180; work and, 4, 34, 51, 106, 152, 160, 161, 163, 166
"tolerated scrounging," 117–18
tools, 1, 10, 50, 98–99, 103, 106–9, 116, 151, 157, 180; energy expenditure and, 26, 56, 100, 112, 159, 171; food and, 4, 61, 63, 65, 66, 80, 81, 96, 113; individuals and, 115, 175; making of, 3–5, 25, 38, 42–44, 54, 87, 101, 107, 151, 160; materials for, 3, 34, 99, 160; as technology, 20, 101, 111–12, 156; utility of, 2, 103, 111, 164
tools, stone: decision making and, 105, 152, 161, 162, 176; development of, 98, 99, 112; energy expenditure and, 18, 48, 123, 172; food and, 58, 113; for grind-ing, 4, 58, 61, 66, 67, 80, 87, 89, 103, 113, 156; hand ax as, 48, 58, 98, 99, 180; raw materials for, 25, 35, 112, 129, 150, 151
trade: markets and, 103–4, 118, 123, 172, 179; networks for, 14, 95, 96, 112, 129, 131, 132, 173; routes for, 113, 166, 179; status and, 116–17, 119, 121, 122, 165, 169

value, 169, 175; of food, 67, 71, 73, 84, 85,
    115; of objects, 47–50, 115–18, 120, 125,
    145, 166, 173, 180; of people, 9, 116, 160;
    social, 37, 64, 93–94, 120, 127, 162, 163,
    164; of time, 135, 146

wherewithal, x, 4, 153, 155, 157, 163,
    164–65, 169, 174
work, 5, 24–26, 87, 148, 172–73, 177; age
    and, 15, 158–60; co-opting, 7, 18, 27, 52,
    69–70, 134, 167–68, 170–74, 181; coor-
    dinating, 18, 93–94, 95, 138, 151–53, 171,
    180–82; as energy expenditure, 4, 18–19,
    51, 134–36, 141, 147, 154, 174, 180–81; food
    and, 53, 59, 85, 163; material culture and,
    98, 101, 103, 117, 123, 164–66; seasonal,
    2, 26, 34–35, 68, 148, 151–54, 162; time
    and, 34, 51, 106, 134, 142–49; types of, 12,
    137–41, 161, 166–68; wage labor and, 103,
    116, 146, 154; "weak ties" and, 138

About the Author

Monica L. Smith received her PhD in anthropology from the University of Michigan and is presently an associate professor of anthropology at the University of California at Los Angeles. She is also director of the South Asian Laboratory at UCLA's Cotsen Institute of Archaeology, which houses reference material and facilities for studying the past of the Indian subcontinent. She has directed archaeological research projects in India and Bangladesh and participated in fieldwork in Italy, Tunisia, Turkey, Egypt, England, Madagascar, and the American Southwest. Smith is the author of *The Archaeology of an Early Historic Town in Central India* (2001), *The Historic Period at Bandelier National Monument* (2002), and *Excavations at Sisupalgarh* (with R. K. Mohanty, 2008) and the editor of *The Social Construction of Ancient Cities* (2003). Her research on archaeological subjects includes the consideration of early state networks, biological models of human behavior, and the role of the past in national identity. At UCLA, she teaches courses on archaeological theory, cognition and material culture, and the development of urbanism.